Sex and Love in the Home

'Much has been written in Christian theology about sex, love, and procreation, but their social meanings and contributions are much more rarely addressed. McCarthy now takes this greatly neglected task, eloquently connecting the Christian household to the common good. All those who want to realise the social vocation of the Christian family will find in this work a rich and challenging resource for understanding and for life.'
Lisa Sowle Cahill, J. Donald Monan Professor of Theology, Boston College

'This book inaugurates a completely new way of thinking about the ethics of marriage and sex. I know of no book on the subject more promising than what McCarthy has achieved here. I think that, as people look back in the next fifty years, they will view *Sex and Love in the Home* as the beginning of an entirely different way of conceptualising not only our lives in and out of marriage but also of how we ought to think about our moral existence more generally.'
Stanley M. Hauerwas, Gilbert T. Rowe Professor of Theological Ethics, Duke University

'Drawing on his own experience of learning how to be a husband and father, David Matzko McCarthy offers wonderfully incisive and readable reflections on the habits of the household – a neighborly space which resists consumerism – and enables sexual relationships to be ordinary, meaningful, and passionate. If you think that all that Christian theology has to say about sex and relationships is twaddle about "complementarity" and "family values", then this is the book for you.'
Gerard Loughlin, Senior Lecturer in Religious Studies, University of Newcastle upon Tyne

Sex and Love in the Home

A Theology of the Household

David Matzko McCarthy

scm press

Copyright © David Matzko McCarthy 2001, 2004

0 334 02946 5

First published in 2001 by
SCM Press,
9–17 St Albans Place London N1 0NX
Second edition published in 2004

SCM Press is a division of
SCM-Canterbury Press Ltd

Typeset by Regent Typesetting, London
and printed in Great Britain by
Biddles, Guildford and King's Lynn

To Sandy Amabel Matzko
Her life teaches the way of hospitality.

Contents

Acknowledgements

I am a husband and a father writing about marriage, family, and the household. My wife asks me, now and then, if my work has changed my ideas about home. My usual answer is that the influence tends to go in the other direction, from home to work. My life as a husband, father, and neighbor has given shape to this book. I am also a teacher and theologian, among other roles like brother and son. Although my answer to my wife's question is more accurate than not (I think), I find it hard to disentangle one set of roles from another. To be honest, it is hard to know where being a father ends and where my role as teacher or neighbor begins. This book project has given me time and opportunity to ruminate on such convergences and to ponder over connections between communities past and present. My life now among neighbors and friends cannot help but resonate with memories of the neighborhood where I grew up. I remember my adventures with Marc Dubois and Gerry Durand. I hear my mother's voice in my own parental directives. Sometimes I hear other parents of my old neighborhood, especially when I am scolding or delighted by the kids next door. I have come to have great appreciation for the men and women of Emmitsburg (where we live now) – for resourceful practitioners like Dr. Bonnie Portier, good neighbors like Samantha Golibart, faithful members of St. Anthony Parish, and various groups that carry on local traditions of service like the Up-County Family Center, Lions Club, and Vigilant Hose Company. Neighborhood sons and daughters, friends and siblings, parents and spouses, old and new are leaving their imprint upon every page.

Given the subject of the book, it is fitting that I dedicate it to my mother, 'Sandy' Amabel Olga Matzko, who was and continues to be a clever household manager. A good bit of my childhood was spent just above or below the statistical poverty line, but we were not poor. On the contrary, we were rich, not only with the things that we needed, but also with good humor and a handiness for making things work and getting by when they did not. Worn out old cars, high utility bills, and homemade haircuts brought conflicts and frustrations that taught us laughter as much as openness to what we could not control. My mother would be called an entrepreneur if she had made any money during her years of economic brinkmanship and ingenuity. Instead, her prudence in dealing with things of the world was put in service to hospitality and the habit of giving things away (Luke 16:1–13). If my mother was going to succeed in keeping us out of trouble (or off a breadline), she was going to be sure to take someone else with us. "Sure as shoot'n," as she would say, we would not be able to enjoy bounty alone. My sisters, Sandee and Sherrie, and my brother Ben share my mother's entrepreneurial talents for not making any money. Among the differences between us, and some of these run deep, we are committed to carrying on the rule of my mother's generosity. When her final days come, may God welcome Amabel, as she has invited many to her table and taken them into her hospitable home.

A whole host of people have been looking after me through the years, and several have made their mark on this book. First, I should thank the Louisville Institute for their gift of the Christian Faith & Life Sabbatical Grant in the academic year 1999–2000. The Institute, based on the campus of Louisville Presbyterian Seminary, is a Lilly Endowment program for the study of American religion. I have been the beneficiary of their good work. I also thank Mount Saint Mary's College, particularly our Provost Carol Hinds, for day-to-day material support and for concerted and fruitful efforts to make the College, in the words of John Henry Newman, "a place for communication and circulation of thought, by means of personal intercourse." I have the good pleasure of engaging colleagues through formal seminars and by casually wandering into neighboring offices, say Marty Malone's, to pick at his bookshelves and brain. Everyday, I wait for wisdom from Carl Glover upon his arrival at the water cooler just outside my door. Everyday, I expect Chris Smith to be dangling an issue in order to hook someone with his hallway conversation and debate. Students have been important to the book as well, especially Katie Staab and Christine Mahoney, who have helped with research and by offering their perspectives on issues of sex, love, and home.

My colleagues in the Theology Department are irreplaceable, each in his or her own way, and together they constitute an interesting 'social body.' I thank Bill Collinge, who has graciously used his skill with words, foreign and familiar, for my good. He has been a great help also in matters of Catholic Social Teaching, Augustine, and the practical wisdom of home. I would like to thank Patsy McDonald, S.H.C.J., for her critical eye on my use of Scripture and her judgments about the project in its entirety. Patsy's intelligence and loyalty have elevated the book. Between Bill and Patsy's talents for words, the two of them provided a last line of defence against my carelessness and incompetence. Surely, some of my errors remain, but without Bill and Patsy, the mistakes would have planted a flag and colonized the text. I also thank Chris McMahon, who was teaching with us in 1999–2000, and colleagues Bill Portier, Jim Donohue, C.R., and Paul Russell for their willingness to play around and test ideas. Paul has been an amiable and interesting office-mate. Jim has been an example of (Canadian) humility and generosity of spirit; his way of life teaches community. Bill P. has enlivened the book. His working-class point of view, love for thinking theologically, and plain-sense about things have given me perspective and courage.

I would like to thank several friends who have helped me from afar. Steve Long, at Garrett Theological Seminary, has been a great help by reading various chapters, and more importantly, for giving a concrete sense that sometimes a friend is rightly called brother, and that brothers and sisters are adopted when friendship endures over time. Robert Brimlow, who teaches in Rochester, NY, and Michael Budde, at De Paul University in Chicago, have offered assistance in understanding modern political theory and the nature of informal economies. Jim Moran, a friend and classmate from high school, has pointed to resources that are indispensable to Chapter 8: The Happy Home. Michael Warren, professor at St. John's University, has provided important insights and resources in understanding the "economy of desire" and "romantic love as passion." Stanley Hauerwas has been a constant source of encouragement to lay the intellectual virtues open to practical wisdom and to transformation by faith, hope, and love.

Finally, I am grateful for my wife, Bridget, and to our children, Abigail, Quinlan, and John Robert. I hope that Abby, Quinn, and Jack will read this book when they are my age and be able to see the profound influence that they have had on their father. While it is customary to thank Bridget for her loving support, I hope to learn greater gratitude for her loving demands, for her care and support that move far beyond me. I am thankful for her ability to sustain community, for her care for the sick (as an R.N.), and for her hope that we will live out, through our everyday life, the adventures of an open home.

Preface to New Edition

SCM Press has given me the opportunity to revise and add material for a second edition of *Sex and Love in the Home*. The chance to revise a book could present a dilemma, but for me it does not. As I imagine it, the typical problem of revision is this. If the book has been useful enough to go to a second edition, then why would an author dare to alter the text? For me, the question is about not revisions but additions. *Sex and Love in the Home* has been reviewed in several academic and pastoral journals, and a common comment has been that topics like cohabitation, non-traditional family and same-sex marriage should be included. These are dealt with in the new, extensive Chapter 10, "Family Miscellany."

The reader can be assured that the book has not been extended simply in order to please its reviewers. Since its original publication, *Sex and Love in the Home* has been used often (perhaps even primarily) in the classroom. The new Chapter 10 is attentive to this location. It includes a great deal of research on topics such as adoption and living together, and is written with the hope of inciting further inquiry and discussion. The book has been described as having a quirky sense of humor. Some have been delighted by the quirks, and others have been distracted. In my defense, I should note that the idiosyncrasies of the text are not extraneous. They represent an intentional effort to match form and content, to show in words the peculiarities and playfulness of home. Additions in the second edition emphasize these themes.

The new chapter highlights the irregularities of family life. I was surprised by reviewers when they demanded comment about "non-traditional" families, such as single-parent households. They did not see the implication of the book's claim that marriage and family are eccentric – that life in neighborhood and home are characterized by overlapping and asymmetrical relationships. The center of the open family (as portrayed in Chapter 5) is outside of the home, insofar as it is part of a web of wider social relationships. Sustaining fulfilling marriages and life-giving families is a common task of neighborhood and church. The new chapter underlines this point. Our task is not to construct self-sufficient families and isolated marriages, but to live as communities that bear the riches of God's hospitality amid the struggles of repairing the broken fixtures of home. The explicit claim of the book is that the ideal of the self-sufficient, nuclear family attempts to avoid the burdens of home repair, and at the same time begins to be closed to the hazards of grace.

Finally, I should give thanks to the families and friends that make our lives rich; to the people of St. Anthony's parish; to the Millers, Samples, and Portiers; to the McCarthy, Zimmel, Devoid, Washington, and Dillard clans; to Carol Hinds, Bill Collinge, Jim Donohue, C.R., and Mary Kate Birge, S.S.J.; to Todd Peterson, our avuncular artist; to Anne Deatherage who makes children of the piano, and to Sheila Dorsey who gives special care to first graders who do not like to read. Special thanks goes to our son Daniel who, after twenty months of consideration, has decided that night time is a good time to sleep.

Introduction

Like the legendary American homestead, the ideal contemporary home has its own acreage and is self-sufficient within. If not sustained by the earth, it has become independent through wages and income. The new suburban homestead, if not separated from others by an expanse of land, has gained functional dissociation. Success, for the family, has come to mean attaining the economic means to contract for services and to avoid practical dependence on neighbors. The same holds within the family. The successful home maintains peace and efficiency through extra telephone lines, single bedrooms, at least one automobile for each driver, and multiple television sets. Our local cable TV company offers a means for every family member to watch his or her own cable station simultaneously. Thank goodness, we will no longer have to fight over the remote control. Detached in practical matters, our home will be free to focus on love and to become a community of affection. As a good family, we will be friendly to neighbors, but we will not entangle them in our problems and practical labors. We will enter common life willingly, but only on a voluntary and leisure basis, through the PTA and youth baseball leagues perhaps. We will be a burden on no one. The ideal home, in other words, is both autonomous and civil, characterized by its self-reliance and social affability. As inviting as it is, such an ideal of home will be challenged throughout this book.

Sex and Love in the Home contributes to current discussions about the home, sexual intimacy and familial love by raising economic and political questions, not in the typical framework of family or "family values", but in more substantive, material terms of the household economy and the polity of my (and probably your) neighborhood. Such ideas as "the household economy" and "neighborhood polity" will be spelled out in detail in the chapters that follow. At this point, suffice it to say that family, typically conceived, sustains an upwardly mobile narrative that is set against informal, interdependent networks of community. I will offer a critique of this closed suburban home and argue for an open, socially reproductive household. When all is said, I will situate a theology of marriage and the meaning of sex and love within the grammar of the dependent household as it struggles within the dominant market economy and the contractual public sphere. I will attend to practical problems, like how our children are being formed by a consumer culture, and I will look to commonplace opportunities for richer, although more strenuous and venturous, community living.

In our time, the typical concept of family functions as an ideal of intimacy, love, and affection. Whether a family is conceived as "nuclear" or "extended", the very idea of family has become nuclear insofar as it is defined by an inward orientation toward its husband-and-wife center. While grandparents and cousins may form a constellation that extends a family, these broader relations revolve around the core of the marriage relationship. Anxious fathers and doting aunts will give congratulations and bits of advice to newly married couples on the matter of "beginning a new family". Seen in this way, an extended family is really a network of autonomous but related families. The marriage, it is assumed, is the foundation of a separate entity. Indeed, the union of two is considered a whole community, closed and complete in itself.[1] According to a contemporary truism, two people who join together in marriage carve out a distinct sphere of life: distinct not only from other families but also from social and economic structures.[2] Husband and wife set up a home, and home, as an ideal of intimacy and love, stands apart from economic judgments or concerns for profit and productivity. Family is, rather, sustained internally by emotional investment. The currency and rationale of the home is unconditional love.

The idea of a household, in contrast, usually has wider social and economic connotations. A family is likely to be conceived as a "household" only when someone is completing tax returns, filling out census information, or answering marketing questionnaires. The household is a matter of calculating dependants, wage earners, and purchasing habits. If family is a sphere of intimacy, the household is simply a place. If family is founded on the heart, a household is built with wood, plaster, and brick, and it is maintained by the arts of plumbing and carpentry. The modern family distributes affection, particularly in opposition to the market and other systems of material distribution.[3] The household, in distinction from family, is a place where time is invested (rather than spent) and where income, labor, and other resources are pooled. The family is characterized by the ideal of unconditional love, whereas the household is subject to external economic and social conditions.[4] The household is fragile and inclined to be dependent upon networks of support, public assistance, and informal financial arrangements.

Ironically, common images of the independent family tend to serve and be shaped by the economic conditions from which they intend to stand apart. The current political debate about "family values" provides a good example. When defenders of family call for autonomy and parental rights, they conceive of the structure of family with the framework of nation-state individualism. A family, in effect, is an individual unit that is distinct and separate from public or social life. It is represented by a "head of household" who, apart from being defined economically, is a generic individual as well. He or she has no specific role in social life, except to maintain the private space of home. In the service economy of late capitalism, the family's essential contribution to public life is its consumption of goods. Dependants within a home are a burden on society unless supported by their productive parents or guardians. While children are a burden, they ought to be under the responsibility and charge of their parents alone: welfare moms and deadbeat dads, as their titles suggest, have become disgraceful public figures and enemies of the common good. Children are an asset to society if they are well behaved and if they consume. Parents help their children become public assets by making their income available to their children. Children, in fact, have become the primary decision-makers for household consumption and the fastest growing market.[5] In effect, the needs of the market and contractual individualism, like the language of family values, undercut the socially interdependent household as an economic and socially reproductive place. Through the family, consumer capitalism and nation-state individualism are reproduced.

Like "family values", common notions of romantic love and sexual desire are assumed to stand outside market rationality and contractual social arrangements, but, ironically, they reproduce dominant economic and social forms. It is no keen insight to notice that love and sex are social and economic currency. Romantic

moments and passionate interchanges are played out in advertisements in order to give personal and social meaning to flavored
coffees and compact cars. Even though it is common knowledge that
sex sells, it is also a prevailing assumption that sexual desire springs
out of us naturally and that romantic connections have a life
and course of their own. This purportedly natural and indomitable
character of desire does not coexist happily with the reality of
marriage and the subsistent social economy of the household.
Passion and romance are believed to defy domestication by their
very nature. Love and desire have the migratory character of growth
capitalism, always dependent upon establishing new markets (or
partners and techniques) for their vitality.

I will argue, in contrast, that the conflict between desire and home
is inevitable not because real sex and love are naturally untamed,
but because desire and romantic love are produced (and therefore
constrained) within a social and economic currency that is set
against the household. Dominant conceptions of passion and
romance are destined to contravene family inasmuch as both the
modern economy and the contractual state have usurped the social
and economic roles of pre-industrial and agrarian households. My
concern is not to challenge capitalism and contractual individualism
as dominant systems (that would be another project entirely).
Rather, I intend to distinguish the social and economic operations
of neighborhood and household from these dominant systems, in
order to provide an alternative landscape for conceptions of sex,
love, and family. Private, suburban "family" is only a complement
to the dominant systems. To provide an alternative, the household,
in contrast to the private family, must be conceived as a socially
reproductive and economically productive place.

The arguments of the book are, in the main, situated in two
different but correlative areas – in the neighborhood and in current
theological discourse about family. Two corresponding lines of
critique are present throughout. On one hand, market capitalism
and nation-state individualism are criticized insofar as they
encroach upon neighborhood reciprocity and the organic (non-
voluntary) character of the household. On the other hand, modern
personalism is scrutinized. In the mid-twentieth century, theological
personalism emerged, in Catholic circles, as a challenge to instrumental and juridical understandings of marriage. Personalism
offered a challenge to the idea that marriage is not good in itself but

produces only external goods like children and social stability.[6] While focusing on marriage as a good in itself, personalism tends to narrow the foundation of family to an interpersonal space (i.e., the couple). This personal space becomes a romantic abstraction when conjugal union is conceived not only as a thing *in itself* but also as a basic social relation *in itself*, outside the practical complexities of the household and other social relations. Like the cultural ideal of romantic love, personalism makes little room for the politics of the neighborhood and the economy of home. Personalist philosophy, along with the modern spirit of individualism, tends to set the household upon a foundation of affective and non-pragmatic (i.e., utopian) relations.

Like the two lines of critique, the book's constructive proposal is set within conversations about the neighborhood on one hand, and Christian theology, on the other. The constructive task for families of our time is to understand how local community works, not only in personal or friendly terms but also in regard to social and economic practices. The theological endeavor is to inquire about our social formation in the language and practices of the household of God. Common life in family and home, for instance, is conceived in terms of a body with non-identical but reciprocal parts and functions, all of which are oriented to the flourishing of the whole and directed to the love of God and neighbor. This conception of the social body is found not only in Scripture (e.g., 1 Cor. 12), but also in the tradition of Catholic social teaching, particularly (but not only) in reference to marriage and family life.[7] When giving an account of marriage and family, it is tempting to present this construal of social life through an ideal of domestic bliss, but it is more important to point to community (to the social body) as it is found amid the ambiguities of our day-to-day activities.

The constructive task is to find sources of common living within our existing ways of life, to train ourselves to be perceptive and wise about contemporary practices and our common endeavors. Positive descriptions of household and family, here, will not depend upon appeal to a golden age, to bygone eras of moral unity and the traditional family, corsets and domestic harmony, father-disciplinarians and doting domestic mothers, the year 50, or 1950.[8] Alternative ways of thinking about sex, love, and family are put into action in the present. By means of practices available to us, we can identify the ways that we are socialized to desire and love in certain ways rather than others, and for certain reasons and motivations rather than others. What do we want to find through sex, and how will we recognize love over against infatuation or lust? After a devastating experience, many of us (me, for example) have thought to ourselves, "Why am I attracted to bad relationships and to people who are not good for me?" With this question, we begin to retrain our desires and our perspectives on love. The question implies another: "How are we enculturated or socialized to love?" In this book, the household is understood to be a basic site of contending socializations and codes of love and sexual desire. The critical task is to depose dominant but inferior systems of formation. The constructive aim is to look toward a "resocialization" where we will be formed in the love of God and "enlarge our capacities for compassion toward others and solidarity in the common good."[9]

In the following pages, I do my best to identify everyday activities of community, but I have been haunted by the worry that my approach depends too much upon the ordinary. Our culture tends to focus on the extraordinary, whether we are looking for beauty and intelligence or considering moral questions through the extreme case, such as euthanasia, assisted suicide, and the like. When we look for the ordinary, we are apt to generalize through public opinion polls, representative samples, and other purportedly disinterested surveys. This sociological approach intends to avoid qualitative or normative claims. It is odd, perhaps anomalous, to point to particular but still ordinary ways of life as exemplary. Highlighting the ordinary is risky, but the hope is that we will find new ways of living where we already stand. The prospect is that we find an adventure in the little things that we do.

An ordinary account of the household, for example, will account for how family is sustained through, not despite, everyday misunderstandings and our interpersonal limitations. In various guides to parenting and family life, examples of reasonable and gentle discipline abound.[10] That is not the norm in my neighborhood. Both children and parents become unreasonable; parents yell and are held spellbound within their own disciplinary monologues. Children learn to weather the storm and to appease their parents without conceding more than is absolutely necessary. In comparison to these ordinary dysfunctions, the ideal family depends upon psychological expertise and works to reach an extraordinary level of interpersonal skill. Parental tirades give way to tight psychological management, as these families, like their self-help manuals, put parenting in a therapeutic model. In the process, family relationships start to fit well in the isolated one-on-one context of therapy. Parenting is conceived as an exclusive parent-to-single-child relationship, where a care-giver guides an individual child through his or her process of development. Siblings are considered not a part of the process, but a challenge to it. They intrude on the seamless therapeutic relationship between parent and child.[11]

This ideal of parenting manuals diminishes the social character of less specialized ways of dealing with children. Withdrawing from the social character of parenting is precisely the goal, not an unintended consequence. The therapeutic conception provides a way to isolate and control childhood development amid communities, neighborhoods, and various influences that parents cannot trust. In this regard, psychological management is both a defensive strategy and a means to offer one's child an advantage over other children. For the purposes of supervision, it provides a narrow context of development, but, ironically, it is apt to produce socially fragile personalities under the guise of autonomy and independence. In a well-managed context, children are raised, unwittingly, to worry about conflict, and as a result they and their parents are more inclined to produce it without resolution. Independence becomes another word for withdrawing and avoiding the complexities of social life.

The open household, in contrast to this ideal family, is a real social space of miscommunication and forgiveness, held together, if at all, by practical ends and intrinsic goods that transcend interpersonal abilities. We often fail; yet, we learn hospitality in recognizing our own insurmountable shortcomings.[12] When faced with the limitations of the nuclear home, we widen the social boundaries of family and household. We blur the lines of interdependence and influence. We lose control, and we have to take the risk of depending upon others, upon teachers, neighbors, other parents, and the like. The risk of interdependence corresponds to the social role of ordinary, not so ideal, families. Theologically speaking, family is grounded not in interpersonal expertise, but in a vocation that cannot be pursued alone.

The contrast between ordinary and extraordinary versions of family has a variant in the fields of theology and ethics. Theologians and moral philosophers tend to overlook everyday motives and intentions for the sake of abstract ideas. Contemporary theologians hold, for example, that sexual intercourse in marriage is an expression of human communion as human beings are created, as male and female, in the image of God (Gen. 1.27). This description, although important, is distant from ordinary matters of marriage, sexual or not. It is a rare moment in everyday life that we intend to express something about our humanity *per se*. The moment would no longer be ordinary and everyday. Seldom are we in the extra-ordinary position of interacting as mere humans. We are brothers and sisters, strangers and neighbors, white and black, Christian and Jew, and the meaning of our interaction is structured by the particulars – by our local histories, social roles, overlapping commitments, and so on. Likewise, matters of marriage and home are ordered not to a grand design, but to concrete tasks, roles, duties, and specific people.[13] I find that, the longer I am married to Bridget Ann McCarthy, the better I am at being her husband and the less able I am to be a husband generally. Bridget and I no longer inhabit a generic place; our mutual "belonging" and shared story give deeper meaning to the simple things that we do.

The same local orientation and limited purview hold for sex in marriage. Through any given sexual act, spouses might express love, desire, generosity, frustration, fatigue, or a manipulative intent, but they will do so in the semantic context of a day, week, a stage of life, and series of specific events, and all set within the broader context of a shared life. Any particular sexual encounter need not say anything earth shattering; it need not point to the fullness or full meaning of a sexual relationship. We need not be completed by our sexual complement. Most sex within marriage is just ordinary, a minor episode in a larger story. One set of sexual expressions may need to be redeemed by another, and can be. One-night stands and passionate affairs, in contrast, need to be earthshaking and splendid because they are the whole story. They are manic attempts to overcome the fact that there is nothing else. The true superiority of sexual intercourse in marriage is that it does not have to mean very much. Expressed sexually or otherwise, our "humanity" is something that accumulates quietly through small steps and comes to us as a whole only when we step back, in order to look back and to imagine the future.

Throughout the book, the everyday will be woven together with a theological "stepping back". In other words, life in the neighborhood will be put in conversation with theological inquiry about such matters as the love of God and the role of the church in the world. This mixed approach may not satisfy the systematic theologian, but it will resonate with the order of the household and, hopefully, with our practical wisdom. I will put together arguments and ideas not as they are formally related to each other, but where and how we tend to use them. At home, when I straighten up our garage, I like to put our garden spades together with snow shovels, rakes, brooms, the sledge hammer, and the ax. All are alike insofar as they have long handles, and they fit neatly together in one place. But within a day or two, I find a spade (apparently my wife's favorite) in its own place just inside the garage door, standing happily, it seems, with the Miracle Grow (which belongs with the other fertilizers) and a few garden trowels (which belong in a small box with other clippers and other hand tools). I no longer protest or complain about my organizational efforts undone. I know that Bridget is right. She accuses me of organizing her tools without reference to their use. She notes that my taxonomy of tools is suited to storing rather than using them. In this book, I take her practical approach.

The structure of the book reflects a common story of love. A young man and a young woman experience attraction and desire toward potential partners. They are interested in a field of options and experiences, but after a time, each moves from general desiring to a specific attraction to a particular person. Each falls in love with the other, and they begin a romantic relationship. The exhilaration and joy of their love leads to a greater depth of care and intimacy, and if their romantic feelings have staying power, the presence of one becomes more indelible in the life of the other. Courtship and marriage follow. They carry on much as before, at first, but slowly they get set in a routine, become more invested in work, household chores, and the tasks of raising children. Before long, they notice that their regard for each other, now, has come to have a different basis. Their intimacy, love, sex, and common interests have changed almost entirely. Their romance has given way to common work. Intimate evenings and fanciful vacations have given way to soccer practice, Happy Meals, gardening, and trips to the zoo. Some couples are able to make the adjustment. If the divorce rate is an indication otherwise, about half of married couples cannot. Some try to recapture the romance; others settle and adjust their expectations. In either case, their lives have passed into the household, where sexual desire, love, and relationships are redefined. Desire is re-socialized.

Following this narrative, the chapters of the book reflect a chiastic structure with the household at the center. Thematically, the book moves from sexual desire and love, to the household, and then from the household back to love and sex. The first part of the book focuses on sex, romantic love, and family within the market economy and the dominant polity of civic and national life. The middle part gives a normative account of the open household and neighborhood reciprocity, in contrast to suburban isolation and the limits of contractual bonds. The third part attends to the alternative and richer character of love and sex in the household, and in addition to "The Order of Love" and "Sexual Practices and Social Reproduction," it includes a chapter on affection and friendship and another pertaining to issues of gender roles, equality, and function. The concluding chapter of the book offers proposals for a theology of marriage and family.

Chapter 1, "Glamour and Good Housekeeping," provides an introduction to themes of the book, particularly the narrative tensions between passion and marriage, and between the politics of the city and the social economy of the church and home. The second and third chapters, "Sexual Desire" and "Romantic Love," discuss our prevailing cultural grammar of sex and love. I have a bit of fun discussing such things as advice from sex therapists and personal ads in *The Washington Post*. I attend to theological and philosophical accounts as well. These chapters show, among other things, that modern passion and romantic impulses are shaped by a flight from the practical bonds of relationships and home. Modern romance is eminently interesting precisely because it is ultimately self-defeating. Chapter 4 proposes that the social and economic framework which produces modern desire and love also animates the closed nuclear family. The upwardly mobile family flourishes in the dominant social economy inasmuch as it becomes externally and internally suburbanized – set apart from the drag of needy neighbors and non-voluntary endeavors. Modern family, ironically, is marked by a flight from home.

Chapter 5, "Two Households," provides a pivotal shift in context from the closed to the open household – from a market economy to personal favors, from contractual arrangements (a service for pay) to ad hoc reciprocation (venison for informal childcare), from limited and manageable interchanges (like a professional lawn service) to open-ended cooperation (like sharing a lawn mower), from the peaceful suburban home to annoying neighbors and the labors of community. The social economy of the open neighborhood is characterized by giving and receiving gifts. In contrast, the closed home is inclined to limit gift-giving not because giving is a burden, but because receiving is. I can give a gift in a disinterested way without expectation of return, but when I receive a gift I feel bound to also receive the giver or to reject the gift. I do not want gifts from strangers or from odd people and jerks whom I do not want to befriend. I am suspicious of what they want from me. In receiving, I am bound to reciprocation, even if my return is a simple thanks or my enjoyment of the gift. I am bound to a social exchange. For this reason, the closed home prefers contracts and payment. These forms of exchange are much more manageable and allow more freedom from binding attachments. The neighborhood economy, on the other hand, binds in excess of the exchange. It is an economy that is open to personal conflicts, social intrusion, and deeper life in community.

Chapters 6 to 11 develop themes important to the household economy. Chapter 6 follows the course of Catholic social teaching on family and home. The tradition's conception of family has developed from an organic fit with culture and state to a distinct social form that is oriented to social transformation. In recent years, family and the household have become important as a site of social reproduction within a dominant economy of consumption and attenuated social relations. I will argue that the coherence of the tradition lies, not in its recent personalist emphasis, but in how personal relations are cast within a social vocation. The familial, in other words, is the political. Following this point, Chapter 7, "The Order of Love," argues that familial love is not an early stage on the way to more mature universal or disinterested love. Rather, the love of family is basic to the love of God, to universal love, and to the church's role as a sacrament of God's love in the world. Chapter 8 discusses productive family relationships and provides a theological (Augustinian) account of friendship. Chapter 10 considers a variety of issues, such as adoption, that help to specify the character of the open household as generative of the kind of social relationships (gift-giving and receiving) that are outlined in Chapter 5. Chapters 9 and 11 situate issues of gender and sexual practices within the socially reproductive household. They move from thin accounts of equality and unity provided by contractual individualism to a richer conception of reciprocity and roles set within common endeavors. Within this frame, sexual practices are shaped by the church's practices of hospitality. The procreative character of sexuality is key to its fit with an outward movement and vocation of love.

The book's conclusion sets matters of marriage and family within the habitat of the household economy. Let an example suffice to introduce the final chapter. This week, I have been spending some time with my daughter, Abigail, at vacation Bible school. I have not spent much time – just about a half-hour when I drop her off and the same when I pick her up. I have had the advantage and disadvantage of looking at the events from the outside. On the first morning, we entered a fellowship hall that was filled with too many happenings to recount. Abigail's teacher had a son clinging to her leg. Children were running about. Animated greetings were passed all around. There were a considerable number of parents – all mothers and grandmothers except a few grandfathers and me. Some adults were talking with each other; others were busy with preparations, and several were helping frightened and shy children adjust to the environment. Teenagers mulled about, some helping, some playing with small children, and others showing obvious resentment. Four women were preparing to lead us in song by practicing a complicated piece. I could hear only bits of it, but I clearly could see their focused coordination. When we began to shout out "He's Got the Whole World in His Hands," I realized that they were not practicing at all. They were enjoying each other's company and an artistic moment amid the chaos. Our song was a digression for them, but for the rest, it was a means to focus our attention. Preschool children went off to daycare with several teenagers, and the various classes settled around designated tables. Vacation Bible school was afoot.

As Abigail joined her group, I looked at her teacher with wonder and compassion. Sheila had volunteered to teach about fifteen kids who were bouncing out of their chairs. Her tasks for the day would require far more depth of character and a far more complex set of skills than what was waiting for me at my office; yet, she would not be publicly recognized for her efforts, would find her patience and composure tested, and certainly would not be paid. Soon, I would steal away to work, which, in comparison, could hardly be called work at all. I was reminded of the ironies of the modern workplace, careers, and life in the so-called public sphere. By and large, work, government, and public administration stand outside the difficulties of social life and the hard work of community.[14] Office, factory, and even manual labor offer the benefits of simple social exchange, comparatively narrow expectations, an immediate and tangible product (money), and freedom from the unreasonable demands of neighbors and children.[15] Traditional women's vocations, such as nursing, social work, childcare, and teaching, are exceptions. These professions, more often than not, are means to extend the skills and goals of care and household management. Abigail's vacation Bible school teacher was doing the same. I went to my office troubled because she was, to use an old cliché, hopping from the frying pan to the fire. Rather than caring for her three children, Sheila was teaching fifteen.

At the end of the week, I asked Sheila how things had gone. "It was a lot of fun," she said. I was skeptical. She admitted that she was anxious and overwhelmed on the first day, but she said that teaching vacation Bible school was indeed enjoyable. I saw indications of enjoyment during the week. Contrary to my expectations, the numbers of parents through the week had not diminished but increased. Sheila was rarely alone with children, and everyone's energy continued to be high. One morning I entered the fellowship hall in the middle of dancing and singing. It was "Pharaoh, Pharaoh, Oh, Oh, Let my People Go," sung to the 1960s tune of "Louie, Louie," by the Kingsmen. I had before me the sight of forty-year-old mothers losing themselves as they moved to the beat – while most of the children either watched in awe or jumped about with futile efforts to keep up. Every morning I watched the musical foursome study and practice their craft, and then lead the group in something far more pedestrian like "Jesus Loves the Little Children." Previously disaffected teenagers were looking more comfortable, happy to interact with little people who thought they were cool.

Vacation Bible school had become a location where several different events were taking place and where, at the same time, common life was enhanced through common work. Although teaching children was the apparent goal, the Bible school was occasion for other kinds of activities and social interchanges. I imagine that members of the quartet are looking forward to next year, but it was not just harmony that made the fellowship hall neighborly. The participants and volunteers were not only parish-ioners, relatives, and friends, but antagonists as well. People share hurts, misunderstandings, and ill-will when they live together closely and endeavor to share their lives. Among our parish volun-teers, subtle frictions remain over passed hurts, and vacation Bible school provided a context to transcend personal disagreements. Newcomers were invited in as well, and unusual personalities found suitable ways to contribute. The common work allowed the teachers and aides to be together in ways that typical friendships would not allow. A thirty-five-year-old teacher and her teenage helper had a fine time working side by side, but they are not going to go shopping together or hang out at the pool. The Bible school represents a particular social economy and opportunities to culti-vate one's identity with reciprocal roles and activities of common life.

The practices of our vacation Bible school are central to the open household, and when theologies of marriage and family render them tangential or optional, the theology is deficient. Catechetical pro-grams and similar parish activities are the basic context for the flourishing of family life insofar as they sustain a socially reproduc-tive economy of church. Community projects such as these cultivate a social economy of reciprocity and provide for complex, although informal, role differentiation and personal identity. They form a training ground for practical skills of community. They establish community in a place, a network that binds over time and in a concrete setting, beyond the participation and passing of individual agents and in excess of mere usefulness. This kind of household space is continually threatened by dominant forms of social management and market utility. Family, as an interpersonal ideal and an unreasonable set of constraints, has become inextricably bound to conceptions of "public" productivity and freedom, and to issues of the so-called private sphere, of desire, affection, role differentiation, and gender. These ideas and issues are treated in the chapters that follow. Theology pertains to issues of our social formation in God's house, and theologies of family life have little worth if they attend neither to the maintenance of neighborhood practices nor to the ambiguities of dominating social forms. The theology of marriage and family is the theology of social repro-duction in the economy of home.

Part One

Glamour and Good Housekeeping

"When Alex and I were dating," explains Dahlia, "I used the passion thermometer to tell me how we were doing." Apparently she and Alex were getting along quite well, until they moved in together. Dahlia "found herself living with a man whose inability to grasp the concept of carrying a dirty dish from table to sink pretty much summed up his take on cohabitation."[1] Dahlia's story is featured in a how-to article in *Glamour* magazine, "Love and Partnership: How to Get Both."[2] The article points to a familiar tension between romantic attraction and practical cooperation. According to Denis de Rougemont, modern romantic love is animated by its conflict with the duties and obligations of home.[3] Social conventions, filial responsibilities, and other institutional obstacles are antagonists in the drama of true love. Marriage, conceived as an obstacle, is the ultimate test. At its core, de Rougemont argues, the logic of romantic love is adulterous, both extramarital and unfaithful to the workaday structure of the home.

Dahlia's case is less extreme and more typical. She finds herself with two conflicting criteria of judgment, one romantic and the other domestic, one passionate and the other pragmatic. The conflict between the two represents a shift in the context of her relationship with Alex, from activities of dating to tasks of cooking and cleaning. In order to sustain love (which lies on the side of romance), Dahlia and Alex will have to adjust or avoid the realities of their new household setting. Although modern romance and domestic life are set at odds, sharing a home, paradoxically, is supposed to follow naturally from passionate love. If cohabitation is a challenge to romance, it is the proving ground of enduring love. Passion and love go together, so that romance will be the route to the happy home. Will love endure for Dahlia and Alex? Will Dahlia's attraction to Alex overcome his unattractive domestic habits? Will she prove her love by tolerating his irresponsibility? Will he change his ways because he loves her? Will love die in a desert of dirty laundry and unwashed pots?

Such questions about love and domestic life are at the heart of this chapter, which aims to introduce a line of inquiry and to generate a conversation about sex, love, and the household. The first part of the chapter considers popular notions of marriage, and the second half presents John Chrysostom, a fourth-century theologian, as a model for the kinds of questions that will be asked in the following chapters. John Chrysostom's work is important, not only because of its theological content, but also because of his distance from us. Chrysostom takes for granted a whole host of ancient assumptions that we as moderns assume we have moved beyond. For instance, he holds that virginity is better than sex and that love is akin to duty. Regardless of whether or not such arguments will convince a modern audience, they can offer a critical perspective from which to demystify our contemporary notions of sexual desire and romantic love.

Chrysostom presupposes that desire for wealth as much as for sex and booze reflects the excesses of his ancient city. He attempts to "re-locate" love and marriage in an alternative place, in the ascetic social economy of the desert monks. This shift in context is analogous to the central themes of this book. The chapters that follow will shift questions of sex and love from the dominant contractual economy to the reciprocity of neighborhood and home. The precise meaning of this shift need not be clear at this point. My intention, in this chapter, is to introduce the problem of "location", that is, of where sexual desire and the quest for love are formed, and to present this problem of formation in social and economic terms. The first part of this chapter discusses the tensions and contradictions of modern romantic love and raises questions about the role of desire in our dominant market economy. It begins with Dahlia's problem, a typical trial of modern courtship: how to get a romantic lover to be a good partner too.

Desire and dirty dishes

The *Glamour*'s article, "Love and Partnership," assumes that, for most of its readers, passion and romantic love are distinct from "shared goals," "feelings of mutuality," and the "flexible giving and taking" which characterize partnerships in work and practical life.[4] Dahlia claimed that, when dating, she used her "passion thermometer" in order to monitor the kind of attention she received from her man. But when setting up house, she wants him to look around instead, in order to see what needs to be done. Weeks ago she was happy with dinner out and a movie, now she wants him to notice the dirty carpet and vacuum it. *Glamour* offers help in closing this romance–housekeeping gap. The article suggests that women use their dating acumen to "trawl" for someone with "partnership potential." "Let his heart melt as he loses himself in your eyes glowing soft and velvety in the candlelight. Your heart needs to remain eagle-eyed, antennae up and quivering . . .," looking for someone who is willing to do the emotional and practical work of "a truly shared life."[5]

When all is said, the *Glamour* "how-to" does not close the gap between romance and home. *Glamour* proposes that, while romancing outwardly, a woman ought not be romantic inwardly. Alex's romance is occasion for Dahlia's pragmatism; he is caught up in desire, and she uses her common sense. As a result, Alex and Dahlia will have conflicting views of their relationship from the start. Both will have to secure what they want from the other through indirect means, role playing, and manipulation. Notice that *Glamour* does not advise Dahlia to look for a man who is looking explicitly for a partner, the kind of guy who would tell a date about his domestic skills and his cooperative orientation to good house-keeping. Such a man is an unattractive nerd. The wise dating-man, when looking for a wife, knows to show his hand only at the last moment, or if possible, lay it on the table face down, never to be seen. What woman would be attracted to a man who is attracted to her because of her partnership potential? Certainly not the *Glamour* woman. She is sexy to men, but secretly pragmatic. The *Glamour* man is full of passion and adventure, but has potential to be "settled" or "domesticated". Both enter the home under the veil of the romantic self. They are not quite what they appear to be.

This tension between passion and home, between the romantic and settled self, does not end after courtship. Housekeeping encroaches upon love every day. Love and lovemaking coincide, but common tasks of everyday life are distracting. While thinking about making dinner, planning tomorrow's schedule at work, and secur-ing a plumber, you are likely to lose the loving feeling. Excuses abound, but "that inability to get into a sexy state of mind, while perfectly natural, is the *real* obstacle to making love."[6] *Redbook* offers help through "16 Ways to Free Your Mind for Great Sex." In the conflict between your to-do list and romance, the stakes are high. Obstacles to good sex must be overcome "because not only is sex essential to your personal well-being, there is simply no way to keep a relationship alive without it."[7] Sex is a vital source of love, and love is the foundation of a good partnership and a happy home. Yet, ironically, practical matters of home militate against love-making. The partnership of a "shared life" is not friendly to love's passion.

The problem introduced here is not only the divergence of romance and friendship, but also the status of the household. It is no coincidence that *Glamour* and *Redbook* provide quick entry into the difficulties of love and living together. Self-help in sex, romance, and home are common in magazines marketed to women – while eroticism and domination of women characterize magazines for men.[8] Despite our contemporary language of equality, women have charge of the home, and they carry the heavier burden in maintaining their relationships with men. Progressives and feminists are dismayed by continued inequities between working men and domestic women, and conservatives like to accentuate the differences.[9] However, both sides agree that women, like it or not, have charge of the home. This leadership of women would be a modern achievement, if the home were not privatized as a mediating institution for more basic structures of economy and state.[10] The household is socially and economically subordinate, so that domestic authority for women amounts to wider social and economic subordination.

While, in ages past, the household was a basic social and economic institution, the modern home need be nothing more than a "free-floating" dyad based in mutual affection.[11] Typically, the modern household lacks inter-generational continuity, and more importantly, it might not last a generation before it is divided and reconstituted through divorce and remarriage. The "family" as "household" is likely to last only a few years. In contrast to pre-industrial settings, the function of family in the modern economy is its consumption, using up household items, automobiles, and the never-ending products children and adults come to want and need. Moreover, modern individualism has loosened personal identity from home and family. We are likely to consider ourselves "whole" or "mature" only after we have left home, in order to decide basic matters of life for ourselves.[12] In short, the modern home has been freed from the social and economic dominance of family and its economic and political authority. The household is no longer a necessary conveyance of land, wealth, and social function. It has been freed, so we moderns believe, for a reformation by love.

Glamour's "Love and Partnership," represents modern conceptions of love and family in several ways. First, love is central, but the concept lacks clarity. Modern love shifts, sometimes without notice, from arousal, to infatuation, to romance, to friendship, and to duty. Some of these loves are considered contradictory; yet, Dahlia hopes to have them all. Poor Alex is probably oblivious. His infatuation with Dahlia has saddled him with domestic duties that he does not understand. Between Dahlia's hopes and Alex's ignorance, a drama unfolds. Emotional and sexual potency are considered the best hope for unity and continuity, if only passion can be sustained in the home. The passage from arousal to cohabitation to dissolution defines the modern narrative of love. Two fall in love, and then, whether or not they wed, they will set up house. The two fall out of love, and whether or not they wed, they will experience a divorce. For the readers of *Glamour,* this passage rises and falls on a woman's skill in "sculpting a partner from the raw material" of a romantic man. Perhaps men are wise to the transition and will do their best to resist. If a man is useless but romantic, he can manage to avoid a great deal of domestic work. In any case, passionate love is the beginning and source, and the household is both love's natural course and its basic challenge. Throughout the drama, sexual desire struggles to be the vitality of love.

Sex and love in the household

The narrative of love and partnership in *Glamour* also impinges upon modern theologies of marriage and family. In contrast to ages past, contemporary theologians emphasize the interpersonal reality of love and intrinsic goods of erotic passion and sexual union. The interpersonal reality of a "Me and You" relationship is considered the basic context of love.[13] In this regard, *Glamour* and the theologians share the idea that true love constitutes the true union between a husband and wife – a union of two who encounter each other face to face as persons. Love between spouses, in theological terms, is considered a unique setting for the experience of self-giving and human communion. Conjugal union gives expression to the original unity of man and woman who are created together in the image of God (Gen. 1.27). Marriage is praised as a community of love in itself, a community of two that generates more love and community.[14] In other words, the love between a man and woman emerges from within the partners; then a marriage is created, and other relationships follow like those between parent and child. Put in story form, boy and girl meet and fall in love; they get married, buy a home and raise a family. Their interpersonal love constitutes their marriage, creates other relationships, and establishes a particular sphere of life called the household.

This priority of love is hard to dispute. Who would argue the contrary, that a marriage can work when it is not founded on love? Apparently unassailable, this key modern principle will be put under scrutiny throughout the following chapters. A counterproposal will be put forward. Love takes various forms, and particular practices of love will fit with the social and economic environment where they are cultivated.[15] In short, environment and a way of life correspond within an ecosystem. In the way that certain plant life flourishes in a rain forest while other species grow in the desert, a fitting habitat is requisite for the germination of conjugal love. When all is said and done, interpersonal love does not create a loving environment as much as it requires existing practices of love as a place to grow. Conjugal love is formed within social practices like those of marriage, family, and household management. The "face-to-face" or "Me and You" love between two people is secondary to these prior social conditions. Good household practices, not romance, will keep love alive. With this argument, the priority of romantic, "Me and You", and marital love is denied, but the priority of love *per se* is not. The context for love is simply broadened and set within the goods of common life.

Basic to modern stories of love is the triumph of love over an arid, loveless environment. Romeo and Juliet have become important to our popular imagination because their love emerges where it should not. Their love seems unthinkable amid inter-family hostility; yet it grows spontaneously and cannot be extinguished, even unto death. A similar, obviously less dire tension is operative in *Glamour*'s "Love and Partnership." Romantic love and cooperative work are incompatible. Dahlia, in order to be true to her love, must make questions of practical compatibility unthinkable. While dating Alex, she is likely to tell her friends that she loves and accepts him for who he is. However, when she and Alex live together, she will turn to the same friends (and *Glamour* magazine) in order to figure out how to change his behavior. Her impulse toward unconditional love contends with the real conditions of their home-bound relationship. *Glamour*'s advice is not to love him for who he is, but to love him for who you can make him become.

While "Love and Partnership" proposes that women remain pragmatic in matters of love, *Glamour* and comparable magazines play the other side of the romantic tension as well. They have an interest in heightening the quest for pure, impractical romance. They do so in most of their articles for no other reason than to offer readers enticing advice and to offer advertisers an enticed reader-ship.[16] Ironically, love is more interesting for us when it is doomed to fail. Failure is inevitable because we must choose either to give up on romance and be practical or to give up on practical concerns and watch our lives fall apart. The challenge to have it all (i.e., love as arousal, romance, and good housekeeping) is the challenge to be the envy of all. Envy, in this regard, may be more important than sex and infatuation. Envy is desire for what we lack because we lack it.[17] Such desire has powerful social and economic currency in our world. If anything, the contradictions of love and partnership keep us wanting more, that is, wanting "to have it all".

An alternative economy of desire

The church, in contrast to the market, has interests in bringing together love, desire, and home. Insofar as Christians are called to love as God loves, the church, by definition, is called to be a habitat where love is reproduced through mutual care, correction, forgive-ness, and reconciliation. While romantic love is set in opposition to practical obstacles, Christian love is a practical working out of dis-agreement and division. We can imagine Dahlia and Alex, in a romantic moment, leaving the dirty dishes in the sink and going out to a fine restaurant in order to renew their courtship. Without domestic distractions, they will be able to talk face to face and gaze into each other's eyes. In doing so, they will attempt to keep love and household on distinct but parallel tracts – or in two distinct places. In order to carry on at home, they will need to leave the house frequently in order to love again. This kind of love is renewed by weekend getaways and expensive restaurants. Christian love, in comparison, is more akin to good household management, raising children, and helping out the neighbors. This not so glamorous setting is often a difficult vantage point from which to speak well of sex and conjugal love.

The standard theological account speaks well of love, passion, and sex, but by and large, does nothing more than assert the unity of interpersonal love, sexual pleasure, and everyday life. In the Introduction, I referred to what I am now calling "the standard account" under the broad heading of personalism. Emerging in the second half of the twentieth century, in reaction to formal and extrinsic accounts of marriage, modern personalism considers the interpersonal, "Self to Self" relationship the basic (and original) context of true love. Love, in other words, is generated by the interpersonal encounter apart from wider social and economic structures. This "Me and You together" is considered a foundational experience. Within this framework, the standard personalist account follows modern trends by highlighting sex and sexual desire as ideal expressions of love. Sex is considered representative of conjugal love, and conjugal intercourse is considered a good and sacramental experience. Through a sexual relationship, we discover our humanity in intimate communion with each other as "Other", and, in the process, encounter God's grace.[18]

This widely accepted account gives sex and interpersonal love profound theological and human meaning, but the context for this meaning tends to be a theoretical nowhere place. The loving sexual union is considered a unique context of total self-giving, and the seed for an expanding context of love.[19] However, this "Me and You" context is conceived as discretely interpersonal. The lovers are defined primarily in relation to an isolated context of two: one Self face to face with another Self. Love, in these terms, is best during those infrequent moments when a couple manages to escape together in order to be alone. In ways similar to *Glamour*'s divide between romantic love and practical concerns, the personalist account assumes a gap between ideal isolation and the practical matters of community and family. Never do we hear about parents too tired for passion. Never do we hear about disagreements or conflicts in an ongoing sexual relationship. We do not hear that our intimate communion may be marked by days of sorrow over a death in the family, by financial worries, or by despair over loss of work. Love is best, in standard modern parlance, when the lovers are abstracted from the conditions of their workaday life. The "Me" and "You" are defined almost entirely in relation to each other. In fact, you and I complete each other. There is little indication that I will discover who you really are as I come to know you in the company of others.

The Christian tradition has emphasized communal love outside of the practices of marriage, particularly love within troublesome contexts, not exotic or heavenly places, but among the poor and amid disagreements and sin. Modern romantics set the meaning of love in the face-to-face wonder of wedding vows, but the Gospels use the image of the wedding banquet, as a place to deal with themes of hospitality and hope for the downtrodden. Love is characterized as a turning around for the unfortunate, as healing, generosity, and most of all, as forgiveness and reconciliation. Grace and forgiveness are basic to the theological drama of love. The stage is not the discrete context of interpersonal love but relationships of the human family and the practical matters of living well in community. The household, in this setting, is where life, love, and sexual union are ordered to common goods and to God. Christian love, from the start, begins outside of me and you, but when contemporary theology conceives of the "Me and You" as *the* original context of love, it has difficulty bringing love and sexual desire back from the impractical and otherworldly sphere of modern romance.

The modern problem of love, then, is a question of its location. Where is the dwelling place of love? When modern personalism sets love in the interpersonal Self-to-Self, it sets love outside broader social and economic constraints. Inter-subjective love is protected within the private harmony of idealized lovers. Modern accounts typically avoid, and preclude, an understanding of love as emerging from the complexities and ambiguities of social life or as a "product" of cultural and economic reproduction. This and the following chapters provide an inquiry about the places and context where sex and love take on meaning and purpose. How are sexual desire and passion produced by the dominant market economy? And how do our common conceptions of sex and love reproduce the forms of desire that perpetuate market and contractual relations? What, in contrast, are the contours of sex and love when set within the context of neighborhood reciprocity, community endeavors,

and household management? How is love formed within the local
economies of neighborhood and household?

John Chrysostom's alternative to the city

John Chrysostom, the fourth-century pastor and theologian, provides a representative example for inquiry about the household.
Chrysostom has become important in recent theology, particularly
his conception of family as domestic church.[20] He offers contemporary theologians a better fit with modern conceptions of marriage
than the historically dominant Augustinian tradition. Augustine's
emphasis on goods external to personal love, namely procreation,
fidelity, and the dissolubility of marriage, led the Western tradition
into the twentieth century, but his influence has waned in the wake
of modern interpersonal concerns. Chrysostom is attractive because
he is less negative about sexual desire and more positive about
conjugal love. His account of marriage appears better suited to the
recent theologies of marriage, which hold that the complementary
union of husband and wife is the foundation of family.[21] Upon close
reading, Chrysostom hardly offers us an account of interpersonal
love. He calls, instead, for household management to be oriented
to the Christian life, to virtue and duty, and set over against the
excesses and self-indulgence of the city.

As a pastor in fourth-century Antioch, John Chrysostom could
not help but speak to issues of the Roman and Christian household.
He was concerned with the Christian family as an alternative and a
hope for a libertine city that walks past its poor and ravishes the
souls of its rich in bacchanalian excess.[22] When denouncing lavish
wedding banquets, he appeals to the common sense, not only of
Antiochene Christians, but of citizens generally. "You are marrying
your wife for the procreation of children and for moderation of life;
what is the meaning of these drunken parties with their lewd and
disgraceful behavior?"[23] As different as John's time is from ours,
much seems familiar. By and large, it is probably more important
for us that wedding receptions be raucous than for them to be
hospitable to strangers. Memorable receptions are expensive and
exclusive affairs.

John's common sense about marriage (for procreation and a
moderation of life) might appear too crass. He lacks our contemporary elevation of romance and seems to reduce marriage to its social

and practical utility. "Honey, will you marry me? You are from good stock and show promise for a harmonious, efficient home." The proposal sounds ridiculous, but if we dare to be honest, household management and child rearing might be closer than exuberant dancing is to the realities of our marriages. While we are inclined to disparage married life for its tedium, countless couples continue to spend their Saturdays watching kids play soccer and their evenings reclining before the television. Do we desire the tedium that we say we hate? Insofar as Chrysostom honors the settled home, his understanding of marriage and home will resonate with some modern proponents of "family values". He seems to picture the household as moral and spiritual sanctuary, a haven of values and social stability. But, we should be careful. His appeal to home ought not resonate too clearly, for as much as Chrysostom was for the Christian household, he was also against the "family values" of his time.

John Chrysostom is concerned to distinguish Christian households from the excessive desires of his home city.[24] He lives in a world where marriage is used as social and economic collateral, a means for maintaining wealth and securing status and social station for good-citizen families. In John Chrysostom's view, the wealth and revelry of the city, of which respectable marriages are very much a part, divide people from God and from each other. We moderns are quick to applaud Chrysostom when he tells men not to seek money when they are about to take a bride, that marriage is a fellowship and union of love, not a business deal.[25] While marriages were arranged for economic and social purposes through to the modern era, we tend to see ourselves differently. Even in the late Middle Ages when a young man might seek out his own bride, however love struck he might be (if he might be at all), it was left to his parents to make binding arrangements through legal and financial haggling.[26] Such intrusions into love are a disgrace in the modern world, so that we are able to look down (happily) on millionaires like Donald Trump, who are rich and famous but unable to commit themselves to marriage without a prenuptial contract. Immersed in money, nothing in their lives is safe from it.

Despite modern hopes to the contrary, personal attractiveness, romance, and marriage are imbued with social and economic meaning. We tend to think about marriage and family in terms of love, trust, communication, and shared interests.[27] Both contemporary

theology and typical self-help manuals depend upon these interpersonal skills for the foundation of a good marriage, and it would
be absurd to find fault with them. Who would be against love and
friendship? For moderns, the home provides a haven outside merely
pragmatic relationships and economic self-interest.[28] Financial
difficulties might challenge our happiness (e.g., he spends, I want to
save) and other values of family (e.g., it is hard to make time for each
other between work and the kids), but money is not considered an
essential part of a loving relationship. It is considered loveless to say
that I want to marry a woman partly because of her potential for
economic advancement, but the fact of the matter is that our social
and economic currency is as much of who we are as our haircuts,
tastes in music, and personal philosophies of life. In a world as
economically determined as ours, it is simply self-deception to think
that attractiveness, interpersonal skills, likes and dislikes are somehow distinct from our inherited social status and our economic
prospects. The amount of money we spend on our personal presentation and appearance belies any claim otherwise. Economic and
social status, however, go far deeper than looks. Our humor,
posture, vocabulary, personal morality, and how we wear our
ambitions are all class cues. Our likes, interests, and identity situate
us on a social and economic hierarchy.[29]

Marriage and family continue to be strategic ventures as we negotiate our social-economic world. If the modern American family is
"free-floating", then its variability and independence are due (at
least partly) to economic conditions that require this free-floating
adaptability. Modern marriage and family cannot be explained
apart from economic and social contingencies, and how these
pressures bear upon cultural inheritance and the like.[30] For example,
working-class families at the beginning of the industrial era were
typically large, in order to sustain a home economy and, at the same
time, to increase the number of wage earners outside the home. The
middle class, on the other hand, was likely to keep offspring to a
minimum in order to invest in education and other requisites for
upward mobility. According to Stephanie Coontz, "reorganization
of family became a means of redistributing economic, political, and
moral duties. Gender differences and new definitions of sexuality
emerged as a major organizing force in society at large and an
increasingly salient aspect of self-identification for individuals."[31]
We should add that the independence of individuals from marriage,

of the nuclear from the extended family, of family from neighborhood, and of sex from procreative responsibilities has been economically advantageous as well. The predominant forms of modern family serve the dominant economy.

For the upwardly mobile, freedom from the household (for men as well as women) is freedom to be bound to the demands of a career. Contemporary forms of sex, love, and family continue to be means of social reproduction, and means of protecting and conveying status and advancement. The difference now is that the modern family, in order to be socially reproductive, operates much like a business or corporation. In order to be economically viable, the modern corporation must be free from anything but contractual attachments to its employees, managers, and local communities. Corporate heads lay off workers and relocate production with great angst. But, as difficult as moving to a cheaper labor market is, they must be responsible to investors. Likewise, in the twentieth century, families began to be created and dissolved in less than a generation – by the kinship equivalent of mergers, bankruptcy, and buyouts. Individuals, in our world, have the astounding power (and burden) to establish and disestablish familial bonds, to attach and detach themselves by legal contract or by force of will if need be. Home is supposed to be where one's heart is, but because the heart can be fragile, we know the benefits of love's independence and adaptability. Family, within the constraints of our contractual economy, is defined by its affective pleasures and its usefulness, both of which are temporary and contingent on personal needs.

In short, our preferences for detachment and independence serve a larger economic and social form. Why is it that families so easily relocate and divide for purposes of higher education and career? How is it that we could imagine a different way? In his time, John Chrysostom gained a critical perspective by looking outside the city. John himself came to his leadership among the Christians of Antioch after six years in the desert, and the life of desert ascetics continued to weigh upon him and his hope for the Christian household. Marriage, in Antioch, represented the norms of the empire, and desert chastity was a relatively new and controversial alternative.[32] From the desert came new ways to organize common life. With the monastic life as a model, Chrysostom "elevated the Christian household so as to eclipse the ancient city."[33] In his *On Virginity*, he gives marriage and monastic self-discipline the same rationale, "to reduce the baseness of our soul and to lead it to perfect virtue."[34] "For even one dwelling in a city may imitate the self-denial of the monks; yea, one who has a wife, and is busied in a household, may pray, and fast, and learn compunction . . . [showing] forth the piety of the occupiers of the deserts . . ."[35] In Chrysostom's view, marriage is good when directed to this end, but sexual continence is better – as human beings are good but the angels better.[36] "Virginity makes angels out of us," insofar as we are made free, like angels, to stand before God continuously and serve him.[37]

John Chrysostom's preference for abstinence is likely to disturb typically modern sensibilities. It is a common claim, in our time, that sexual pleasure is a basic necessity for true human fulfillment. This modern form of sexual orthodoxy imposes its own forms of sexual restrictions.[38] The virgins among us, for instance, are often considered immature, less worldly-wise, and incomplete selves. Those who grow old without "sexual experiences" are believed to have been denied a key feature of any truly good life. John's preference for virginity may strike us as odd, but the oddness of it may offer a new way to understand what we do. We need not take up his asceticism, but we may benefit from his critical attitude toward the city. Taking a perspective outside the city among the desert virgins, Chrysostom offers us the insight that sexual expression carries the logic of social life. The role and meaning of our sexual desires will cohere with our social and economic impulses. Chrysostom's preference for virginity and the church's call for some to live a celibate life cannot be reduced to personal options or set of lifestyle choices. They cohere with the social fabric of a community. Sexual practices carry a social form.

Theologically, John Chrysostom locates the beginning of marriage, along with the beginning of the city, after the exile from Eden. By doing so, he redefines the civic common sense that he used earlier against revelry of wedding banquets (i.e., the commonsense view that marriage is for household management and the generation of good citizens).[39] Christian marriage, John proposes, is primarily for the purpose of avoiding fornication, restraining desire, practicing chastity, and living well before God.[40] If a good marriage is characterized by good household management, the household will be oriented to the city of God. Here, John's shift from civic marriage to desert piety is obvious; "for like a dam, marriage gives us an opportunity for legitimate intercourse and in this way contains the flood of sexual desire. It deposits us in a calm sea and watches over us."[41] In effect, the household ought to cohere with the tranquility of the desert soul, resting in friendship with God and with the peace of those pure in heart. Within the household, sexual desire can be oriented to the harmony of common living.

Chrysostom's desert attitude is directed not so much against sex as it is against the constraints imposed by our desires, our desires for riches as much as for sexual pleasure. "Sex is not evil," he holds, "but it is a hindrance to someone who desires to devote all her strength to a life of prayer."[42] He takes a common ascetic view that sexual desire, like the love of luxury, is liable to bind us to worldly troubles. Likewise, Chrysostom believes that the household ought to be directed to God's peace rather than the wrangling that comes with the pride of the well-to-do and the corruption that reigns in the city.[43] Chrysostom understands sexual desire (*eros*) as a positive force which binds a man and a woman in unity. Desire is a way that creation leads us to love. Chrysostom holds that the working of *eros* within us is completed in the affection, honor, and friendship (*agape*) of common life.[44] For John, marriage is a mystery of love; that is to say, it is a mystery of Christ and the church (Eph. 5.32). Life in Christ does not exclude desire but directs it to the unity of the social body.

John does not hold that interpersonal love *produces* a marriage, but that marital love *is constituted* within a social body, founded upon a more fundamental embodiment of the church and by social relations (duties and obligations), which are the fabric of love. Chrysostom advises suitors to seek a spouse of good virtue. He assumes that if the roles of husband and wife are performed well, harmony and love will take root and abound.[45] He calls members of the household to attach themselves through a love that requires detachment from the city. In a homily on Matt. 25.31–41, John emphasizes his usual themes of prayer and a life dedicated to God. To this, he adds not only the customary exhortations based on Matt. 25, such as service to the poor, feeding the hungry, and visiting the sick. He also adds a call to imitate Christ, to see Christ in the poor of the city and to follow them in Christ's poverty: to accept injustice without revenge, to reject envy and hatred, and to lower ourselves from our lives of luxury. Although Chrysostom's asceticism is distant from us in many ways, we can profit from his distance from the city and his attempt to relocate the household and to redefine its social significance. Chrysostom looks to the household as a social embodiment of faithfulness, in the household of God.

Conclusion

John Chrysostom's desert perspective provides critical distance from the social economy of Antioch. From the outside, it is clear to him that Antiochene practices of marriage and household simply sustain the polity of what he understood as a profligate city. Modern conditions are quite different insofar as the economy and social contract are generated and sustained outside the home, but the relation between desire and the city are much the same. Like the market economy and nation-state politics, typically modern conceptions of love, sex, and family are formed outside the home as well. Few of us would claim to learn what to desire from the pages of *Glamour* magazine, but our poor Dahlia and Alex reveal a common contradiction between love and home. Romantic love begins and is cultivated outside the household – in pleasurable and friendly places of trade and consumption. The dating-scene and common meeting places, for instance, are market landscapes (e.g., malls, movie theaters, and restaurants).[46] Coming from the outside, romantic love is expected to provide a foundation for the home; yet, on the other hand, marriage and family life are expected to deaden passion and the vitality of love. Within the modern economy of desire, the household is our desert. If John Chrysostom looks from the polity of the desert in order to criticize the city and citizen-household, the next two chapters will critique modern sex and love from the economy of home.

2

Sexual Desire

Introduction

In a recent television ad for the Honda Civic car, we observe a young man captivated by several women in bikinis. He is walking through what seems to be a deserted parking lot, and they are playing volleyball on the beach. Walking straight but mesmerized by the women on his right he bumps into a Civic (which appears as suddenly to the TV viewer as it does to our young man). Once he makes contact with it, he is enthralled. Without taking his eyes off it, he makes his way around the sporty sedan. Walking backwards while staring at the Civic, he bumps into a young woman in a bikini. Women on the beach or a Civic, they produce the same fascination and desire.

The commercial reminds me of the classic Corvette ads featuring a busty blonde sitting on the hood of the car. It might seem that the message is, "Buy the car, get the girl,"[1] but the Honda commercial reveals the subtlety of market desire. These ads evoke a code of desire where feelings of longing and impulses of unfulfilled desire are transferable. The Corvette and Civic ads use the image of sexual desire to conjure up a set of feelings. Once sexual yearning is produced, the ads create a sense that we are missing something we could have. The point is not "Buy the car, get the girl," but "You lack the car, you lack the girl." "You do not have the new Honda, and your desires are unfulfilled." The ads trade on producing a frustrated desire.

While Chapter 1 has raised questions about social and economic landscapes of love and marriage, this chapter considers the sexual grammar of our dominant economy of desire. The man who is captivated by women, bikinis, and Honda Civics is a representative image of this economy. Volumes could be written about the automobile (in American culture) as an always moving place-in-itself, as a means to rebel against convention, and as a romantic transport to other worlds.[2] This chapter regards modern sexual desire as precisely the same. The first part of the chapter considers the anxiousness of prevailing forms of desire and their connection to a typically modern conception of self. The second part deals with a common theological account that attempts to stabilize the sexual self, and in the process, to secure marriage as the basic location of desire and the true self. In the end, I criticize this common approach insofar as its understanding of sexual communication transcends everyday problems and opportunities of living together, enduring another's bodily presence, and sharing tasks of the home. Like the migratory economy of desire, the typical personalist account of marriage isolates a deep personal truth in the sexual act-in-itself. It continues to define desire over against home. This and the following chapter on love suggest that a wider conception of the household economy is required to make good sense of love, marriage, and sex.

An economy of sexual desire

Contentment is a problem for modern conceptions of sex and sexual desire. Sex is considered a basic expression of the true self, and sexual experiences and fulfillment are goods of life for which we struggle and strive. Virginity, in comparison, is more likely to bring embarrassment than honor. The age is gone when people will not own up to their sexual activity.[3] We are obliged, it seems, to worry about our sexual fulfillment, if we hope to be healthy, mature, and whole. In the prevailing sexual market, fulfillment does not last long. Once comfortable and content, we are inclined to worry that we have lost our sexual drive. In short, sex is necessary to the contemporary self, and we are necessarily anxious about it.[4] Most people would disagree with the claim that "sex *ought to be* unsettling." Most would hold, on the contrary, that sex ought to be pleasurable and free. Nonetheless, pleasure and freedom bind sex in their own way. Our culture tends to conceive of sexual pleasure not as bringing calm but as increasing excitement and desire. Sex is bound to be restless.

In the prevailing economy of desire, moments of satisfying pleasure ought to give way to a need for more, so that common standards of good sex are frequency, technique, and the power of pleasure to create a need for more. Years ago, a common boast among my school buddies was to have "done it." Now, a common brag among couples my age is to have "done it all night long." This thirty-something boast strikes me as odd, as something equivalent to a thirty-eight-year-old father bragging about drinking too much. He would not wear the excess well. Likewise, would not a deep and contented sleep be the best end to a satisfying sexual encounter? The boast of repeated orgasm seems out of place among those in the settled life of marriage until we note that being "settled" is precisely the problem. Marital familiarity, routine, and a secure sense of belonging bring a sense of satisfaction that threaten the vitality of sex. Sex, amid home life, becomes domesticated rather than free; comfortable rather than exciting. A criterion of the healthy sexual bond, within and outside of marriage, is frequency. Need is a measure of health.[5]

According to a contemporary truism, sex is best (i.e., most pleasurable) when new and unexplored. Novelty is a critical feature, for instance, in Alan Soble's philosophical defense of what he calls the pleasure model of sex.[6] His connection between pleasure and novelty is simple. If our own pleasure is central to the meaning of sex, then sexual interaction with another person ought to bring some set of experiences or sensations to us that we are not accustomed to having. In other words, Soble argues that masturbation is essentially the same as paired sex except that we are more likely to become bored with ourselves. "The allure of touching the other," he holds, "lies in its novelty."[7] Because self-stimulation is essentially the same as paired sexual pleasure, the allure of masturbation might lie in innovation as well. Soble suspects that "men and women are ingenious in devising new methods for masturbating, to produce either new sensations or old sensations in new ways."[8] However, even when not a new sensation, masturbation remains, for Soble, a paradigmatic sexual experience on a par with sexual relationships. He defines all sexual pleasure as an autoerotic experience. Sex is defined by personal sensations. By describing sex this way, Soble gives weight to the notion that "good sex" requires new techniques, new partners, or new sexual dramas. If a person is not seeking out novel pleasures, he or she is better off alone.

Soble holds that autoerotic monotony might be quite pleasurable, insofar as some people gain pleasure from receiving sensations that they know they like best. Who knows what a person likes and how to attain it better than the individual himself? If efficiency and consistency are pleasurable, then masturbation is the most effective route to satisfying one's desires. According to Soble, sex between long-term partners might be interesting in an analogous, but derivative way. The touch of another might become as familiar, direct, and effective as touching oneself.[9] In this case, paired sex is an extended version of masturbation. A couple's sexual routine is likely to be more of a bother than autoerotic stimulation and more likely to fail in achieving its goal because the relationship will bring extra-sexual complications. Masturbation is superior inasmuch as it is straightforward in its orientation to pleasure.

Soble's defense of masturbation might strike the reader as sensationalist and unusual, but his arguments are philosophically sophisticated, and he is not looking to be merely provocative. If sexual relationships bring pleasure, Soble argues, they will bring something new within the sexual experience itself. His account of autoerotic practices is not ordinary, but he uses the argument to present very common understandings of sexual pleasure, excitement, novelty, and the boredom of routine. His analysis seeks to be careful, open, and honest about pleasure. He challenges us to think about sexual pleasure with consistency and to overcome the illogic of our unexamined traditions and social conventions. Why, he asks, is masturbation considered either shameful or a joke when it is so common and so commonly enjoyed? Soble wants to make our theories of sexuality consistent with our practices. In doing so, he articulates a basic sexual grammar of popular culture. Pleasure is central to sex and fulfills personal desire. Desire is enlivened by novelty and adventure; therefore, sexual pleasure is constantly threatened by domestication, boredom, and marriage, which is by definition sexual monotony. Exclusive sex between an exclusive pair is characterized by a lack of novelty and best suited to those who are not interested in sex at all, to those content with married life. Settled sex is for the sexless.[10]

Because sexual desire is enlivened by the new and improved, dissatisfaction is key to this grammar of good sex. The need for novel pleasures is accompanied by a need for ceaseless sexual yearning, so that if a person is contented, he or she ought not be. In an age of access, sexual interest and excitement are depressed by the availability of one's sexual partner. "When you get comfortable with your lover, you feel as though you can get laid whenever you want.

And that's the problem."[11] Vigorous sexual relationships require a healthy bit of sexual tension and frustration, in order to "put the thrill of first-time sex into your long-term lovemaking." The meaning and power of sex come with the question, "Will she or won't she?", with the "thrill of the chase," with "the feeling of being all sexed up with nowhere to go." Good sex requires that we re-create situations of discomfort and the frustration of unconsummated passion.[12]

Those skeptical of this advice should take note: it comes from purported experts, from Barbara Keesling, Ph.D., and Susan Block, Ph.D., both seasoned sex therapists and successful authors. Whatever their credentials, they make a good living giving advice. Block is a radio talk-show host and author of *The Ten Commandments of Pleasure*,[13] and Keesling is author of several books, including *Getting Close: A Lover's Guide to Embracing Fantasy and Heightening Sexual Connection*.[14] Both authors deal with the problem of sexual malaise, with the loss of desire, and a lack of interest in sex. They consider this lack of interest the most prominent and formidable challenge to "healthy" sex.

Block's ten commandments offer a set of rules for couples who have let their sexual infatuation fade. "They have kids, work gets hard, life gets tough, reality sets in. And they let love die."[15] Block does not shy away from making a clear connection between sexual pleasure and love. Love is passion. Block holds that a loss of desire is natural to lasting relationships, so that the natural course of relationships is also a loss of love. A natural disconnection sets in amid the tasks and trials of everyday life. The tenor of all her commands is to relocate a couple's relationship back to the pre-sexual, pre-relationship stage. The key to passion's revival is to begin a sexual encounter that will end in frustration. Foreplay in public is a good idea. Block suggests that "deliberately planning activities that preclude sex [will send] the old tension tingle down his spine." A weekend visit to grandmother's house can become "a frenzied game of musical chairs."[16]

In *Getting Close*, Barbara Keesling endeavors to help women sensitize themselves to sex, to the end that they can sensitize their partners as well. She tells the story of fading desire as a loss of the sexual self. "Every woman I know," Keesling points out, "wishes she had a more vital connection to her sexual self, and a more vibrant connection to her loving partner."[17] Keesling proposes that the real sexual self is already within, but, at the same time, she also assumes that a loss of self is a universal problem. A woman *ought to* worry if she is satisfied with a sexual relationship that is merely good enough. So much more is possible; she ought not be content. Keesling outlines a regime of sexual training in order to remake the sexual self: first autoerotic techniques, then fantasy, and finally sharing the newfound eroticism with one's partner. First, the initial autoerotic techniques train and pique the senses. In this stage, Alan Soble's theory of sex turns out to be true. Second, lessons in fantasy cultivate the sexual imagination and produce sexual frustration, using a method that Keesling calls "Fantastius Interuptus."[18] In the final stage, a woman brings her partner into her realm of unfulfilled desire.

When all is said, sex, particularly for women, is hard work.[19] While sex is assumed to be natural and basic to the self, one must labor to reproduce desire. Men's magazines and popular literature on sex diverge from this sexual work ethic to the degree that they develop an ethics of access. A recurring theme, here, is the fantasy of the extraordinary woman who *wants* sex from average guys. She is ready, and she desires to give access to all men. Along with this theme of effortless sex, a complementary (or contradictory) work ethic for men pertains to fashion, body, and ways to get what you want (i.e., sex) from women. The male sexual ethic is directed to creating opportunity and access to otherwise resistant women, who continue to be responsible for the greater measure of sexual work. In magazines for women as well as men, women are objects of sexual desire. *Mademoiselle* and *Cosmopolitan* are clear in their advice to women: you will not become properly sexualized without careful self-analysis and adaptation. You must make yourself desirable. For men, sex is both ordinary and an achievement; for women, it is both achievement and tool.

Three broad themes of this sexual work immediately come into view. First, work, mainly for a woman, is required to have sexual desire or to be in touch with one's inner passion. Often, no explicit reason is given for the need to feel sexy or to be sexy, but it is implied always that sexual desire makes life happier, contributes to one's well-being, and is necessary for mental health. Sexual labor can be pleasurable in itself insofar as the work is directly linked to consumption. Sexual work is usually tied to a product, sometimes a type of product like lipstick and sometimes a company (e.g., www.salsafreak.com), but more often than not a specific name-brand is part of the pitch. "Let your skin shine. Rub on glimmery flecks of rosy gold with warm, floral-scented Lancôme Huile Pollen Shimmering Face and Body Oil."[20] It is important to note that these endorsements do not make vulgar connections between cosmetics and catching a man or woman. These products help us get in touch with our inner passion.

The second theme follows. Once passion is cultivated within, it must be sustained in sexual relationships through careful attention to one's own behavior and environment. A woman can direct a man's behavior, and vice versa, through certain actions that will invite desired reactions. Perhaps, a liaison will be as easy as "learn[ing] how to spot the woman who wants you for your body – and just for tonight."[21] However, in the main (and particularly for women), hard work and care are required to ensure the vitality of sexual relationships. Oddly, we must learn to be conscious of our sexual dynamics in order to try "just acting on our erotic impulses."[22] What comes naturally does not come naturally to us. If being intentionally impulsive is not contradictory enough, various techniques are offered to help us conjure up or produce natural impulses.[23] Techniques for inciting passion are matched by techniques for enhancing the sexual exchange: such methods as baths and massages for example. Sexual techniques allow a flight from the ordinary, like stripping your bedroom of personal items and adding expensive sheets and a bottle of champagne in order to create a hotel atmosphere.[24] It is best to pretend to be away from home.

Finally, sex is part of an over-all strategy. A sexual relationship has its own narrative progression that will either parallel the romantic relationship or run at cross-purposes. While men seem to be concerned with methods for enhancing sexual relationships, women are often advised to use sex as a means, as a tool, for cultivating romance. The surprising news from a *Mademoiselle* readers' poll is that a woman would do well to wait ten dates before sex, although she will have to wait much longer for "I love you."[25] On one hand, sex is enticement, but on the other, one should cultivate friendship and romantic love first. Sex does good work, but it has to be used with good timing and style.

How much credence should we give to the sexual landscape of sex therapists and philosophers like Alan Soble?[26] Or a better question: How seriously does anyone consider their advice and assumptions about sex? Some readers, perhaps, do accept this sexual world at face value, but it is likely that most give critical consideration to magazines, sexual self-help, and various popular attitudes toward sex. For the sake of argument, it is best to assume, it seems to me, that most people do not see themselves in what they read but, nevertheless, see something worth reading. How to interpret popular culture remains an open question, as I realized after my wife told me that our neighbors, married with children, secured a babysitter and drove out to a quiet road a few nights ago in order to have sex in their truck. Excitement for some and discomfort for others, their sexual adventure is definitely something to talk about. The draw of the sex experts may be their wisdom (who knows?), but I expect that most take their advice in good humor. Even if most readers take a superior attitude, even if we set ourselves above the techniques and hapless people who need such help, we still enjoy reading about it.

In other words, the sexual landscape of contemporary culture is a market, for entertainment and consumption, pleasure and play. Although popular culture is *just* a market and not necessarily true to what people do or believe about sex, the market is shaped by a public grammar of sexual desire that taps basic modern truths: sex is exciting, good, fun, healthy, ephemeral, and elusive. Sex dies in the routines of home. This sexual grammar is constituted by a market that overlaps and fits with other markets, such as TV, film, music, publishing, cyberspace, travel, cosmetics, clothes, jewelry, beer, food, liquor, and sports. Most of these products and markets also tap into our desires for ephemeral and elusive pleasures. Elusive pleasures and experiences can be had in the product, in low-fat chocolate cookies, through exotic vacations, or in giving a diamond ring to a lover. There is nothing out of the ordinary about the prevailing landscape and language of sexual activity; it is simply market time and space. Consumer capitalism is less about what we have and more about desire for what we lack.[27]

Market space is nomadic, and its time is short, so that sexual relationships can never be vital at home, where common life is stabilized, domesticated, and extended over time. The household is a subsistence economy, where relationships flourish in an equilibrium that does not depend upon a search for novel pleasures and new sexual experiences. In market time and place, desires for pleasure and sexual fulfillment will be characterized by a powerful anxiety about what we lack, about gaining access to what we do not have. We need to keep up with new possibilities for enjoyment. Restlessness in this regard is essential to sexual vitality, so that a contented couple *ought to be* anxious about the loss of passion. Their enduring relationship, they ought to expect, has deadened their desire for more desire. Thank goodness for Viagra. Notice that romantic and passionate places are usually contrived, through weekend getaways, fantasy, and make-believe hotel rooms. We must escape the home or be sexually lifeless. We must invent the unexplored in order to locate sex in novel places.

The dominant economy of desire unsettles the self. The migratory character of desire is produced by a contradiction of our freedom. Contemporary access, availability, and freedom of expression must be protected; otherwise desire is constrained. Yet, settled partners are too accessible; they share their bodies too readily, and they are open to each other too freely. Something must be withheld; new terrain must be explored. The invention of novel pleasures begins from within, with an ever elusive sexual self. To be vital, desire must wander about homeless, so that domesticated relationships will have to "carry" desire internally, in each person's capacity for new sensuous delight, in his or her deep passion center. That is to say, sexuality will be located in the unexplored depths of the individual psyche and not, first of all, in the social space of everyday life. Likewise, sexual consummation seems to have no real "sexual" time. Orgasm is a timeless moment. The movement of desire is sustained by striving through unfulfilled moments of passion.

When characterizing modern sexuality, historian Philippe Ariès presents similar contradictions.[28] First, he suggests that there is no discrete domain of sexuality but a pan-sexuality, inasmuch as sex has become an element in all spheres of life. Economic transactions, politics, and the workplace, if not imbued with sexual tensions, are porous and susceptible to the advance of sexual power. Ariès' second suggestion is that sex stands alone in its own sexual sphere. No longer bound to procreation or the household, or to friendship and love, sexual desire is free to pursue its own end. According to Ariès, sex is understood to be the "consummation of the deepest urges, allowing a man and woman to experience total fulfillment during the moment, lived like an eternity, of the orgasm."[29]

Ariès is pointing to a modern love for and democratization of sheer pleasure, but he may be offering too much clarity here.

Although orgasm and sexual pleasure are objects of veneration, the "consummation of [our] deepest urges" is more elusive, and total fulfillment more vague than the physical stimulation of orgasm. Sexual fulfillment is an aimless, liminal moment. It is assumed to defy utility and convention. It happens in an instant, and then it is gone. Insofar as fulfillment is elusive, sexual expression has been attached not so much to attainable pleasure but to a quest for the inner self.[30] Passion is a means of being personally connected, but it is seldom sustained naturally. Insofar as sex stands alone, its fulfillment is more distant than near. The consummation of our sexual desire stands over against us, characterized more by a lack of fulfillment than satisfaction.

The contradiction of contemporary sexuality is this: When sex pervades everything, something is missing from all. Making sense of this contradiction is not a manageable endeavor, but much can be gained by understanding the migratory character of modern sex, its homelessness and the fact that our sexual desire turns into dissatisfaction when it finds a resting place, when we find a home. In our time, sex is considered a birthright of sorts (perhaps a human right) insofar as sexual expression is considered a fundamental and unavoidable aspect of personal identity. Sex is more important than ever. It is good in itself. Sexual expression is self-expression, and to deny sex is to deny ourselves. However, it is not necessary for any given sexual encounter to express "who we really are." Sexual expression does not require personal investment; sex may leave us hollow, bored, used, abused, or frustrated. None of these mishaps undermines sexual desire, on the contrary. Less than complete, we are simply set on the road to needing more.

The economy of marriage and home

The practices of marriage represent an alternative to the dominant cultural codes of sex and desire. According to predominant conventions, sexual desire, by its very nature, defies domestication. Sexual vitality is believed to be unsettling and ill-suited to home. Recent theology, whether conservative or liberal, cannot help but highlight basic differences from the prevailing sexual economy. Marriage, in theological terms, is thought to illuminate the essential meaning and natural ends of sexual intercourse. Sex is never "just sex," and desire is never just desire for its own sake. Within the thought and practices of the church, sexual activity is shaped by our desires for unity with another person and by the duties and gifts that come with sharing our lives. In contrast to the market form of desire, marriage sets the meaning of sex within the environment and practices of housekeeping. In this context, sexual vitality has less to do with novel pleasures and more to do with sitting together at the kitchen table and sharing a meal. It has less to do with exotic night spots and more to do with sharing a bed night after night, year after year. Sex is our bodily coming to belong with another who knows us like no other. Sexual relationships have less to do with fleeting moments and more to do with the passage of time. Marriage, in short, sets our desires in household time and place.

One of the main concerns of contemporary theology is to consider the true meaning of sex in terms of the interpersonal unity of marriage. Interpersonal unity implies the procreative goods of marriage, as well as our full sharing of life, opens us to the creativity of love. Each act of sexual intercourse is invested with meaning that transcends the mere physical union of bodies. Sex is regarded as symbolic of a more deeply personal (i.e., spiritual, social, and psychological) relationship. In a word, sexual activity is considered an expression of the "whole" person.[31] Likewise, sexual desire is thought to be emblematic of our desire for "wholeness."[32] "What we yearn for sexually is a symbolic representation of what we need in order to become whole."[33] This yearning, then, is associated with the institution of marriage: with an enduring commitment, faithfulness, and an intimate sharing of life.[34] When I am moved by passion, I want to give my whole life to my beloved, and I want to receive my loved one fully. Sexual desire moves us toward a complete unity of selves.

The chief problem in this personalist account of sex is, not that it goes wrong, but that it says too much to be right. Every sexual act is defined as full and total, so that sex has no room to be ordinary. The act of sexual intercourse, in this theological framework, transcends its particular meaning in time, in order to reveal the complete contours of our two-in-one-flesh humanity. With this total union of body and spirit, sexual relationships are lifted out of the everyday activities of marriage. The everyday meaning of sex, in contrast, is extended through the day-to-day ebb and flow of common endeavors, joys, and struggles of love in the home. Not in an instant, but over time, we come to belong. In this regard, no sexual act represents a total self or full relationship. Rather, what we do today gains its meaning in relation to yesterday and what we will do tomorrow. For sex to have depth, it needs extended bodily communication over time. The transcendent personalist account, on the other hand, runs ahead of the day-to-day. Every act is understood to ritualize "a fully shared life" and the "total self-giving" of spouses.[35] This ritual context suits a honeymoon or anniversary day consummation, but I dare to say that our everyday bodily presence is far more subtle and patient. Those who believe sex is earth shattering will put it out of marriage.

Premarital sexuality

The category of "premarital" makes little sense to many contemporary considerations of sexual ethics. Alan Soble, as noted above, makes the category of self-directed pleasure fundamental, but most focus on the values or structure of a relationship.[36] Moral philosophers tend to ask questions like, "Does the sexual relationship provide an honest interchange of self?" or "Is the relationship characterized by equality and respect?" These questions are not believed to divide marital from premarital sex. It is certainly imaginable, for instance, that sex outside of marriage could be honest, while a husband and wife could be deceiving each other. Sex in marriage is not always good; this point is common sense. Nevertheless, the divide between premarital and marital sex remains critical for the theology of marriage. The "pre" of premarital sex obviously points to sex before marriage, but in a broader sense, "premarital" sex represents a basic instance of "non-marital" intercourse. Non-marital sex is practiced outside the socially established commitments of marriage, and it is vague, at best, about its communal responsibilities and its lines of social support. The description "premarital" says something else about non-marital sexual activity. Sex-before-marriage suggests that sexual activity precedes a commitment of partners to share their whole lives. Theologically, an emphasis on sex within marriage implies the opposite. A self-giving of partners comes before, and makes possible, the fullness of sexuality. The categories of "premarital" and "marital" sex are fundamental to how the theological tradition thinks of sex in terms of a fully shared life and the total self-giving of husband and wife.

This theological framework is synthesized and represented well by Vincent Genovesi, in his *In Pursuit of Love*.[37] Perceptively, Genovesi begins to spell out the relationship between sex and marriage in a chapter titled, "The Issue of Premarital Sexuality." He argues that love is the context for sex, rather than vice versa. He dismisses the notions that sex "makes love" and that sex is evidence of true love. Love is not produced by a sexual relationship, even a long-term one. People share love, but only in certain kinds of loving relationships do we express our love sexually. According to Genovesi, "true love is distinct from physical sex. Genital sex, in other words, is not the primary language or ultimate proof of love; rather, for Christians, the greatest proof of love is caring for others even to the point of self-sacrifice: we have no greater love than to lay down our lives for our friends (John 15.13)."[38] Genovesi makes use of this "laying down our lives" as an index of true love: self-giving. Sex is a distinct kind of self-giving, and as distinctive, it fits with the special character of marital love, in the love which finds "expression in the mutual pledge of a lifelong commitment."[39]

Put strongly, Genovesi holds that the act of sexual intercourse, in itself, implies an enduring, intimate, and sexually exclusive union of spouses. He explains that "the only time sexual intercourse tells the truth is when it signifies that two people have united themselves as one to start a new life together."[40] He supports this claim by describing the human being as a unity of body and spirit. In the modern world, a prevailing dualism sees sexual intercourse "as nothing more than the joining together of two bodies, which can bring happiness and pleasure to the internal occupants of those bodies but which leaves those occupants (the human spirits) largely unaffected."[41] Rejecting this dualism, Genovesi explains that body-to-body contact is the touch of persons. Sex is an activity of the spirit and personality as well. "Sexual intercourse is a sign of total, unreserved giving of self. At the moment of orgasm, the individual's personality is lost in an interpenetration of the other self. Sexual intercourse is expressive of one's person. To be authentic and not a lie it must correspond to the existing relationship between persons."[42] Further, Genovesi connects this sexual self-giving to a permanent or "total" union. It serves to "physically symbolize" a mutual and unconditional responsibility for one another.[43] In sexual intercourse, a partner says, "Not only do I care for you, but I also want to take care of you. Not only do I respond sensitively and

physically to you, but I also want to be responsible for you unconditionally."[44]

Genovesi's connections between sex and marriage are attractive
insofar as they give sexual intercourse an essentially nuptial character. It is important to note once again that Genovesi represents a
common personalist approach to sex and the theology of marriage.
Sexual intercourse is understood as a communication between
persons, where selves are "totally" given and received whether or
not the partners intend to express themselves in this "whole self"
relation. The sexual act is, by definition, total self-giving. When the
partners do not intend to give themselves entirely, the sexual communication is a lie. When a couple does not hope to share a lifelong
covenant, the gift of self is eventually taken back. A cost–benefit
exchange is hidden under the guise of a gift. In premarital sexual
relations, we are making a bodily promise, but refusing to do so
with our full personhood.

This common personalist conception union is deceptively abstract
and figurative rather than concrete. In other words, Genovesi talks
about embodiment, but he is interested almost entirely with the
spiritual meaning that the body symbolizes. He wants to counter a
dualism that imagines sex to be only physical, but he subsumes the
physical into the intangible aspects of a spiritual commitment.
Consider an alternative. Genovesi could have defined the act of
sexual intercourse in reference to a day-to-day bodily presence
between partners. Sex could be defined in the context of sharing a
home, sleeping in the same bed, caring for each other in times of illness, trusting, and desiring each other's non-erotic touch. In short,
sex could be put in the context of sharing an enduring bodily
belonging. This alternative is insufficient for Genovesi because
spreading the meaning of sex over the course of a lifetime does not
lend itself to a clear definition of sexual intercourse in itself. Each act
of sexual intercourse would not have to be "total" self-giving (or
even enjoyable) inasmuch as any married couple has the time and
opportunity to try again next time. Married couples have the freedom to say "that bit of sex was not so good." The "total" is conceived only by looking back over a marriage as a whole. One can say
to the other, "As far as I can tell, we have given all we have." This
option is inadequate for Genovesi insofar as he expects to outline a
single meaning of every sexual act. He gives the body a meaning that
transcends our day-to-day embodiment.

Genovesi and other personalists are quite clear that their understanding of the body is figurative. Sex is understood as a symbol, ritual, and sacrament.[45] By making sex symbolic, a single sexual act is made to represent a lifetime friendship between husband and wife. In fact, the symbolic meaning of the sexual act is narrowed further to genital contact and finally to the moment of orgasm, where we lose ourselves completely in union with another. In line with Philippe Ariès' comments about modern sexual romanticism, sex becomes a distinct sphere of meaning, a liminal moment that transcends time and space. In the instant of orgasm, a complete self-giving is achieved. Certainly, as a symbol or ritual, sexual intercourse is understood to be a concrete physical act, but as a ritual act it is akin to the "I do" of the wedding ceremony. Sex is considered the bodily "I do." It is a defining moment. Ironically, this totalizing moment makes day-to-day sexual embodiment semantically superfluous. Each act of sexual intercourse is assumed to have immense meaning, but a single act carries the meaning of the whole so that continuing embodiment adds nothing. Once a couple proclaims their nuptial "I do's," they will not say the same words in that ritual context again. They might renew their vows or declare their love, but it is not likely that the incredible defining moment of the original "I do" will ever be experienced again. There is only one first night (fortunately for some of us). Genovesi's theory sets everyday embodiment in an impracticable situation. Sex "just because," which is one of the great opportunities of marriage, will never measure up.

When sex is given this transcendent meaning, it is taken out of quotidian life in the household. The apostle Paul proposes that husband and wife should have sexual intercourse "just because" one of them (not necessarily both) is full of pent up desire (1 Cor. 7). Other occasions of "just because" are imaginable: because we can, or we want to. It is part of our routine, or how we belong; we love each other, or we are physically attracted. There is a multiplicity of "meanings" or things that might be communicated through any given sexual act. Some might express spontaneous joy, friendship, or a deep connection. Others might turn out to be melancholy experiences, and important precisely because they express that something is not quite right. Some sexual acts will have a reconciling effect, and it is quite possible that, on occasion, a bit of anger or alienation is revealed. Sex might not fix anything, but be the source of a problem.

The concrete effects of sex within marriage are variable, and the unevenness is not at all a burden or threat to the unity or stability of a sexual relationship. The cumulative effect of the multiple meanings and experiences is that two people share a common life that makes possible a whole range of bodily expressions and a profound sense of bodily presence. In these terms, sexual activity belongs in marriage, not because every sexual act means everything, but because sex says so many things, and isolated acts say so little. Sexual intercourse might, on occasion, have a symbolic import. Given the right circumstances, sex might speak of the whole person and an entire shared life, but as a concrete embodiment, sex means what it happens to mean day to day.

Within Genovesi's framework, my "just because" seems to open the way for sex outside of marriage, but I have turned the criticism around. His personalist theory puts sexual intercourse, in its essence, outside the basic practices of married life, set apart from practices of living side by side, working, managing a home, raising children, and cooperating with neighbors. Although he begins with the claim that a personal relationship precedes and gives meaning to sexual intercourse, he quickly shifts to the "transcendent sexual act" which then symbolically and semantically precedes the actual living out of day-to-day life. Sex is given a "wedding day" and "honeymoon night" context of meaning; it represents an original promise. By contrast, sexual intercourse within marriage is, no doubt, part of the founding promises, but its context is a couple's everyday embodiment. The honeymoon night inaugurates a relationship, but the day-to-day tasks of mutual support and sustaining a home are the real stuff of marriage. These criticisms of Genovesi do not imply that sex in marriage lacks distinction, but only that its meaning cannot be established through an account of sexual intercourse that transcends who we are in our home-bound time and place.

Sharing a home

After Genovesi develops his personalist conception of the sexual act, he turns, somewhat awkwardly, to what he calls social sensitivity. Sensitivity implies concern and responsibility. It is Genovesi's soft term for the fact that marriage is a social institution that carries social roles and makes possible a socially significant friendship between husband and wife. From his notion of social sensitivity follows a sacramental understanding of marriage. This sacramental character within common life means that conjugal love reflects God's enduring faithfulness, conveys that love and grace, and is expressed through a vocation in community.[46] Genovesi's transition to social sensitivity is awkward because he attempts to make this wider social context internal to the meaning of the sexual act in itself, but he actually indicates that his conception of the "transcendent sexual act in itself" is unnecessary. It seems that sex is held together by broader social practices. Social sensitivity "suggests that intercourse should occur within the context of marriage, which is a social institution designed both to assist a couple in living their vocation as lovers and to offer them some protection against the enemies and abuses of love that arise from immaturity and self-centeredness."[47] Here Genovesi widens the landscape, which is what I intend to do mainly in Parts Two and Three of this book. Before that constructive proposal, we will consider the cultural code of romantic love.

3

Romantic Love

Introduction

"What are the essential ingredients for a long, happy marriage?"
When asked this question, psychiatrist Vance Fitzgerald responds
with a pragmatic description that will strike many readers as
nothing less than clinical.[1] According to Fitzgerald, the ideal couple
"must first be blessed with good health, long life, and a normal
aging process. One or both will possess marketable skills so that
their family will enjoy a decent income. They will be able to give
birth or to adopt the number of children they decide they can
accommodate emotionally and financially." Fitzgerald imagines
that the ideal pair will have worked out these details prior to
marriage, with a dispassionate assessment of the prospective
partner's "assets and liabilities" and a sense of marriage as a
contractual agreement. In addition, the spouses will have "approxi-
mately equal intelligence" so that they can share interests and
friends. "Both spouses will have attained the maturity characteristic
of the young adult level by the time they marry," and will be able to
achieve a level of "interpersonal intimacy . . . during the first stage
of their marriage." Fitzgerald's ideal couple "may or may not have
gone through that time limited quasipsychotic state of being 'in
love.' If they have, they recognize it for what it was, at least in retro-
spect, and will value their genuine if less intense affection more."
Each spouse will be able to "count on the other." They "will meet
each other's needs most of the time . . . [and] over time the deep and
genuine affection and respect this happy couple feel toward each
other will tame any hostilities they feel."[2]

Fitzgerald's intended audience, the readers of *Medical Aspects of
Human Sexuality,* will expect scientific detachment from him, but
the rest of us may be troubled by his reference to being "in love" as
a psychological malady. At the same time, we are likely to agree

with his good, common sense. Fitzgerald is asked to describe a "long, happy marriage" not an exciting or romantic one, and we might agree that being in love and happiness are not always the same. Fitzgerald intends to describe a couple whom "most outside observers" would point to as happy. His couple lives a good life. Each attains and secures what he and she want on social, economic and personal levels, and they do so in good company. Each experiences the pleasures of marriage that come with pursuing and attaining a certain kind of life.

Fitzgerald's notions of marital happiness do not make for stimulating reading. He gives us a pair of everyday people with no frills. Their marriage is hardly remarkable. Fitzgerald provides a generally accepted picture of marital happiness, that, to the dismay of many, will not necessarily include what most of us consider the exciting part, the enlivening movements of love. This disconcerting problem will be the focus of the chapter. Similar to the approach of the previous chapter, we will enquire about the dominant social economy of love as passion. Critical to this economy is a desire to establish personal connections, a clear sense of belonging, and a deeper self-knowledge through relationships of love. Like the economy of desire, modern love deals in restlessness and frustration. I am not pointing to a romantic love that is self-sacrificial in the early modern sense.[3] Love as passion, in the contemporary sense, is considered a means to cause commitment, unity, and mutual responsibility. Ironically, it is set against the solidarity that can be had through workaday common endeavors, inasmuch as the goal of love as passion is to sustain its connection through nothing other than the love of connection itself. People are likely to conceive of "relationships" as based, not on a pursuit of common goods, but on the activities of having a relationship as a good in itself. As a sphere of activity and a separate sense of connection, this romantic love does not sit well with us, and it is certainly inhospitable to home.

Looking for love

In her *Consuming the Romantic Utopia*, Eva Illouz asks a random sampling of Americans to respond to three fictional love stories and then to tell about their own most memorable experiences of love.[4] The first fictional story is a romantic drama about a chance meeting on a train, love at first sight, and a precipitous marriage. The second and third stories do not include descriptions of passion or declarations of love. The second tale takes the pattern of an arranged marriage where a man and woman are "matched up" and, after a time, come "to the conclusion that their relationship was good and healthy enough to make a good marriage." The third story tells about two young professionals who date for a few years, seem "to get along well" and feel good together. They decide to marry, and do so after one receives a professional promotion that assures a secure future.[5] When Illouz's interviewees respond to these stories and then tell stories of their own, inconsistency is the persistent theme. They think that practically minded companionship is best, but they want passion.

All of Illouz's respondents recognize the first story as typical Hollywood, as a made-for-television romance, with its immediate attraction and irrational love. Most agree that the romance does not represent real life or true love. They criticize the story as "a myth of love at first sight," which in reality turns out to be an infatuation with undesirable consequences. The second and third stories, by and large, receive a more favorable reading. These stories are considered more consistent with the practical wisdom that love follows out of friendship and that loving relationships require time and work.[6] Illouz's interviews take an unexpected turn, however, when she begins to elicit personal love stories. Although the made-for-television romance is rejected by most as merely fiction, *all* the respondents use its basic pattern as a standard to tell and to judge their own experiences of love.

According to Illouz, the interviewees tell their personal love stories in the compressed time of the contemporary cinema. They tell of immediate attraction and short-lived affairs. They recount romantic adventures "cut off from the entanglements of and connections to everyday life."[7] They speak wistfully of distant events, irrational magnetism, and chance sexual encounters. It is as though they were composing their own fictional tales. Illouz notes the oddness of their romantic standards. The romantic story is recognized as flawed when set in the abstract or experienced by someone else; yet, romance is preferred when the respondents are asked to take the question of love personally. Regardless of their objective standards, the interviewees identify love as mere emotional and psychological intensity.

Illouz argues that this standard of romantic love fits with an economy of consumption, where pleasures are intense and transient. This is an economy of desire, where passionate relationships are sustained by reproducing and extending passion indefinitely. Love arouses the self. The promise of desire is that we will come alive and transcend the ordinary. We will discover a deeper self that is not available in the regular course of life. Illouz points out that this preference for romantic love is incompatible with what continues to be common sense about companionship and happiness. She explains that "the contemporary romantic self is marked by its persistent, sisyphean attempt to conjure up the local and fleeting intensity of the love affair within the long-term global narratives of love (such as marriage) to reconcile an overarching narrative of enduring love with the fragmentary intensity of affairs."[8]

With Illouz's respondents in mind, I went looking for love in the personal ads of *The Washington Post*. I suspected that the personals would give a picture of untamed desires, but I was surprised to find that the personal inquiries and requests are heavily weighted, not toward romance and passion, but on the side of friendship and the long-term relationship (i.e., the LTR). Without a clear sense of the demographics, I had assumed that the personals were a medium for trysts and affairs; not so. Consider the following examples.

> Marriage-minded military officer, 35, 5'8", 140#, seeks Oriental female.
> Handsome Italian SWPM [single, white, professional male] ISO [in search of] dancer/cheerleader type SF, 18+, for wintertime fun and LTR.
> DWCPF [divorced, white, Christian, professional female], 54, loves life, enjoys variety of activities, fit, tired of being alone.
> Attention: SBM [single, black, male], 35 to 40s, w/small kids. SBF w/young child, ISO someone to share activities.
> Attractive BF, 33, seeks tall, professional WM, 35–45, for friendship.[9]

With the proliferation of newspaper, Internet, telephone, and brick-and-mortar dating services, it is obvious that these agencies are needed by people in search of companions. The variety and specificity of the ads are cause to wonder: What do the advertisements tell us about the real "product," that is, the people behind the ads and the loves they are looking for?

Personal advertisements seem to be written in a cultural code, where important matters are expressed in images and implied narratives. Our marriage-minded military man seeks a woman with an Asian lineage. But what kind of love is he after? Is "Asian" a code word for non-Western attitudes toward marriage? Is he after the modern man's dream of an exotic yet deferential wife? Or has he done military service in the Orient, and does "Asian" indicate a contrast to the Caucasian women he now encounters everyday? How about the handsome Italian man? His request for a "dancer/cheerleader type" is certainly loaded with social expectations. I imagine him watching hours upon hours of sports on television. Tired of all the women in his life, he cannot help but notice the beautiful cheerleaders who enthusiastically support his world of competing men. Is he looking for a girl who looks good doing the splits and has a "Rah, Rah, Go Team" attitude toward her man?

Our divorced female (DWCPF, loves life, enjoys a variety of activities) shares more with these two men than it may first appear. She seems open enough, offering no criteria for potential companions. She is just tired of being alone. However, there is something suspicious when a person asks for nothing in particular, yet still is alone. Does she live on an island? Is she unable to find a friend at work, in the neighborhood, or park? Like the military officer's "Asian," and the handsome suitors "cheerleader," this woman's "tired of being alone" seems to be code for, "I am looking for someone whom I do not encounter in *my* life. I cannot seem to make a connection with the many men that I know." It is likely that these same uninteresting men will be answering her ad, which is the disappointing reality of courting the readers of a newspaper that you read yourself. Amid people at home and work, they are alone as well. They all need something new. A similar flight from the ordinary might be behind our BF's request for a professional WM. In a racist world, her practical options may be limited to Black men. What does she want from a WM that she cannot get from a BM? Perhaps something besides the same old thing, a chance to enter a different world.

The personals, by and large, make very modest requests that, apparently, are not easy to fulfill. Certainly, it is not difficult to be "Asian" or a "cheerleader type" or to "enjoy a variety of activities," but it is hard work to be wife or friend, a long-term partner or the antidote to someone's loneliness. The ads assume an air of casual distance, but they imply a desire for a close connection. The mother (SBF) in search of a SBM with children distinguishes herself in this regard. Her request is even less demanding than the rest, but her utilitarian approach to companionship will narrow the field to a brave few. She merely wants to share activities, but who would dare? Why would a person need to place an ad for a companion to join her and her children for an outing? What is she really looking for? A sadness and cultural dismay are palpable in the pages of the personal ads. Can we not find the simple matters of love and friendship where we are and with the people we know? Already knowing them is not the problem, but how and why we know them.

Looking for love, according to Niklas Luhmann in his *Love as Passion*, is looking for a personal connection.[10] In the context of modern individualism, our personal identities are shaped, not so much by social duties and station or by the social reciprocity that status and responsibilities confer, but by a less structured system of personal exchange and intimacy. Luhmann argues that passion is first of all, not an emotion, but a culture code for communicating personal identity and establishing one's individuality in relation to the social (and too often impersonal) world.[11] Love as passion is viewed as an indomitable force that creates a personal connection that is utterly different from relations in the workaday world.[12] We want someone to be close to us. More importantly, we want someone to want to be close to us. If we share work with a co-worker, we share an experience of love and closeness with the lover. Love is a sphere of activity in itself. Luhmann calls this sharing of love for its own sake the "mutual reflexivity of desire," a mutual desire to be desired.[13]

The personal ads, in this regard, do not request extraordinary people or unusual behavior, only basic types (like a dancer/cheerleader) and common, but shared activities. The ads function, in the main, to identify others who want to have a relationship for the purposes of having a personal relationship. What the personal ads offer is an exchange based, not on shared interests or common character types, but on a common desire to establish closeness, to be separated out from the rest and identified personally. Desires for specific personal qualities and interests are important but secondary to this personal connection, to intimacy for its own sake. Relationships at work or among associates and neighbors may be constructive and beneficial, and they might be loving in the sense that they are sustained by mutual regard, care, and cooperation. These "working" relationships may connect us to others, but they are insufficient for love. They may bring us together, but they are not directed to carrying on through the very feelings and deep experiences of being connected.

Lovestyles and landscapes

In order to see the personals ads from a personal point of view, I logged onto *The Washington Post*'s "Personals Plus" web-site (www.relationshipnetwork.com). The online service allows you to browse the ads "based on category and relationship type" and to narrow "your search based on some characteristics about the person you'd like to meet." I am a man seeking a woman. I would like to meet someone for dating, as opposed to someone with similar interests. I am looking for someone between the ages of 30 and 40. I decided that ethnic background would not matter, but I limited myself to those who identify themselves as Christian. Education level? Some college. Children at home? Doesn't matter. Non-smoker please. These categories and characteristics narrow the field, but they do not tell me what I really need to know. What I want to know is the kind of love relationship I might be getting into, what love-personality, what style of life, and what will I receive in return.

Among my top matches, the teaser lines ranged from "seeks fellow night owl for daytime/late night frolicking" to "SuperMom . . . pretty, witty, full of pity (passion) . . . ISO, [tall, handsome] SuperDad," from "A beautiful SWF, 33, bl/bl, thin, seeks 6'+, very confident, successful, funny SWPM" to "Caribbean Queen ISO loyal subject." The brief descriptions draw the outline of the relationship-styles relatively well, but I imagine any personal connection is a gamble. Nevertheless, the teaser lines do provide a landscape: I could imagine myself frolicking about the town with an energetic woman, settling in at home with Mrs. SuperDad, laughing at a fine restaurant with my bl/bl (my blond-haired, blue-eyed) beauty, or tip-toeing around my supine Caribbean queen. Actually, being a loyal subject to the Caribbean queen is a stretch, but the other story lines would suit me just fine. The difficult question is whether or not I could survive the relationships that the short episodes represent.

The different landscapes say a lot about particular hopes for a relationship, and about the possibilities of love in the market setting of personal advertisements. Each story line represents a technique for making a personal connection. Frolicking about the night, for instance, is probably a metaphor for a relationship high in emotional energy but low in emotional investment (at least at first). There is nothing more exhilarating, perhaps, than the safety of cultivating a relationship away from home. In contrast, SuperMom is fearless. The man who steps over her threshold will have the door shut behind him. Clearly, the night owl and SuperMom represent different modes of connection. In this regard, John Alan Lee proposes that we think about love in terms of what he calls love-styles (equivalent to lifestyles) as a way to link notions of love with behavioral patterns, with emotional needs and types of attachment, and with socio-economic frameworks.[14]

Lee is particularly interested in ideologies of love, that is, in the cultural common sense about love that is embedded in structures of social life. He presents a convincing case that "the dominant stream of ideology in love and sex today seems to be exactly the same as in politics and economics: the market economy."[15] The market ideology bears upon us when we are looking for "the best possible deal," when we hold potential partners up to an explicit or informal check list (e.g., is there passion between us?), and when we wonder whether or not we should invest time into a relationship. Lee's proposal is convincing because it is hard to imagine doing otherwise. Even when we fall in love, which might be considered as fortuitous as winning the lottery, we are required to make choices about investing wisely or spending wildly until it's gone. We assess the value of another person, and we calculate the goods and outcomes of love.

John Lee does not resist the market; rather, he gives expression to its ideology insofar as he assumes that lovestyles present themselves as an array of choices for our consumption and that our own proclivities for one style or another are determined ultimately by our personality traits and personal preferences. In other words, lovestyles are (or ought to be) consumer driven. Lee argues that lovestyles are innumerable, but he outlines three primary and three of the most important secondary forms.[16]

The three primary lovestyles, eros, storge, and ludus, are ideal types and seldom seen in their pure forms. Eros emphasizes sexual desire and physical appearance. It "is a conception of love centered on an expectation of intense emotional and physical attraction to the beloved." Storge is akin to companionate love. It "is the ancient Greek conception of a quiet and friendly attachment." Finally, the ludic lover is out for fun, experimentation, and personal gratification. He or she follows a playboy ethics, where love is considered a game to be played and enjoyed "without jealousy or commitment to a single partner."[17] These lovestyles are likely to be expressed in various combinations: the intensity of eros, for example, when mixed with the calculations of the playboy lover results in what Lee calls manic love.

Along with mania, Lee's secondary lovestyles are pragma and agape. Agape is not erotic but is inclined toward surrender and self-giving. Because it does not fit with the logic of the market, Lee does not have much further to say. Mania, as just noted, is a combination of erotic intensity with a need for the predictability and the control of the playboy. Mania is nothing other than romantic love. It is obsessive, possessive, and anxious, but it is also spontaneous, vital, and transformative. Mania, according to Lee, is the predominant Western form. Unlike early modern versions of romantic love, it is "a falling for another" that is hardly selfless. One becomes a slave to love, let's say, with an expectation of personal fulfillment. We are helplessly in love, but we make clear demands, the most important of which is that our beloved be dependent, vulnerable, and helplessly in love as well. In a romance, we hope to lose ourselves in passion, while at the same time we have the contradictory belief that our lives will be made happy and our selves made whole. Pragmatic love, also prominent, is the opposite of romantic love. It combines the emotional balance of ludic calculation with the friendly attachment of companionate love. The pragmatic lover is utilitarian. He or she plays the field and commits, cautiously, to the most compatible partner.[18]

According to Lee, lovestyles are matters of skill and learned through experience, but they are also tendencies that we find within ourselves. Lovestyles are choices open to us within the limits of our personality traits. I may tend toward the high self-esteem of the erotic lover or toward the frustration of my manic needs. Lee explains that, when all is said, people tend to "enjoy different lovestyles at the same time, or one after the other . . . For example, you might love one partner in a friendly way (storge) and be passionately attracted to another's beauty (eros) . . . Few lovers are pure examples of any given lovestyle. As with choices of color for clothing and decoration, most people mix and match lovestyles. After all, any of these lovestyles is available in our media."[19] Availability is key to Lee's market framework. He wants me to have my frolic about the city with one lover, a SuperDad experience with another, and opportunity, if I desire, to kneel at the feet of my Caribbean queen.

The trouble, for Lee, is that cultural common sense (i.e., a dominant ideology) together with its complementary social arrangements works against freedom by privileging one lovestyle over another. This critique of ideology fits with Lee's own market view. Ideologies become a problem, according to Lee, when they limit the free flow of lovestyle exchange. Lee does not seem to notice that the "free market" of love is a dominating ideology itself. He imagines the free market to be bound to privilege no lovestyle and no set of social arrangement in particular. In this regard, the personal ads, whether online or in the newspaper, provide his paradigmatic location. The advertisers are able to define themselves without a substantive, everyday context while at the same time utilizing common social indicators and cultural cues (like picking products off a shelf). The market of love allows the military man, the handsome Italian, the frolicking night owl, and Caribbean queen to create a drama and setting that are probably unfamiliar in their ordinary lives. The market ideology makes the LTR (the long-term relationship) a matter of invention and self-creation.

As unreflective as Lee is about his own standpoint, he does offer interesting insights about the social construction of love. He considers romantic love (mania) the dominant love-ideology of modern society, fitting well with the ethos of consumer capitalism. Lee hypothesizes that romantic love influences our everyday lives with a power that is comparable to our reigning scientific and political ideologies.[20] Romantic love is apprehensive; it seeks to possess and consume. "Manic love keeps the thoughts and even the body of the lover very busy." The lover is filled with desire for another, absolutely moved by his or her beloved. The down side of this wonderful romance is that the needs and joys of ordinary life fade. The romantic lover may forget to eat, and he or she will certainly not care to sleep. The benefit of manic asceticism is that "the lover is drawn out of him or herself into a world of feelings probably never known before . . . [T]he lover discovers just how deeply she or he is capable of feeling for another person. Mania rouses full expression of emotional capacity. It can be good to know you are capable of such intense feeling for another person."[21] Romantic love, it is thought, makes for the truest interpersonal connections.

Romantic love has ideological power insofar as it is framed as a means for social transcendence, through the force of an individual's desire. Romance is a route to upward mobility. Through the force of the lover's will social norms are overcome and redefined. The noble plebeian, a bodyguard let's say, falls in love with a fragile pop star.[22] A penniless American, aboard the Titanic, falls in love with a young woman of the impenetrable moneyed class.[23] A virtuous prostitute, in *Pretty Woman*, falls for a heartless financier.[24] In these scripts and countless more, from *Love Story* to Disney's *Aladdin*, romantic love proves its wonder by overcoming obstacles, particularly those of social convention and economic class. This story line fits with the modern narrative of individual self-invention. If we only follow our passion, our dreams will be fulfilled.

Romantic love establishes a hierarchy which overturns wealth and power. Truer is the love that does not conform to norms of status and social utility. Love breaks with custom and convention. Romantic plot lines are written so that the lower social partner (the poor man or prostitute) is worthy, while the lover of higher status is flawed and/or imprisoned. The rich are hollowed out or trapped by their money. The pop singer needs protection from the cost of fame; the rich young woman is trapped by a purely pragmatic courtship, and the prostitute's financier needs to find his own heart. Not only are social conventions overcome by the will of individuals, but individual worth is redistributed by one's measure of love. In the movie *Titanic*, the young woman's rich fiancé is presented as nothing but an insensitive chauvinist, and the poor man is a tender adventurer and romantic pioneer.

Ironically, this redistribution of status by love leaves real divisions of class and power as they are. Because romantic love is about individual fulfillment and self-making, there is no real social reformation. In fact, romance turns out to have a pragmatic bias. Love, in other words, tends to settle on the side of advantage, money and prestige. Perhaps the prostitute will enjoy her man's wealth, but she will do so by leaving her old life completely behind. She will be able to leave her squalid apartment building and her irresponsible, self-centered friends. Her lover's credit card and the woman it makes her are undeniably romantic. In the case of *Titanic*, the poor man will die for love, and the rich woman will be freed by his love from a pragmatic marriage. For romantic love to do its anti-utilitarian work, it must cost the poor man. The lover must die, and the calculating rich ex-fiancé must carry on as before. Freed *by* the romantic lover, the young woman must be free *from* him as well. Otherwise, romance would end with the distasteful matters of his ordinary working-class life. The romance would not make sense if she were to leave a life of riches only to do dishes and mop the floor for a poor man. With the lover dead, their love can endure evermore in a de-structured social moment.

Romantic love is a cultural grammar. It is a way of experiencing closeness and seeking fulfillment that corresponds to a broader code (or a narrative) of pleasure, success, and consumption. In the ideology of the market, falling in love makes a relationship true, so that we can distinguish our attachment to another person from our desire and consumption of things.[25] Passion, it is believed, takes us beyond choices into the necessity of personal desire.[26] Romantic love is spontaneous and based in emotion over against utilitarian rationality, cost–benefit analysis and other means of rational control. Through passion, we can find the depth of who we are, apart from roles, duties, and merely functional relationships. The fundamental aspect of romantic love is not passion itself, but the idea that love is a sphere of its own, that love itself is a self-sustained connection.

Advertisements for someone to share parenting activities, or for a man to relieve loneliness, or for an Oriental female seem to be hollowed by their external and utilitarian criteria. Like expressions of romantic love, they are signals of a desire to re-create ordinary life; yet, these requests for practical compatibility appear to make romance impossible. It is thinkable to request companionship or an LTR, but is it possible to make "professional" a criterion for someone you will love? Does love calculate income or social status? Is love in search of a category like the SBCM or the DWPF? Although pragmatic judgments seem to contradict the abandon of falling in love, utilitarian coolness is the market complement of romantic love. Love and pragmatism must be separated, but one resolves the tensions of the other. We endeavor to make deep connections and to make them safe.

Marriage and romantic love

Marriage is untamed passion made safe, which, of course, puts the vitality of love at risk. Marriage becomes a basic limit on the movement of passion and its inevitable resting place as well. As family has been differentiated from the economy and political institutions, it has become inwardly directed and defined by its affective cohesion. "Love as passion" has become its own sphere, and this autonomy of desiring has come to define modern marriage and family. "In the course of the nineteenth century," according to Niklas Luhmann, "the barriers to a marriage based on 'Romantic' love were taken down and thus had an effect on what was now seen and desired as 'Romantic'."[27] The industry and social position of family have been minimized so that the reasons for marriage have become concerns of individuals. People must decide whether or not to begin a *new* life together in their own sphere of affection. The critical question in the modern world is whether or not there are good reasons to be married at all. In this context, "love became the sole legitimate reason for the choice of a partner, and all those moments of passion that were threatening, that endangered existence and put life and death in the balance had to be filtered out."[28] Marriage intends to institutionalize the benefits of romance and Lee's mania: we are connected to another, and our emotions and sense of being are aroused. We discover a deep capacity for sharing our lives with another.

Romantic marriage corresponds precisely to the "transcendent sexuality" of the predominant theological personalism (discussed in Chapter 2). The standard personalist account proposes that sex connects the "whole person." Parallel to their theology of sex, personalists attempt to out-romance romantic love on its own terms. If the self is roused in love, then marriage offers the total self-giving and unity of selves. Consider an example from a prominent writer (and Catholic-cultural icon) in the United States. Andrew Greeley, in cooperation with his sister, Mary Greeley Durkin, provides a good inter-subjective description of falling victim to love. Greeley and Durkin hold that falling in love is a humanizing encounter. We are inclined toward isolation and self-serving autonomy, but love as passion calls us "to move beyond ourselves. Our beloved becomes the focus of our attention. Our self-complacency is shattered. Our independence is threatened. Yet we make no effort to resist the attraction."[29] Such passion moves us beyond reason, beyond our principles of autonomy, and beyond our need for security. "We delight in the discovery of this other person and experience a desire to be with her or him for the rest of our lives. We are overwhelmed by the thought that another person feels the same about us."[30] In response to this experience, we desire to commit ourselves entirely, to care for another "for richer, for poorer, in sickness and in health, till death do we part."

While they focus on passion, Greeley and Durkin include elements common to those who conceive of conjugal love in less passionate terms of companionship. In Dietrich von Hildebrand's theology of marriage, for instance, the story of love begins with the isolated self.[31] Spousal love is presented as original, as emerging through the inter-subjectivity of two in order to establish a foundation for a new community. This inter-subjective interpretation of marriage gives romantic meaning to marital companionship. The companions turn their relationship inward. According to Hildebrand, "conjugal love in itself constitutes a completely new kind of love. It involves a unique mutual giving of one's self, which is the outstanding characteristic of this type of love. It is true that in every kind of love one gives oneself in one way or another. But here the giving is literally complete and ultimate. Not only the heart but the entire personality is given up to the other."[32]

Hildebrand is concerned to distinguish marriage from mere companionship. If friendship, traditionally defined, is walking "side by side – hand in hand," marriage is gazing "face-to-face," an I–Thou. If friendship is oriented to common social goods and the good, the marriage partnership is unique because, unlike typical partnerships that are based in common work or an outward vocation, the marital union is self-directed. It is love reproducing love through an activity of inter-subjective love. Conjugal love "tends to . . . a community where two persons constitute a closed union . . . a relationship in which the regard of each one of the two parties is turned exclusively upon the other."[33] This inter-subjective account of conjugal love is romantic in its refusal to define partnership in terms of the virtues or character of the beloved. Love is conceived as a formal interchange of subjectivity without reference to whether or not a good partner is needed for a good partnership. It is the very losing and gaining of self that establishes the context of love.

While it may seem that Greeley, Durkin, and Hildebrand are

appealing to a common experience of love, they are not making reference to the kind of love, closeness, and solidarity that sustains a home. Their stories of love imply a typical trial of modern romance. Although we have cultivated our love throughout our courtship, through gazing into each other's eyes under a moonlit sky, we may not be able to sustain the side-by-side of sharing a household, working for each other's good, and sustaining the goods of common life with friends and neighbors. Great lovers do not necessarily make for good housekeeping. In the dominant mode of desire, it is likely that our focus outward (beyond the face to face) will be experienced as a dissipation of the inter-subjective love we once shared. Love and passion die once partners settle in at home.

Hildebrand focuses on companionate love and Greeley and Durkin on passion, but they share an appeal to the formal qualities of "total" self-giving. Their idealism sounds wonderful, but it encourages a sense of loss, frustration, and failure. The "total" marriage would have to be so heroic as to carry the weight of a total self, or the self would have to be shallow and one dimensional, so that it could be completely unveiled in a single relationship. In either case, their understanding of nuptial union resonates more with private moments of passion than washing the dishes, dinner with the in-laws, cooperating with neighbors, and managing a home. Their account is romantic in its apparent otherness from the everyday world. Their theology of marriage draws a picture of the transparent private self, where "he is different with me than he is with any one else" or "we get connected only when we have time alone." The unique face-to-face love brings us outside of ourselves, but it has no clear connection to the side-by-side nature of quotidian endeavors.

One striking result of theological romanticism about marriage is that it actually takes the joy out of the regular course of things. We must always be looking beyond for moments of self-discovery, liminal experiences, and total abandon. In order to understand enjoyment and struggles of sex and love in the home, a different approach will have to be taken. We will have to set ourselves to cultivating a social landscape that reproduces love and passion of a different kind. The social economy of home will be the topic of Chapter 5. Beforehand, in Chapter 4, we will enquire about the common conceptions of family and household that make romantic love so attractive and convincing.

4

Family Values

Introduction

Actor Gwyneth Paltrow and musician Chris Martin were wed recently. The couple have done their best to avoid public notice but their courtship, Paltrow's pregnancy, and their impending marriage have been making the news for several months. When the rich and famous fall in love and marry, we want to know all the details. We want to be part of the excitement. Why? According to celebrity-watcher, Marite Burwell, "When it comes to love and the grand march down the aisle, we're fascinated with what charmed celebrities with unlimited money and show-stopping resources can do."[1]

Gwyneth and Chris hold the promise of an idyllic life together. Although they will have to deal with intrusions of their fame, they have few barriers to enjoying the perfect marriage. They can live in London, wed in Santa Barbara, and honeymoon in Los Cabos, Mexico. They are attractive and successful, and they have a beautiful baby. They will be parents for all the right reasons (i.e., for the quality time). Surely, they will hire a well-qualified nanny and tutor for their child. Surely, Gwyneth and Chris will not be washing loads of laundry, feeding the baby, and cleaning up the kitchen before setting off to work at 7.00am. Ordinary people are fascinated because the actor and rock star are living a dream.

The celebrity marriage is a contemporary genre that sustains, within family, a modern conception of desire and love. Paltrow and Martin have the opportunity to join together only for love and passion. Each is financially and professionally independent and there is no social or practical reason to marry. Their marriage is gratuitous. It is not a practical necessity, but an opportunity to prize each other as we want to treasure them. Their married life will be set apart, at least in my mind, from everyday concerns. I do not imagine them discussing how to reduce their electric bill or whether or not their mini-van has another year of life left in it. The celebrity marriage is valuable to us, I suspect, because it is free from practical matters that tend to obscure unconditional love.

This chapter considers the kind of social and political life that this unconditioned conception of marriage and family serves. This family of private affection has emerged as family-based political and economic functions have been replaced by the modern economy and the rule of the nation-state. The first section of the chapter will consider the efforts of legislators and agents of government to protect the self-sufficiency and independence of family, for our benefit and for the health of the nation. I will suggest that by making the family an independent entity, it is reduced to a political individual with its own interests and, in the process, governed from the outside. In response, many call for a return to family values, in order to protect the autonomy of the family once again; yet, this counterargument sustains the politics of the useless (i.e., loving) home. Within the politics of the modern state, family cultivates a detachment from household relations. We must transcend the home. This logic of detachment will be the topic of the second section of the chapter. The final section will turn to the representative image of the upwardly mobile suburban home. Regular people may never have the chance for celebrity, but the promise of the suburbs is a key step toward the dream of a marriage set apart.

The value of family

Since 1996, the President of the United States has been proclaiming a Sunday in July to be Parents' Day. Apparently, Mother's Day and Father's Day are not enough. Mother's and Father's Day follow on the heels of Easter and pass through May and June as pivot points for a commercial calendar. As a father, I find my day in June to be an interesting combination of filial affection and hardware. The economics of this special day is simple. Mothers receive flowers and tender greeting cards on their day, and it's hammers, staple guns, and power drills for Dad. On the same day that I am enjoying recognition at home, various advertisements suggest that I am better off tinkering alone in the garage with my tools. I cannot help but be suspicious that Father's Day sustains a construction of fatherhood that is more useful to the market than to my life at home. Perhaps another day for parents is necessary. In any case, Parents' Day is a politicians' holiday. It is an opportunity for leaders of state to speak in a ceremonial tone and with reverence for the governed population.

Parents' Day represents civic life. It is not likely that this solemn occasion will become a popular institution in the twenty-first century, but the federal government's interest in parenthood and family will continue. Concerns for family and child rearing have become requisites for gaining and executing the public trust. If Parents' Day becomes an institution, it will be carried on the tide of a common political construction of family. First instituted by William Clinton, the tradition of Parents' Day has been carried on by George W. Bush. Although they disagree on fiscal and military policy and are on opposite sides of the "culture wars," they are of the same mind about family.

On Sunday July 25, 1999, for instance, President Clinton starts his tribute to parents by stating undisputed principles. "Parents are the foundation of the family and a cornerstone of community life in America. They instill the values, attitudes, and guidance children need to become strong individuals and caring citizens; we turn to our parents for the unconditional love and encouragement we need to make the most of our lives and to contribute to the life of our Nation."[2] In 2001, President Bush agrees that "as parents we provide our children with the love and support they need to grow up to be caring individuals and responsible citizens. The care we express and the values we instill help our children achieve their greatest potential and ultimately determine the future of our Nation."[3] In 2003, he adds that "parents have the important responsibility of providing for, protecting, nurturing, teaching, and loving their children" and that these values that bind families also "help define us as a Nation."[4]

Sensitive and encouraging statements by Presidents Clinton and Bush warm the hearts of just about everyone. Across the political spectrum, family is a moral center, where we are loved and where we learn both compassion and civic responsibility. The home is an environment of unconditional acceptance and encouragement. Unconditional love is nothing other than an inner desire for deep personal connections (see Chapter 3), and the loving family, as a result, is considered the inner foundation of social and political life. I take this formula to be putative common sense, and I expect that many readers will wonder what I might propose as an alternative. Should there be no family at all? Should civil servants be the agents of affection? The Parents' Day formula of love and governance seems indisputable.

However, we ought to see at least hints of inconsistency in the claim that a loving home is the foundation of good government. The politically vested household of the ancient world has been replaced, in modern times, by a home founded on love between husband and wife rather than social alliances and financial exchanges between families. Money and politics ought not be the foundation of the modern family, and preferential love has no place in the rule of law. Love comes from within, but governance and patronage come from the outside, from the modern state to the individual. Nonetheless, loving family and modern nations are complementary. The loving family is assumed to stand apart from politics, but it functions as a mediating institution, which conveys both the aims of government to the individual and the participation of individuals in projects of the state.[5]

By assuming a place outside economy and power, modern love sustains the social order. Family, religion, and the Boy Scouts should cultivate both citizenship and individuality. If thought by their members to be ends in themselves, then such groups are considered sectarian, authoritarian, and oppressive. The *ancien régime* was a government of families, where the patriarch was given final authority over those in his household, whether they were educated, sent out to work, loved or abandoned. Such authority is intolerable to us moderns who judge parenthood in terms of its service to the order of the state under the banner of the individual.[6] It is common sense, for instance, that individuals might be required to kill and die for their country, but it would be ridiculous if the same were an obligation of family. It is common sense that a nation will grant its citizens special rights and care over against foreign peoples and resident aliens, but similar preferences, when granted to sons and daughters, are considered evidence of a family's basic social inequities. These inequities of family are justified by love but limited and corrected by the state.

In their Parents' Day addresses, Mr. Clinton and Mr. Bush present this typical modern perspective. They offer the customary mixture of public and private languages, of national vitality and unconditional love. They blend the public language of the autonomous individual with a private language of the parent–child bond. They speak, on one hand, of responsible, productive citizens and, on the other hand, of children who need care and guidance. Family, as it is used by US presidents, is a political concept that connects these two moral languages in the same way that autonomous parents are connected to their dependent children. Family is the political means through which dependent individuals are joined to productive ones, so that, in practice, the basic unit of society is not family but the independent individual.[7] The family is steward to the state, and it will perform its function well if familial relations serve the dominant market economy. Children enter the public sphere primarily as consumers who dispose of their parents' income.

The family unit, in this regard, is treated by modern government as though it were a single individual (i.e., the head of the household who represents a single economic entity). Whether liberals embrace "new forms of family" or conservatives grieve for the "traditional" home, the logic is the same.[8] Modern political organization assumes an implied contract between free individuals. The nation-state, therefore, cannot make regular practice of engaging dependent individuals directly. In its modern conception, the social body is a fraternity of autonomous agents, and political community is primarily an anonymous association of self-interested persons.[9] The state ought not tell us what is good for us (as parents do), and it is certainly unjust for lawmakers to treat some individuals (rather than others) with the preferential treatment of family. The modern state attempts to grant freedom by limiting its role in deciding matters of everyday life (e.g., choosing a home and neighborhood, schools and piano lessons, television or reading). Such decisions are considered the right of parents for their children. In this way, family is a social unit that offers a means for dealing with non-autonomous (and therefore quasi-social) individuals through those who have an immediate relation to the state.

The political family unit and the notion of its economic "head" define the household externally. Rather than household management or filial duties, modern families have political and market relations at their center.[10] This concept of the home is a modern peculiarity that we have come to take for granted. We define the head of the household as the person who earns wages, who is away from home most of the time, whose primary role is distinct from the home, and whose identity as wage-earner has no necessary relationship to a role as father, mother, husband or wife. If someone is a housekeeper, she (usually she) is considered not its head or manager but a dependant. This assignment of roles is curious. In practical matters of life, the homemaker is, in fact, the head of the household, and the wage-earner helps sustain a home that the housekeeper manages. Our political "head of household" governs home from the outside.

On Parents' Day Mr. Clinton pledges to produce "strong individuals and caring citizens," and Mr. Bush looks to cultivate "caring individuals and responsible citizens." It should be no surprise that the declarations are the same. Both pronouncements are consistent with the peculiar modern conception of home. Both make reference to their administrations' programs that support family: health care, tax cuts, and education. Whether on the left or the right, the government, as a matter of course, intervenes by (1) imposing a financial bond between wage-earning parents and their dependants, (2) providing aid and training for productive civic life, and (3) alleviating child rearing burdens through public education. Family, in return, offers a means for parents to cooperate in civic life by raising "responsible citizens of tomorrow"[11] and "America's future leaders."[12]

Many have objected to these "liberal" interventions into family, but conservative disagreements lie, not in reference to the family's mediating function or the nation-state's right to intervene, but in how the political and economic role of family is sustained. Both sides situate family between the poles of individual and state, and between autonomy and civic order. Conservatives have substantive disagreements with liberals about the nature of family and its internal workings. Against progressives, they argue for "an idealized form of the nineteenth century middle-class family" with the father as final authority and the mother as homebound care-giver.[13] They express great despair about a reigning "therapeutic" ideology in schools and various cultural trends that undermine the decision-making power of parents.[14] These substantive disagreements between liberals and conservative are real, but in order to fit with the modern polity of government, the arguments must be translated into procedural proposals. Liberal and conservative disagreements about family correspond to their debates about government's bureaucratic role in the market.[15]

One side calls for government assistance, and the other for freedom from intrusion, but their differences are only a matter of emphasis. Liberals call for regulations and government cooperation, while conservatives strike out against big government and promote the unfettered market economy. Both are committed to market autonomy, and both call for intervention when the rules of the market are violated. Conservatives begin with a *laissez-faire* orientation to economic matters, but like liberals, they are obliged to impose upon the market when laws of fair trade and taxation are broken. Likewise, a *laissez-faire* approach to family is proposed as a means to give autonomy to the "traditional" family and, by doing so, promote family values. Nevertheless, conservatives, like liberals, recognize the responsibility of the state to ensure that children have a nurturing home.[16] Parents are free to educate and raise their children within the domain of good government, which determines standards for the parental role by legislative and legal processes and carries them out by executive agencies. The poles of individual and state are firmly in place.

In this political construction of family, the household functions as an emotional unit where love, nurture, and mutual care are distributed, particularly to children and other individuals who are not agents in social and political life.[17] Social, economic, and political life function differently. The public sphere is constituted by free, self-interested individuals, and its basic context of exchange (whether political or economic) is an encounter between strangers who form contractual relationships for mutual benefit. Autonomous individuals are the basic unit of society. Children, in contrast, do not make basic lifestyle decisions. They do not earn their living, buy homes, or decide how to be educated. Regardless of merit, they receive financial benefit and personal care from others. Precisely for this reason, US presidents, Democrats and Republicans speak of family in terms of unconditional love. Love is unconditional in relation to politics and the market because it makes no social or economic sense.

Family has the function of performing what our economic and social organization cannot – a natural and necessary (or at least what seems to be an inevitable) set of affective bonds. Family is responsible for sustaining personal connections, for reproducing love as a deep feeling, and perpetuating the exchange of love as passion. As a context of nurture and affection, the household cannot be allowed real social and economic currency. Families ought to produce good citizens, but they cannot be allowed to undercut basic economic and political relations.[18] Insofar as family functions according to preferential treatment, it is thought to represent social and economic injustice, nepotism and unregulated monetary exchange. Familial love establishes preferential relationships and unequal means of economic distribution. For this reason, its social role must be defined from the outside. Family values, oddly, are a means of regulating family because the household represents a network of relations which undermines political and economic life.

Detachment from home

The market economy and modern political organization imply a corresponding family form that sustains its own undoing. Presidents Clinton's and Bush's reference to the home in terms of national vitality and unconditional love are entirely representative in contemporary life. The family is an interpersonal affair. The modern home is characterized by mutual care and a currency of affection, but it is interesting how strongly statecraft impinges upon the practical working out of what is assumed to be a private, interpersonal realm. Although the attachments of family may be considered natural and necessary, they are ultimately an obstacle to moral autonomy and public life. In this regard, the successful family, or the family-in-good-working-order, fosters detachment from home.

A standard narrative of family is offered in John Rawls' *A Theory of Justice*. Published in 1971, the work is a watershed in contemporary political philosophy. The greater part of political theory in the decades since its publication has been either commentary on Rawls or intentionally set in relation to him.[19] Although he does not represent the spectrum of political theory, he does articulate the modern problem of family. His political construction of family parallels the themes outlined on Parent's Day. On one hand, Rawls suggests that civil society depends upon some form of family, while on the other, his theory of justice, as fairness, is set against the inequities of inheritance and nepotism. His theory is set against family-bound inequalities among citizens, some of whom are born in wealthy households rather than poor ones. On one hand, he assumes that the family and parent–child relationships are natural givens, while on the other he suspects that some other arrangement for raising children would be more consistent with the requirements of justice.[20]

Although few will accept, in its entirety, Rawls' theoretical construction of what he calls "the original position," most assume, with him, that political justice requires detachment from the bonds, private motivations, and preferential treatment of family. Family, it is agreed, produces an economic and social lottery. It transfers power and money by means of sentiment and a disregard for social cost and benefit. The brightest children of the rich are given advantages they do not need, while their dim-witted siblings are given what they cannot use. Family, it is assumed, defies justice. At the same time, most also agree that good families are necessary in order to cultivate our capacity for justice and compassion. Between disinterested justice and preferential family, Rawls must balance two incompatible conceptions of human moral agency.[21] He does so through a narrative of moral progress.

Rawls' discussion of family is placed in the last part of *A Theory of Justice*, in a chapter titled "The Sense of Justice." His conception of justice is developed earlier in the book, particularly the first part, through his heuristic device of the original position. Rawls asks us to imagine a handful of "original" individuals who are set to the task of developing principles of justice. The individuals are "elementary" persons insofar as they lack knowledge of their own economic class, social status, natural abilities, conceptions of the good life, psychological make-up, and rational life plan. These original individuals do have knowledge of general facts, possibilities, and limitations of existing economic and social life, as well as common knowledge of human motivations and moral capacities. In other words, an individual in the original position lacks only information about who he or she is and about anyone in particular. Therefore, the original individual is equal to others because each, in effect, is anyone and no one.

Although the original position imagines self-interest to be a person's basic social motivation, the original individual has no means to conceptualize preferential treatment for himself or herself. This point is critical. Rawls promises to separate the principles of justice from the interests of anyone in particular, but the possibility of this separation is founded on the idea of a pre-social self who has conceived of his or her interests prior to the substantive relationships of social life. In effect, Rawls follows in the classic liberal political tradition (along with Immanuel Kant) that conceives of self-interest as natural and as socially and politically corrupting. The very idea of self-interest has no content, so that all self-interest and social life are set at odds. Self-interest is viewed as a necessity, but all such interest, whatever the content, is given a bad name. Rawls' "original" individuals are able to think fairly because they are asocial.

In this regard, the original position represents a rational justification of inequities that have developed historically and, of course, contingently.[22] There never has been a time when people in modern society have actually been equal. There have always been the powerful and weak, the rich and the poor, the politically articulate and the disenfranchised (*de facto* if not *de jure*). Rawls uses the original position to imagine not only a time and place where people are functionally equal, but also a way that they would, from their regard for their own interests, rationally commit to real-world inequities.

Rawls imagines that our society is put together through an implied contract, so that the basic inequities of common life can be justified only as a rational construction for the good of all. According to the implied contract, we all have already agreed (through the fact of our membership) to a structure of common life. To be agreeable and rationally acceptable, the structure would have to provide the best prospects for each individual's self-interest. Based on rational self-interest, the system would have to represent a reasonable acceptance of social and economic inequities. Rawls proposes that individuals in the original position would agree that "all social primary goods – liberty and opportunity, income and wealth, and the bases of self-respect – are to be distributed equally unless an unequal distribution of any or all these goods is to the advantage of the least favored."[23]

For the sake of argument, let us assume that Rawls' rational construction has been achieved. If so, our real political work has just begun. In order to sustain Rawlsian inequities, modern society will have to cultivate a strong commitment to its original contractual arrangements. This is not merely a problem for Rawls. It is a practical problem of modern social life. How is it that self-interested people will overlook their real but arbitrary disadvantages for the sake of a common conception of justice? When a person finds him or herself in an inferior social position, how will she come to support justice and struggle on without envy? She will have to be able to say, "In principle, I am equal to others, but I have less real opportunity and fewer advantages. I am poor and earn low wages, but the system that we have is best for all." Rawls must show how individuals who benefit the least from his conception of justice can transcend the basic self-interest that the original position assumes as a given. Rawls needs a "sense of justice" that his anonymous "original position" cannot provide.

Insofar as family represents shared identity and common goods, it becomes the location to tell the story of a transition from self-interest to concern for the whole. Family always precedes its youngest members who encounter the "whole" from the start. Family knows no "original" position. It is this lack of anonymity that makes a "sense of justice" possible, so that Rawls will be able to narrate the detachment of the original position as an end rather than a first principle. He is pressed to outline a cogent moral psychology "whereby a person would acquire an understanding of and an attachment to the principles of justice as he grows up in this particular form of well-ordered society [realizing the principles of justice as fairness]."[24] "Attachment" to principles is an appropriate description, as Rawls will show how attachments within family produce and give way to detachment, that is, to an attachment to abstract concepts rather than those implied in one's own social position.

Rawls proposes that agents mature by passing through two stages, the moralities of authority and association, and by settling into a third, the morality of principles. In this regard, it is no accident that he depends upon the work of Jean Piaget and Lawrence Kohlberg.[25] Kohlberg, for instance, defines moral maturity in terms of individual autonomy and a commitment to abstract principles (like Kant's categorical imperative) that transcend particular moral rules. Kohlberg's stages point to the superiority of Rawls' conception of public justice and the setting of the original position. The original position achieves fairness in principle by excluding personal commitments. In the same way, Rawls' morality of principles offers freedom from loyalty to anyone in particular and freedom for an anonymous conception of justice. If the original position is where justice is best conceived, the moral man is better off without the attachments of family and friends.

It is also no accident that Kohlberg's moral psychology is commonly understood, at least since Carol Gilligan's *In a Different Voice* (1982), as an account which privileges the developmental narrative of boys and men. According to Gilligan "male and female voices typically speak of the importance of different truths, the former of the role of separation as it defines and empowers the self, the latter of the ongoing process of attachment that creates and sustains the human community."[26] Gilligan gives notions of justice over to the boys, and speaks instead of an ethics of care. The distinction fits well into modern conceptions of public and private spheres, between civil society and family. In any event, Gilligan invigorates the idea of a woman's way of being and knowing in contrast to standards established by the dominant, public, male sphere.

Gilligan's theory gives expression to the liberal feminist dilemma. Do we seek liberation through escape from the bonds of the household? Or do we bind social life to the home, offering the healing touch of domesticity to public life? At the same time that many liberal feminists argue for a personalist or relational ethics, they also seek to transcend the relational vulnerability of the household. While they argue against the impersonal character of the male/public sphere, the protections of contractual arrangements become the best solution to the problems of home.[27] Women ought to enter marriage, in the manner that men do, as autonomous individuals who have their primary interests defined outside of home, in the public sphere.

Liberal feminism has conceptualized equality and freedom as liberation from the home. This dilemma may be more liberal than feminist, for Rawls and his liberal ancestors are faced with the dilemma as well.[28] The modern privatization of home presents this dilemma first to men. Political liberalism, with its distinction between the social contract and the natural home, uses the distinction between public and private, male and female spheres, as the solution to the dilemma.[29] Contractual arrangements and procedural goods of the public sphere depend upon the organic and substantive goods of the household. Love for one's wife and children at home provide a rationale for competition and self-interest in the public sphere. Likewise, Rawls' moral psychology instantiates the contrasting needs of contractual theory. Modern political theory depends upon family at the same time that it needs to transcend it.

The first two stages of Rawls' moral psychology are set within the home. The morality of authority is suited for a child's pre-rational development. Although authority is given top billing, this stage of life depends upon relationships of trust and love. Prescriptive rules of behavior and prohibitions come to the child from the outside, from the power of parents, but this imposition of power will promote moral development only when it is set within a context of unconditional love. Good behavior will be facilitated not primarily through fear of punishment but by relational attachments. Parents will have to engender trust. They should be consistent in their moral requirements and demand what is appropriate to a child's ability. Love encourages emulation, so that parents must be examples worthy of admiration. "In this way they arouse in [the child] a sense of his own value and the desire to become the sort of person that they are."[30]

The second stage, the morality of association, is set within organic social networks, where an individual will inhabit a particular role, which has a reciprocal but not equal relationship to other roles and stations. Such an association need not be family, but family is representative. "At this stage, the family itself is viewed as a small association, normally characterized by a definite hierarchy, in which each member has certain rights and duties. As the child becomes older he is taught the standards of conduct suitable for one in his station. The virtues of a good son or daughter are explained, or at least conveyed by parental expectations . . ." In other kinds of association, "one learns the virtues of a good student and classmate, and the ideals of a good sport and companion." Such moral ideals extend to adult life, and "the content . . . is given by the various conceptions of a good wife and husband, a good friend and citizen, and so on."[31]

The morality of association provides a training ground in moral reasoning. Roles and duties are not chosen, but neither are they external to the agent. As a person develops in her role, she begins to understand the complex interplay of roles and duties, the intricacies of cooperation, and the wider aims and purposes that make her own actions intelligible. Not only that, she begins to understand the roles and stations of others and will be able to see things from their particular points of view. Moral reasoning, here, is subtle. By understanding others – their goals, motivations, and the like – we will gain a greater understanding of our place and the good of the whole, and we will be able to act with even greater confidence and proficiency. If we understand the system to be just, then bonds of friendship and trust will be deepened. Criteria of behavior, both positive and negative, will be internal to the basic structure of relationships, common goods, and the reasoning which coheres within. Moral goods will begin to be conceived as human excellences, and goodness or justice and fairness are embodied in persons and relationships between persons.

Rawls' final stage of moral development moves us beyond attachment to particular people or groups. Like the morality of association, the morality of principles includes an affective (personal) engagement and a set of commitments, but, here, the objects of our moral sentiments are, not social and contingent, but first principles like those derived from the original position. Rawls expects that the morality of association will cultivate an adequate understanding of the principles of justice. However, the morality of association is limited, first, as a grounds for moral motivation and, second, as a referent or purview of justice. First, the morality of association locates our agency within social roles and duties, and as a consequence, it is "upheld by social approval and disapproval" and motivated "largely from . . . ties of friendship and fellow feeling for others and . . . concern for the approbation of the wider society."[32] The second point follows. We cannot be friends with everyone in public life. The citizenry is too large, and bonds of affection too attenuated.

The morality of principles "seeks to extend the conception they [i.e., particular associations and schemes that affirm our good] embody to further situations for the good of the larger community."[33] To this degree, the morality of principles corresponds to the conception of an original position, where all are represented through no one in particular. Our attachments of association have their place, but the object of our moral sentiments is independent of social contingencies and therefore free to refer to all humanity. Rawls seems to imply that association and principles do not present different types of justice, and for this reason, "the sense of justice is continuous with the love of mankind." The problem is "that benevolence is at a loss when the many objects of its love oppose one another."[34] The principles of justice, as they are detached from concrete affections, are able to guide us when our friendships and commitments within social roles and duties cannot.

We arrive at a sense of justice through an analogy of kinship, friendship, and love, while the original position is structured by rules of self-interest, anonymity, and detachment. Rawls holds these divergent models together by a developmental scheme that begins with attachment of people and ends in principles. He offers no means to move in the other direction, from a conception of justice to a just family. In *A Theory of Justice*, Rawls makes vague reference to the family as "just in some form," but his concept of justice is such that he has no means to follow through on this claim. In his later *Political Liberalism*, he admits that he cannot follow through. He simply prescinds from the question. He must withdraw from the issue of the just family insofar as his theory of justice depends upon family more for its inequities than its amenability to the original position. Ironically, inequities of roles, station, and function in the morality of association are not simply tolerated but required to cultivate a sense of justice.

The social commitments established by the original position and the morality of principles are not conceived as "attachments of association." In this way, Rawls is able to give the contractual nation-state the appearance of universality, as though our duties as detached citizens serve no one in particular. Detachment is assumed to serve only the original-rational plan, but in the process, the nations of privilege gain further advantage, and the global economy continues to privilege the rich. The inequities that are rejected when produced by family are justified when produced by the nation-state. Rawls could be read as a careful and methodical chauvinist of the American intelligentsia. Family simply represents a primitive form of social organization and a parochial sense of identity. When individuals become distinguished and intelligent, they detach themselves from home.

The suburbs

While political theory works with a contrast between government and family, the wider logic of nation-state individualism and contractual social arrangements give shape to the modern household. The Presidential Proclamation of Parent's Day and Rawls' theory of justice share a pattern. Family is a bond of love, a context for the care of dependants, and a setting to form those unable to think for themselves. The household functions properly when its network of attachments and distribution is directed toward wage earning, self-reliance, contractual agreements, and rational detachment from the contingent social arrangements of home. Home provides a distribution of unconditional love, but as "unconditional" its form of exchange must be regulated by an external economy. This political conception of family is found as well in the dominant narrative of social advancement and the dream of the suburban home.

The dream of the suburbs is a self-sufficient home, inhabited by affable kin and graced with plenty of yard to provide a buffer between neighbors.[35] The aim of suburban life is to choose a home and neighborhood where we can be happy, where people work hard and respect the ways of others, and where families get along on their own and come together for recreation and leisure. In the good neighborhood, we cooperate willingly. We volunteer our talents and free time, and in this way we contribute to civic life. The great pleasure of home ownership is freedom and autonomy. We are free to establish our style of life. We establish ourselves apart from (but perhaps much like) the homes and neighborhoods where we were raised, and we enjoy a reasonable distance (but not total separation) from our roles as little brother or dutiful daughter. We will be free and self-sufficient in a quiet neighborhood, friendly and safe, away from crime and the traffic of the city and apart from the demands and competition of the workplace. Our bonds at home and in the neighborhood are affective. We are likeable people who sincerely enjoy each other's company.

The dream home has similar spatial dimensions, and family life has an internal emphasis on leisure and voluntary association as well. Typically, upward mobility corresponds to greater personal space. The poor share beds, while middle-class families are likely to limit offspring to the number of available bedrooms, one per child. Everyone needs his or her own domain. It is interesting to consider whether or not the common space in a home is voluntary and recreational, something equivalent to the neighborhood park (where every family has a yard as well). Are common meals obligatory, and do family members mingle in the kitchen afterward? Or do people "see" each other primarily in a central room while actually watching television? Are the TV-room and other common spaces made optional by outfitting each bedroom with its own TV, personal computer, telephone, and (we can only hope) its own bathroom as well?

Inasmuch as the middle-class family is bound together by mutual affection, forms of interaction that minimize work and interpersonal aggravation are a great help. The good home is suited to relaxation rather than work, and a mark of success is the means to contract services for the home, such as lawn care, house cleaning, snow removal, plumbing repairs, home improvement, and child care. If I do not have to push around the lawn mower or harp on my daughter to do so, we can play catch in the backyard. Or I can read, and she can shop. If I do not spend all Saturday fighting with the garbage disposal, I can go to my son's soccer game. Or, I can watch golf on television. Microwave food and McDonald's hamburgers are great time-savers as well. After a hard day at work, it does not make sense to labor over the stove.

Suburban harmony flourishes with leisure. Because day-to-day home life must fit with the day-to-day matters of wage earning and work, vacations provide important opportunities for quality time. Upwardly mobile families seek a bond of affection similar to romance. Vacations to Disney Land and other recreational activities allow time to highlight and cultivate the modern family's love. Love is well served by escaping the confines and practical tasks of home. The affective goal is to enjoy each other's company because we are moved inside to do so. Our busy lives push us apart, but as hard as it is, we make time for each other. This is love as passion: our time together is occupied by the activity of spending time together. The affective connection is the activity. Sensitive fathers in the last quarter century have set out to correct the old practical ways of the past. We spent time with our fathers while raking the yard or painting the house. We have "relationships" with our children.

The suburban home represents the separation of the family from wider social life. The special image of the suburbs is representative. The internal structure of a household is divided into discrete private spaces with voluntary activity in common areas. The market value of a home in suburban America, for instance, is likely to hinge on matters like the quality of neighborhood and the ratio of rooms to bathrooms. While an image, the suburb is also a historical reference to the aspirations of the modern family. Individuals aspire to have a marriage based in romantic love, to begin a new family that is structurally isolated from the demands (and noise) of neighbors and clan, to bond with one's children, not out of duty, but through friendship and the parent–child equivalent of romantic love, to cultivate a haven amid a world of work and competition, and to establish equality between women and men through equal access to that world of competition and work and meaningful activities outside the home.[36]

The upwardly mobile family minimizes the social character of the household, and it is quite successful in fulfilling the modern political ideal of detachment from home. The suburban family is able to understand itself in terms of what is believed to be its essential affective bond. The irony, of course, is that this kind of emotional self-understanding is founded in great part on certain (middle-class) privileges of income and social status. Rawls' "morality of principles" is a privilege of progress. If his "morality of association" is simply a stage through which individuals pass on their way to maturity (and rational detachment), its character as an "organic social network" is also simply a stage in the narrative of the successful household. "Organic" is inferior to voluntary and contractual. The successful family minimizes those characteristics of association that Rawls thinks distinctive of family, such as assigned (not chosen) roles and duties, reciprocal (but not equal) relationships and stations, common goods that take precedence over individual interests, and moral criteria that are internal to the social structure of relationships.

We grow out of home. The upwardly mobile family frees itself from neighborhoods where people want to borrow the phone and from other constraints of cooperation, such as sharing yards, driveways, gardens, and childcare. Parents are likely to tell their children stories of apartments and neighborhoods past, of checking in on the elderly couple next door, of the loud footsteps of upstairs inhabitants, of crying babies and hospitality from lonely neighbors. The key element to these stories is social intrusion by neighbors who would not be chosen as friends. The corresponding achievement of the good home is privacy and voluntary social exchange. Internally, the successful family will minimize cooperative tasks, like cleaning up messes that are not one's own or preparing dinner for all, and it will emphasize individual advancement (paying for the best education) and individual interests (sports). It is likely that as children become adolescents and teenagers, jobs and extra-curricular activities will mean an end to shared meals and vacations. Family is a social setting we seem to need, but we are forever passing through.

Part Two

5

Two Households

Introduction

A few years ago, my wife, children, and I moved into our current home. The move was a trial that we do not care to repeat: a new teaching position for me, a job search for my wife, strange schools, unfamiliar people, and almost four hundred miles separating us from our former lives. One of the more difficult tasks of the move was looking for a house to buy. We thought that we knew what we wanted; apparently we did not.

In the old neighborhood, we were used to spending our evenings talking over the fence with neighbors. In fact, our yards and houses were modest enough to allow conversations with neighbors a few houses away without raising our voices. We had to get along, and we did. We shared meals, took care of neighborhood children, bought groceries for others if they needed something when we were going to the store. I could water my next-door neighbor's tiny garden from my own backyard, and I often did. With this family, we started a tradition of gathering together for Easter dinner, along with whatever extended family we had with us that year. Certainly, there were problems in the neighborhood (e.g., noise and roaming dogs), but on the whole we lived well as neighbors. Nevertheless, when we moved, we vowed that we would settle only for a house with a sizeable yard, to give us a little more space of our own.

We took great pains over our search for a new place to live. In *Helping Ourselves: Family and the Human Network*, Mary Howell articulates well our apprehensions. She notes that community "is feared as much as it is sought . . . For many of us the idea of 'community' is tied to a fear of losing what little control we seem to have over the business of our own lives . . . Thus, family has become the agency of our independence."[1] We were looking for a friendly neighborhood without the need for everyday contact or inter-dependence. Contrary to our original plan, we bought an old row house. It came within our price range, and its well-formed character appealed to us, its odd-shaped doors, high ceilings, and random layout of rooms. The price of character, we have discovered, is not monetary. For instance, our narrow backyard has a long wood-frame apartment building bordering its entire length. Children in the second-floor tenements next door often tease each other by throwing one another's belongings into our backyard. The older children taunt our little ones. The back of our house extends beyond the row of houses, and creates a peculiar situation where we could, if we cared to, converse with some of our neighbors from dining room to dining room. On the other side of the house, I have become used to the uncomfortable practice of waving at our neighbor through the closed kitchen window. This is not the home we were looking for.

This chapter has a biographical subtext about our being pulled into relations based on proximity and mutual concerns. The under-lying story is not my own; it is about the life of neighborhoods and networks of households amid a dominant grammar of self-sufficiency and independence. Howell's *Helping Ourselves* will figure prominently in the chapter. I discovered the book after following through on a passing reference by Christopher Lasch in the posthumous *Women and the Common Life*.[2] Lasch notes with regret that this work by Howell, published in 1975, has not been taken seriously if it has been read at all.[3] This lack of interest is understandable. Howell proposes, as will I, that ordinary practices of local interdependence are the substance of a complex system of interchange and a rich community life. Howell's proposal might appear uninteresting because we are accustomed to trivializing the social character of home. When taken seriously, neighborhood systems may be too adventurous for most of us, as Howell suggests. In any case, the little things in the neighborhood are likely to usher in great social change. The chapter begins with an inquiry about where the home is located in contemporary life. After an extended discussion of Howell's picture of the open family, I will conclude with an account of home economics as a complex system of exchange that deepens and extends common life.

A tale of two households

Ours is an age of contradictions. Although close to 50% of marriages end in divorce, the number of couples vowing never to part is strong and steady.[4] Parenthood is honored more than ever, not only by mothers but by fathers as well; yet, successful people minimize time spent with their children.[5] In response to this confusion, it is tempting to locate the home in some ideal time and place, among ancient Christians, European nobility, the American homestead, peasant farmers, the rising middle class at the turn of the century, or "Leave it to Beaver" reruns.[6] Even if we could will ourselves into a different era, our ideal family may not turn out to be bearable, or supportable as a practical reality. In his *Making of the Modern Family*, Edward Shorter begins with a blunt reference to the "Bad Old Days" of the pre-industrial age, when family was still "held firmly in the matrix of a larger social order."[7] While we might be wistful for days gone by, for inter-generational continuity and the stable home, we ought not overlook the ease with which the household has given way to cultural change and broader social and economic structures. The family we have fits who we are.

Shorter points to three basic moorings of the traditional family: a sphere of kinship, local community, and a historical continuity of habits and social practices. In contrast to the moorings of old, he refers to the modern family as a "free-floating dyad" that creates and dissolves itself at will and is characterized by its adaptability. According to Shorter, the traditional family was constrained by its attachments:

> One set of ties bound it to the surrounding kin, the network of aunts and uncles, cousins and nieces who dotted the old regime's landscape. Another fastened it to the wide community, and gaping holes in the shield of privacy permitted others to enter the household freely and, if necessary, preserve order. A final set of ties held this elementary family to generations past and future. Awareness of ancestral traditions and ways of doing business would be present in people's minds as they went about their day. Because they knew that the purpose of life was preparing coming generations to do as past ones had done, they would have clear rules for shaping relations within the family, for deciding what was essential and what was not.[8]

Shorter's description of traditional ties is illuminating, but his image of the modern home as a "free-floating dyad" is deceptive if we assume that we can simply cast our lines to the dock in order to secure ourselves, once again, to networks of kin, community, and time.

Like other historical and contemporary studies, Shorter's history of family indicates that traditional links have not really been cut; rather, they are dangling free, still dragging around fragments of what once was their moorage. Generations past are still remembered. Walking about as a McCarthy, I know that cultural heritage is often cause for Irish Americans to think of each other as kin, at least vaguely. This kind of generational continuity, although part of our lives, seldom has practical consequences. Most of us carry on our heritage through rituals that distinguish us (e.g., St. Patrick's Day parades); yet, we have little practical memory or tolerance for what ruled the daily lives of our ancestors.

Among its wide variations, the household and marriage did, at one time, have important social and economic functions, from treaty-making among European nobility to financial agreements and civic/religious commitments among seventeenth-century Puritans.[9] From the New England farm to the Boston tenement house, from plantation to the urban estate, the household sustained an economy, structured the wider social relations of its members, and provided the basic outlines of their identity and future, by passing on land, trade, wealth and station – or not. Today, the household still has powerful influence in determining a son or daughter's cultural literacy and prospects for social mobility.[10] The modern formula, in this regard, is a purely economic one: "It takes money to make money." In order to protect and promote the economic advancement of their members, middle-class families, for instance, have reduced family size and increased hours of work outside the home.

Like its precursors, the modern middle-class household has an economic strategy. It differs from its predecessors insofar as it has been dissociated, at least in theory, from our common language of economic utility. As noted in the previous chapter, the family's economic strategy is structured outside the home. At the same time that the modern family seems unable to resist invasion by market rationality and utilitarian contracts, it is defined in contrast to dominant forms of social relationships and economic canons of growth and profit.[11] Although as economically minded as ever, family, most assume, ought to lack an economy.

With the progress of modern industry and market rationality, "affection and inclination, love and sympathy, came to take the place of 'instrumental' considerations in regulating the dealings of family members with one another. Spouses and children came to be prized for what they were, rather than for what they represented or could do."[12] When money-making and social position take leave of home, sentiment fills the conceptual void, providing a rationale for marriage, in romantic love, and for our relationships to offspring, in the intensity of the mother–child relationship.[13] With the rise of industry, the world of production and politics comes to be located in the public life of men, while women are thought to sustain the emotional and moral sphere of home.[14] At the same time that the social and economic character of the household is degraded, family is honored for its non-economic, non-utilitarian relationships.

In the process of becoming "non-economic," however, the household becomes a center of consumption. Relationships between spouses and between parent and child become product- rather than production-oriented. As indicated in previous chapters, domestic life, on its own dull terms, is considered inhospitable to romance and must be remade and enlivened by floral scents, whiter laundry, and skin that challenges time, by leisure, exotic vacations, and expensive nights out without the kids.[15] At the same time, the focus of the household becomes its children, who take advantage of a protracted childhood, require high emotional investment, and are considered priceless to the degree they are beyond calculation of financial investment and return.[16] For those with means, monetary expense may in fact be a measure of emotional assets, not in a vulgar sense of buying love, but in a more systemic orientation that puts the benefits of wages out to the service of the consumptive household. Growth capitalism provides ever-increasing standards for good parents and the expanding plenty of the family. Affection, for all classes, carries a financial burden; monetary resources are the making of harmony at home.

Contractual social relations and market utility shape the dominant narrative of home, but on this standard, many households do not succeed. The ideal suburban home brings the benefit of social autonomy and various pleasures of leisure, but many aspiring families do not attain self-sufficiency and security. The middle-class family, by and large, is motivated and structured by a therapeutic individualism that advances the economic interests of its members while cultivating love and compatibility through non-utilitarian activities (i.e., fun).[17] But there are households (perhaps most) that occupy spaces outside the dominant narrative, on the fringe, or at an intermediate point between failure and success. The aspiring homes are bound to networks of dependency but always looking forward to the freedom of contractual arrangements. Such households continue to sustain informal and subsistent economies, and these networks of exchange lie between contractual arrangements, on one hand, and the sentimental home, on the other.

One example is the family farm, where the household is structured as a productive rather than consumptive set of relationships.[18] On a farm in Rocky Ridge, Maryland, Dennis "Buck" Wivell was raised as the youngest of thirteen children. When asked why his parents had so many children, Buck does not reply with comment about their love for children or their preference for large families. He points out, laconically, that his parents needed a lot of help on the farm. Buck's dry response does not indicate that he has had a better childhood and that his family enjoys a deeper bond. On the contrary, he is more likely to evoke sympathy than envy or admiration from his classmates. After graduation, he will leave them scratching their heads when he does not take his degree in accounting to a high paying job in the city. At this point in his life, he will tell you, he prefers manual labor. Buck's life on the family farm may not survive the market privileges of mass production and corporate farming, and Buck himself stands within the economic and social world of other American twenty-two-year-olds. But he is outside of it as well, and it is this other side of the household that, by necessity rather than lifestyle choice, pushes beyond the sentimental character of the modern home and represents a different kind of social formation.

Some analogies can be drawn from research on informal economies. Through her ongoing study of New York City's informal economy, Saskia Sassen-Koop proposes that the conditions of late capitalism, with its polarization of high- and low-paying jobs and its devaluation of labor, actually "induce the growth of an informal economy in large cities."[19] The middle-class boom after World War II brought a standardization of consumption and production. Now the impetus for uniformity is waning, along with the manufacturing industry and its capacity to afford a middle-class wage. The formal economy, in other words, depends upon an availability of resources and level of wages that it cannot sustain. These tensions within the formal economy create favorable conditions for the cheap, flexible work of unlicensed enterprises and informal labor arrangements.

The ugly side of the informal economy is the exploitation of workers in sweatshops and the like. The positive side is the strength of neighborhood sub-economies, usually found among immigrant communities, that provide local goods and services for a local price. According to Sassen-Koop, "certain aspects of the informal transportation system are illustrative, notably gypsy cabs servicing low-income immigrant areas . . . [as well as] certain aspects of the construction industry, especially renovations and small-store alterations or construction."[20] Often these enterprises will expand, from their local base, to a wider constituency in response to outside demand.

Community and kinship seem to be the difference between sweatshop abuses and advantageous illegal work. Outside the formal economy, household and neighborhood appear to make the difference between exploitation and mutually beneficial agreements, between economic captivity and cooperation. Unregistered workers who enter the work force in an "individuated and dispersed manner . . . [are] extremely dependent on the labor market supply and demand forces entirely beyond their control."[21] They have few protections and suffer the lawlessness of the informal economy. The economically privileged exploit the weak. Immigrant and ethnic enclaves, in contrast, tend to shield their members from the forces of the wider economy. Workers outside the rule of law are sustained by the rule of community and home. The household, in this regard, functions as a structured (albeit "non-public") economy where laborers and entrepreneurs, as husband and wife, brother and sister, share work and profits as they share a home.[22]

The relationship between the formal and informal economy suggests that we may not have to look outside the narrative of the upwardly mobile household in order to find a different kind of home. In the way that pressures of the formal economy create conditions for informal arrangements, the market conditions of the contractual, affective home produce conditions for different kinds of household economies based on establishing ties to neighborhood and wider networks of productive association. The narrative of suburban isolation and self-sufficiency will continue to be attractive, but for many, practically unattainable. The example of the immigrant enclave is interesting because it points to practical bonds of proximity and necessity, rather than lifestyle choice. In a similar way, many households are faced with the necessity of defining themselves as part of a neighborhood that must cooperate for mutual benefit and common ends.

Between the dominant languages of the disinterested market and private, sentimental attachments, there are spaces where a social fabric of reciprocity, roles, vocation, apprenticeship, and practical wisdom is sustained. These spaces are not suited to replace the dominant economy, and by their nature they will not become national or global systems. Neighborhood economies, inasmuch as they are restricted, offer a different grammar and richer possibilities for personal identity, common life, and an ordering of love. It is a mistake to champion an alterative economy as productive of romantic harmony and cheery affections at home. Because more profoundly social, this kind of household diverges from the ideal of the placid suburban home. As interdependence increases, more occasions arise for disagreements, hurts, and unresolved disputes. Those who have attained suburban autonomy will cringe at the noise, the demands of neighbors, and the annoyances of depending upon others. Family members may aspire to upward mobility, but these households will function, in large part, in terms of a local or subsistence economy.

In order to sustain themselves, members of these "subsistence" households establish and maintain informal connections, bartered agreements, and relationships of mutual benefit. There will be a local currency of skills, like welding or sewing, and informal standards of exchange, such as pies for plumbing. Many of these associations are asymmetrical and interpersonally difficult, and they will be tolerable only if balanced by a broader network and a wider sense of reciprocity between households. For balance to be maintained, these informal systems need the passage of time. Differing once again from the suburban dream, these homes will not provide a self-sufficient emotional economy. Spouses and children will look beyond the walls of their homes for friendship and intimacy, not when the family system breaks down, but as a matter of its good working order. I will use Mary Howell's simple designation of these kinds of households as open families rather than closed.[23]

Closed families

Closed families represent what Howell calls "the mythical standard of the 'ideal' for contemporary U.S. life."[24] The closed family understands its health and well-being in terms of emotional and financial independence. Pointing to the same kind of household, I have used the spatial image of the ideal suburban development: homes set apart in a neighborhood tied together by recreational interests and practically oriented to the outside world through contracted services, salary/wage-earning, and consumption.[25] Another useful conception is the ideal of the nuclear family, defined by narrow lines of kinship and a clear boundary between inside and out. For nuclear households, most kinship relations, grandparents to grandchildren for instance, are considered either positive or unacceptable intrusions, but always as external relationships. The nuclear structure also allows for a simplification of roles, such as father as breadwinner and mother as homemaker, or spouses simply sharing the two roles. In either case, housekeeping as a "role" is clearly divided from productive activity. Children are, in effect, accidental to the system; they have no operative role except as objects of investment (of time, money, emotions). The average nuclear family of four considers at least half its members as irrelevant to its practical maintenance. Its independence is sustained from the outside.

The closed family's self-sufficiency is largely dependent on professional expertise and bureaucratic managers. A principal goal of contractual government in the modern state is to make families independent (see Chapter 4). Contracting services from professionals and government agencies offers task-oriented, temporary relationships that are free from unpredictable entanglements. I would rather hire a professional to paint and repair my windows than the teenager down the street. In the latter case, I risk involvement in the project. I will have to give detailed instructions to the adolescent along with an avuncular sponsorship of her work. Making demands of a professional painter is less risky because our relationship is limited to a contract. With the teenager, we would have to develop something akin to friendship or a uncle–niece relationship, and I would probably end up making an alliance with her parents whether or not the job goes well. They would walk by the house attempting an innocuous look as they examine my windows with pride. If there is trouble, I am likely to find a parent planted in my yard for an interminable "teaching moment." Worse, it might be me out there teaching basic skills and a good work ethic.

If my car will not start, and my neighbor offers to help replace the starter, I will wonder what his help will cost me, not in dollars but in time, patience, and some future-but-not-yet-conceived payback. At the least, I will owe him gratitude. I might grumble when I write a check to a mechanic for a couple hundred dollars, but the nature of the transaction is clear and formal. My neighbor's offer is not businesslike and self-contained; it is an open-ended neighborliness. It is a risky gesture of friendliness between people who are close enough to see each other and to depend upon one another every day. If I had been stranded on the side of the road, I would gladly accept assistance from a good samaritan who, after helping me, would drive off never to be seen again. Intercourse between neighbors is different. My neighbor's benevolence is part of an ongoing relation, or it might establish a relationship. We will get to know each other with our hands under the hood, and not only that, he will eat up time with incessant jabber about something about which I have little interest (like cars or car racing). I become vulnerable: we will have a relationship that is not mutual, set out in terms of his giving and my receiving. I surely would prefer the independence offered me by the professional mechanic.

Professional expertise and bureaucratic management are also attractive because they present themselves as neutral and scientific.[26] Nowhere is the professional more prominent in day-to-day life than in matters of childcare and education.[27] A family therapist, childcare supervisor, teacher, and social worker have professional certification, and because detached from their clients, they are expected to have more skills and better judgment. Professionals do have a great deal to offer, but their social position privileges bureaucratic knowledge. A woman with a high school education, who has been taking care of children for twenty years, has much less currency and credibility than a young professional, especially if the older woman is not articulate and has not been paid (or paid much) for her twenty years of work. In any respectable business or public institution, the twenty-five-year-old with a degree in social work will be managing the forty-five-year-old wage-earner. This older woman knows children, while the younger has certification as an expert.

In addition, bureaucratic neutrality and detachment give priority to controlled space. Certified daycare is often assumed to be more trustworthy than informal home care. There is something reassuring about dropping off one's child at an authorized facility as opposed to a living room. More importantly, the public space socializes children into public life. In his pre-kindergarten program, our son learns that sharing is fun and makes a person feel good inside. This might be true in places where sharing is optional, a matter of amiable relations, or in a contractual setting where social agents are assumed to have a prior and more fundamental independence. At home we teach our children that sharing is necessary (because at home it is), whether they like it or not, whether it feels good or not. At home, sharing a toy is not a matter of happy recreation as much as it is an instance for learning the habits of sharing a bedroom, a kitchen, burdens, and responsibilities. Sharing is a basic grammar of common life. Sometimes it feels good and sometimes not. Sometimes if it makes us feel good inside it is not sharing: sharing, for example, vulnerability or suffering. Sharing in the household is difficult because it is a concession that we are not in control, that our personal possession is limited by common goods.

Sharing is a benign example. Another is the effort to encourage children to take great pride in being unique as though uniqueness *per se* were an achievement and a social contribution. If the student who is uniquely disruptive in class were equally as clever, she would raise an interesting objection from the time-out chair. "I was just being me." Sharing-as-fun and uniqueness-as-essential-value are simply methods of bureaucratic management. They are means of managing relations between individuals who do not share substantive goods and common ends. It is interesting that our public (contractual) socialization depends heavily on cultivating a moral psychology predicated on the isolated self and a pre-social conception of self-interest. I am my own unique category of person, and my motivation to engage in common life (to share) precedes a social conception of the self and personal benefit.

Amid a household economy, it seems to me, constraints are far less psychologically intrusive and personal identity far richer. I do not have to like what I must do, so that I have far more emotional and psychological latitude. When forced to reconcile, I remember the disdain with which I would say, "I am sorry," to my brother. Such contempt is out of bounds at school. In the home, my identity is shaped within a distinct economy of relationships and functions, and as a neighborhood becomes more functionally complex, the system cultivates distinctiveness. Households are similar only by analogy. Bureaucratic management, on the other hand, attempts to make social relationships uniform. In this regard, uniqueness must be emphasized as a counterweight to the systemic uniformity. The closed nuclear family, with its simplified roles, allows for the same kind of bureaucratic regularity. Family comes to mean clearly specified duties of parents to their children, so that there will be hand wringing when no one is present to play the "father" or "mother." Some of the best people I know are psychologically askew. The closed family helps to standardize emotional health, and it certainly makes theories of family therapy easier, where personal character and psychological maladies, for instance, can be identified according to birth order or to the personality types of one's parents.

Bureaucratic management and professional expertise fit with the polity of nation-state individualism and the dream of the suburban home. By assuming a neutral stance, bureaucrats can offer services without overt encroachment, while at the same time reinforcing the family's implied contract with the state. The government's requirements are minimal and usually appear to be benign. They amount to complying with professional guidance offered through the schools, from standards for vaccinations to definitions of abuse and neglect. Most parents manage to steer clear of trouble, and are left alone. Some argue that the state's relationship to the family is a subtle but pernicious management of child rearing and the like.[28] Such arguments are disquieting in their own right when they suggest that family ought to be an autonomous space. The intrusion of impersonal management is precisely this movement toward self-sufficiency. Contractual politics reduces the home to a private place, and in doing so, undermines the possibility of alternative social forms. Taking public servants at their word, we ought to worry that aid to families through public schools and other programs are oriented to the independence of the home. Professional and contractual services allow us to control our associations through contracted and thin social agreements and clearly defined tasks. The contract reduces conflict and the logic of ongoing, day-to-day dependence. It keeps social complications at a minimum, along with coinciding networks of reciprocity and informal relationships of interdependence, subsistence, and mutual aid. The threat of dominant forms of political and economic exchange is that they are inhospitable to the hospitality of home.

The closed household simply shifts its system of dependency to shallow, episodic relationships and deeper monetary (consumptive) demands. The closed family perpetuates a state of affairs where contractual arrangements, bureaucratic management, and professional expertise appear more dependable and available because informal dependence and reciprocity are, by definition, a challenge to the closed home. When I hire a painter rather than apprentice my neighbor's child, she will be inclined to believe that scraping, puttying, and painting are esoteric tasks. Will she ever know what a putty knife looks like? Or the difference between paint and primer? Or what her car's starter looks like? How to make flaky crust and apple pies? Replace screens and window panes, extend the life of her mattress, ground electrical outlets, grow string beans, or know when to plant potatoes? After generations of suburban advancement, when contractual services begin to characterize the home, everyone will become an expert, a professional. The skills and habits of household management will come from outside the neighborhood and home.

Household networks

Open families have loose and porous boundaries, whether they are thought to be nuclear, extended, traditional, or untraditional.[29] If the closed nuclear family is a cultural ideal, failure to succeed is likely to necessitate an openness. For example, the closed structure of one middle-class family was destabilized by divorce. After the father left, the mother decided and her teenage children agreed to take in a boarder in order to maintain their home. The teenagers were embarrassed about such an undignified arrangement. To make matters worse, the most promising tenant (an older man and friend of a friend) found their house attractive because he hoped to run a part-time upholstery business out of their large garage. As compensation, he kept track of repairs around the house. After a protracted adjustment period, the family members came to accept their household composition, even with their tenant's eccentricities, phone calls from a guy who knew a guy who needed upholstery work, and an occasional stranger in the kitchen. Sometimes an annoyance, sometimes full of good humor, home life began to take on a formative story of its own, the kind worth telling generations to come. It is interesting that we tend to think of such arrangements as part of the failure, rather than the success, of the home.

When Mary Howell, in *Helping Ourselves,* accounts for the expanding network of the open home into kinfolk, friends, and neighborhood, she focuses upon unpaid services and non-monetary (but still economic) exchange. In this regard, the tenant mentioned above began to be seen as an odd uncle, who paid rent but whose relation to the home's economy could not be reduced to a monthly check. So when the oldest child was married, she was not quite sure what to do with him. Should he sit in one of the family pews? Doesn't he count at least as much as Aunt Esther who is coming up from Florida? Kinship is fraught with these kinds of functional ambiguities and arbitrary preferences. When a friend sold me a dependable car for three hundred dollars (almost a gift), I gave my old car to my second cousin whom I hardly knew and who lived, my mother told me, about ten miles away. Later, he decided to give the car to his sister, whom I knew a little better. Sometime after, while visiting my mother, I was surprised to see my cousin pull up into the driveway in my old car. To tell the truth, I was happier to see my car than her, but even happier to see my beloved brown Toyota and my cousin together. I was happier still to know that she was keeping track of my mother (her great aunt), and it dawned on me that my mother had plotted out the series of exchanges long before. My second cousin drives out to see my mother in my old car; certainly a mutually beneficial relationship.

Howell defines kinfolk as "persons with whom we feel a bond of long-term commitment."[30] My relationship to my second cousins is an interesting case. We do not see each other often or know each other all that well, but we have a strong obligation to each other for mutual assistance. We understand ourselves within a network of interdependence, however distant and infrequently used. I would, for instance, open my home to them and their children, and I cannot account for this commitment simply out of fond affection. We are family, and family implies a kind of material (along with an emotional) exchange. Howell notes that mutual aid expands our circle of kinfolk. "Sometimes a friendship is so stable over time that it seems like a kin bond; friends sometimes act as if their commitment to each other to exchange services were as firm an obligation as it would be for a brother or sister [cousin, aunt or uncle]."[31] Howell observes that it is not an intensity of feeling that distinguishes mere friends from kin, but practical dependence and patronage.

Relationships to kinfolk (not merely blood relations) are "part pleasure and part prickles," part shared history and part misunderstanding, but definitely a web of commitment to mutual service over time. Howell continues:

> With kinfolk we are close to, we most often exchange such services as child care, loans or gifts of money, nursing care for those who are ill at home, visiting and cheering for those who are ill in a hospital, sharing sorrow and giving comfort at times of death, preparing food for special occasions or as a gesture of help. We also exchange special knowledge and skills – plumbing or carpentry, know-how about medical, legal, or educational problems, access to work opportunities, and experienced savvy about the manipulation of bureaucratic agencies like the telephone company, the school system, the outpatient clinic of the local hospital, or the welfare office.[32]

Kinfolk also gossip. Either in day-to-day conversation or while gathering for birthdays and holidays, they repeat shared stories and keep up with who is doing what and who is having a tough time with whom and with what. This gossip, albeit not always charitable, provides the lines of communication for the "exchange-of-service network." It is not idle talk; it is different from pernicious "office gossip" that is not directed to practical help and the good of others. Kin keep track of each other, and in such a network a person's identity is shaped by a web of relations that exceeds private or isolated household units.

Howell's definition of kinfolk includes lasting commitments of friendship, but she identifies "friends" as those with whom we have more temporary relationships. As with kinfolk, she points to the practical nature of friendship, to mutual service and unpaid work, to cooperation and common life. For Howell, friendship differs from kinfolk insofar as "exchanges of service" are more variable, less clearly defined, more voluntary, and more vulnerable.[33] Friendship has a greater dependence on proximity and accessibility. When we change jobs or schools for instance, friendships from the old setting are likely to fade. They do not survive the distance and are crowded out by people and responsibilities in our new life. This "occasional" quality of many friendships has its advantages. We build relationships that correspond to practical matters of everyday life, at work, at school, in task-oriented associations, and while coaching football. To this degree, friendships are clearly based in mutual service, and they link us to even wider networks. "Because all our friends bring us into potential contact with their own networks of kin and beyond, our access to an informal system of exchange of unpaid services is greatly increased through our friendships."[34] The challenge of friendship, in terms of mutual help, is to carry on the means and standards of exchange that tend to have a more natural feel among kinfolk. What is the point at which we ask for fair return, before we start feeling used?

Howell also locates practical exchange in the neighborhood. If kinfolk are defined by enduring commitments and friends by shared activities, neighbors are those with whom we share a place. "Their proximity allows an enormous potential for exchange, and opportunities for repeated contact make it possible to develop trust. The varieties of service that can be exchanged between neighbors are almost endless."[35] Neighbors may or may not be kin, and they may or may not be friends. However, they have a common standpoint: their common neighbors, houses, yards, streets, sidewalks, and soil. Neighborhoods depend upon a common respect for habitat. When families or individuals dishonor the place, through neglect or violence, they breed distrust and fear, and they destroy a neighborhood. Some housing environments are constructed with a disrespect for the human habitat, when families are crowded into projects and when parks are paved over so that no one needs to take responsibility for upkeep. Other environments are built to circumvent trust, by spacing houses a safe distance apart, by fencing and gating the development, or by achieving a (de facto) economic or racial segregation.

If a neighborhood is a habitat, then it is a joint endeavor. Some neighbors make their cooperation formal, through neighborhood associations, food cooperatives, and community centers. Some neighborhoods rally around specific goals, like closing down the drug dealers or raising money for playground equipment. The day-to-day activities of the household are cooperative as well, such as shoveling snow, mowing lawns, keeping track of children, rides to school and choir practice, fixing flat tires and dead batteries, moving furniture, borrowing tools, finding a use for hand-me-down clothes and old desks from the attic, sharing storage space, gardening, finding a good dentist or an electrician who will work outside normal hours. Neighbors reprimand each other's children, and they keep spare keys at each other's houses. They gossip as well. This is how they will know that Mr. Cameron was admitted to the hospital and that they will have to mow his lawn, pick up his mail, and get the bills to his daughter. Neighbors get reputations for cutting hair well, for generosity or stinginess, and for drinking too much. Neighbors know who needs what and who can be depended upon for something else.

Kinfolk, friends, and neighborhood are three distinct, but sometimes overlapping, kinds of networks. Each open household is dependent upon all three, in different ways and configurations. One household might lack relationships of extended family and have more contact with neighbors and friends who function as kin. Another family might have neighbors who are kinfolk or who are co-workers and friends. In any case, the critical feature of the open home is its practical dependence on a wider network of exchange, particularly in relation to a dominant cultural and economic narrative that gives privilege to the isolated, self-sufficient home. To this degree, the distinction between open and closed family is more definitive than distinctions between nuclear and extended or one- and two-parent families. Open families, whether single-parent, extended or nuclear, have a similar orientation to the household economy and are able to minimize the dependence on salary/wage earning, professionals, and constraints of the formal economy.

Home economics[36]

Last January, we in the mid-Atlantic United States were hit with a few unusually heavy snow storms, and we enjoyed the media hype and hysteria usual for areas unaccustomed to deep snow. Grocery shoppers descended upon milk and bread like locusts, and just about every business and institution that could close did. Sitting in our front room while our children made use of their deliverance from school, I caught a glance, through the window, of snow spraying upward. With a closer look, I discovered our neighbor from about five doors down pushing his snow-blower up and down the sidewalk. As far as I could tell, our neighbor, Carl, was clearing the walk from corner to corner, providing a service for at least seven families. I should add that our town council has mandated sidewalk snow removal. There were about ten inches of snow on the ground, so Carl's task was formidable and much appreciated by all, I was sure.

I began to wonder about his motives. Was Carl just looking for something to do since he could not go to work? Was the snow-blower a new toy? Were we doing him a favor by letting him play on our section of the sidewalk? Was he happy to have a heavy snow in order, finally, to justify the purchase (to his wife perhaps)? Was he simply being neighborly? Would he feel used if we did not thank him, and how much thanks did he need? What, I wondered, could I do for him? His generosity just hung in the air obliging me to respond, but I was not sure how. So I peeked my head out the door and gave him a self-conscious smile and nod. I gave a similar nod and a hello the next day along with a thanks, but the magnanimity of his act still hung in the air.

Our good neighbor's benevolence had a similar effect on others. The next day, after a dusting of snow, another neighbor was out clearing the same stretch of sidewalk with his leaf-blower. Like the first neighbor, his preference for a display of mechanical force blurred the line between play and work. His abuse of the power tool created a situation where it was unclear whether or not he was performing an altruistic act. A few days following, after another few inches of snow, enough to cancel school but not work, a third neighbor's two boys were sent out, shovels in hand, in order to take responsibility for the corner-to-corner expanse of walkway. I began to wonder if clearing only one's own section of sidewalk would now be taken as an offense.

When would my turn come, and would my turn mean shoveling snow or doing something else? Both of these questions, first about timing (when?) and next about the form or opportunity for my own expression of neighborliness (what benefit might I bestow?), are key to a basic pattern of household exchange between kinfolk, friends, and neighbors. No one responded to our good neighbor by writing him a check or by dashing out of the house to help him. In either case, he rightfully would be offended. If he were obviously struggling with a shovel, that would be a different matter. Given his mastery of his task, our duty as neighbors was to accept and appreciate his kindness. What would I be saying to him if I rushed out of the house to clear the snow with my shovel before he was able to finish my section of the sidewalk?

There would be no insult, of course, when Pam Kavanaugh sent over a dozen cookies the next day, not as payment but because she happened to have made a double batch. Sam, her eight-year-old boy, told me the story as though it were an adventure. He had helped his mother make cookies. He arranged them on a plate. He wrapped them in cellophane, and he walked them over to Mr. Carl's house with the message (obviously rehearsed) that he and his brother had been making cookies, just for something to do, and wanted to know if Mr. Carl would like to have some. No offense would be taken after the two following snows, when Mr. Carl would return from work to find his own walk cleared, first after just a dusting of snow and then after an inch or two. I expect that when the next heavy snow falls, we will expect to see him out with his snow-blower. Our expectations will have the character partly of a hope and partly of an unarticulated obligation. Carl is now the heavy snow remover (among other things). In one sense, his benevolent use of his snow-blower will always be understood as a gift; yet in another, it would become part of a pattern of reciprocity, part of the neighborhood equilibrium whereby we sustain a certain status among others and exchange benefits.[37]

This kind of neighborly gift exchange is distinguished from buying, selling, lending, and leasing by its temporal structure and by its lack of standardized currency.[38] The counter-gift is deferred, so that, through the lapse of time, a kind of forgetfulness and a shift in context allow the return-gift to take on a gratuity of its own. Baking cookies with one's children in order to occupy them during an idle day establishes an occasion where the excess of cookies (rather than snow removal) is reason for the gift. This means of exchange might appear to conceal the payback; on the contrary, it reveals exchange as social (that is, mutual) self-interest and, in the process, names the social self as a gift. A gift comes back to the original giver not as payment or compensation, but as a social gesture and benefit that carries with it the mark of the giver. Social reciprocity is maintained, weaving a social bond, cultivating standards of neighborliness, and shaping the status, identity, and particular niche of the good neighbor. Gift exchange is not leveled to a common currency, but is sustained by difference and by an inequality of exchange that has its equilibrium within a wider social network. One to one, single party to party exchanges are rare. Instead, a series of overlapping non-identical gifts take on value and balance in an intricate constellation of wedding showers, baptisms and first communions, three-bean casseroles for grieving families, rides to work, babysitting, informal childcare, and hand-me-down clothes.

We may give our gifts as unmerited and unconditional, but it is a mistake to confuse gratuity with a lack of reciprocity.[39] The temporal structure of gift exchange and the non-identical gift hold gratuity and reciprocity together, and by doing so, make gift-giving a *continuing* possibility. Put another way, the gift is expressed fully only when it mediates shared life. A gracious overture to a stranger, for instance, is truncated if he or she remains outside. Full gratuity is oriented to inviting the stranger to sit at one's table as a guest. Although highly regarded, the anonymous gift is giving cut short and controlled. Giving implies preferential treatment, a being-chosen, that either comes as an invitation or confirms an existing relationship. Gift exchange, reciprocity, doing something for another, and accepting assistance are media through which relationships take shape, through which they take on their particular character.

The birthday gift is a common example. Birthday gifts among adult siblings are reciprocal, even though gifts are not given with the intention of securing a gift in return, and there is never a moment of parity. There is no end point at which someone tallies the score. As one birthday follows another, one imbalance is overturned by another (or sometimes not). The gift exchanges, like the ongoing relationships, are never complete. Gifts are not identical or comparable, and sometimes no gift is given at all. Some asymmetries remain and reflect different roles and stations within the network of kin. Seen over time, the cycle of gifts will represent the particularities of that specific circle of reciprocity: who's the glue, who's on the periphery, who makes more money, who likes to spend, who gives the thoughtful gift, and who depends upon whom for what. The same can be said about relationships between spouses or friends. We do not offer identical contributions to our relationships; we are not identical people, and our relationships will be characterized by asymmetries particular to us, which amount to our own personal equilibrium. Likewise, on a theological level, God's grace establishes a distinct kind of reciprocation. Grace is utterly gratuitous, and it is the basis for sharing not only communion with

God but the love of God, which makes possible an active, loving return to God and love for others, even one's enemy, for God's sake.[40]

Networks of kin, friends, and neighbors have their own internal logic and course of development. Unpaid services and reciprocity of the household should not be taken as merely an informal imitation of paid and contracted services. The nature of the transaction is different. The exchange of work and assistance may take the form of bartered agreements or monetary compensation, but the base from which these arrangements emerge, insofar as they are set within the open household and neighborhood, is the reciprocity of the gift. The household economy has its foundation within the temporal structure of common life and the ad hoc currency of the non-identical gift.

One day last Spring, my neighbor Chris strolled over while I was putting in replacement windows. He wanted to know if I planned to replace any more windows. I did. He wanted me *to let him* find a good deal on windows *for me*. That was how he put the matter. I would be doing him a favor by letting him help me. He suggested that he would be offended if I went off and bought the rest of the windows retail. He had a friend who had a contractor's license and could get me the windows wholesale. He was persistent (I suspect that he appreciates the hospitality we show to his children). It seems that Chris' offer was part of neighborly reciprocity, but with an interesting economic twist. He was offering me a privileged route around retail, undermining the rules of trade and taxation. The transaction would be much like the neighborhood's support of part-time labor and services. If you need a carpenter, you ask around for someone who will work in the evening after work. You pay cash. The down side is that you might have to wait a few weeks or months, and you will have to do some of the work. The informal system can be painfully casual.

An interesting question is whether or not these transactions violate basic rules of economic exchange. Does informal work violate union rules? Is the wholesale window connection something like insider trading? Insider trading is wrong because it contradicts the proper functioning of the market. If I act on privileged information about the future of a company and its stock, I disregard the very rules of fairness that make the market work. In fact, my success depends upon those rules in the same way that the effectiveness of a lie depends upon principles of truthfulness. If lies were the rule, not even truth would be trusted. Insider trading works precisely because it is a deception.

The household economy is different. The offer of wholesale windows and black-market carpentry is consistent with our neighborhood reciprocity. The neighborhood is a network of privileged access, personal favors, and most of all, gratuity. Access and gratuity might in fact work in the other direction. If a neighbor or cousin were starting her own business, I might give her more work than I need, pay her more, and encourage others in the network to do so. In this case, we would be giving her a privileged step up in relation to the wider market (something that seems equivalent to price fixing). In this way, the open household cultivates a sub-economy underneath the contractual, impersonal, and individualist constraints of the dominant system. It is natural for networks of kinfolk, friends, and neighbors to do so inasmuch as their social bond and rules of exchange have an entirely different character. On the one hand, the bond is personal and requires preferential treatment and trust. On the other, exchange must always be incomplete and therefore have the quality of a gift that holds the social body together in a temporal sequence of reciprocity.

Housework

In our capitalist economy, housework makes people, primarily women, vulnerable.[41] Housecleaning, grocery shopping, cooking, caring for children, mowing the lawn, and organizing community endeavors constitute the housekeeper's long hours of unpaid labor. Housework is not productive in the dominant economy. No distinct product is manufactured, nor does monetary compensation accrue by punching a clock, by position or salary, or by service rendered. To the degree that value is determined by the market, housekeeping is nearly meaningless. Housekeepers acquire little worth, few assets, and scant means for economic independence. In a world where power and cultural capital are structured outside the home, housework diminishes one's personal and social standing. The homemaker is left with no means of self-sufficiency, no credit rating, and no résumé.

Modern economic life has developed along gender lines and between different spheres of activity, between male productivity and a woman's work in the home or home-like work, such as nursing care, any work with children, and housecleaning. Empirical evidence continues to bear out the vulnerability of women and the home. Working women continue to earn considerably less than working men; twice as many elderly women are poor, and more than half of the households in poverty are maintained by single mothers.[42] The compromised status of the home and homemaker is matched, ironically, by the vulnerability of modern work, of salary and wage earning. The working class has no control over the availability of work and secures little or no loyalty from employers, unless employers are willing to make non-economic commitments. Even the professional or successful modern household is supported by a very shallow foundation, by one or two incomes without which the family's home and lifestyle cannot be sustained.

The upwardly mobile family responds to wage vulnerability by narrowing and closing off its borders, by minimizing the household economy, and by redoubling its focus on wage earning and contractual arrangements. The aspiring home is sustained and advanced by minimizing entanglements at home: its time-consuming tasks, its peripheral (non-nuclear) relationships, and the less efficient system of neighborhood reciprocity. However, except for a rare few, this strategy of narrowing boundaries is self-defeating. The home is secured, but there is little time or reason to be there. Household management, then, loses its legs, loses its rationale, and the housekeeper is no longer interdependent but simply dependent and socially inconsequential. The market economy makes voracious demands upon our time, whether we are wage earners or salaried professionals, and home life becomes a competing interest.[43] Except for special occasions or planned quality time, the household becomes part entertainment center (i.e., oriented to leisure), part bedroom, part closet, and a place to heat (but not prepare) food. Housekeeping begins to look more like working as a dispatcher or air traffic controller, managing arrivals and departures.

This chapter is central to the book, but I worry, as we come to its end, that its content seems trivial. Such matters as snow removal and hand-me-down clothes are hardly exceptional practices. The apparent insignificance, however, reveals a great risk. Ordinary practices of community threaten to draw us in and bind us within everyday practices of a richly shared life. My examples are modest because the encroachment of market utility and its thin social

relations is so clear. Upward mobility and the promise of contractual politics are nothing if not safe. The open household requires
a sense of adventure and a willingness to welcome the unknown and
to entertain the unmanageable. If we let down our guard, neighbors
will be entering our homes as though they belong there. An interesting contrast to suburban mobility is a recent downward movement
among the middle class. Malia McCawley Wyckoff and Mary
Snyder, for example, offer a self-help guide, *You Can Afford to
Stay Home with Your Kids*.[44] The movement's focus on child rearing is not new, as it is basic to the conception of the closed family.
The book's suggestion that the household can be something other
than a locus of consumer capitalism is not new either. Many of
the authors' practical suggestions are common knowledge (and
necessity) in working-class homes and for homemakers who continue to work for wages and sustain their homes through an
informal economy, reciprocity, and frugality.[45] The interesting
aspect of *You Can Afford to Stay Home* is its theme of conversion,
not only converting the consumptive household into a subsistent
one, but also a conversion of a family's "worldview." We will be
transformed by the way of home.

6

The Social Role of the Family

Introduction

Kathleen and James McGinnis, coordinators of the Parenting for Peace and Justice Network, propose that "families are called to be nothing less than God's instrument for the transformation of the world."[1] Allow me an understated response. It is challenging even to imagine that their claim has any relation to what goes on in my house. Nonetheless, their bold statement represents a common theme in recent theological discussions of family. Modern political thinkers, like John Rawls, have consistently asked (at least in theory) whether or not the ties of family ought to be abolished entirely. The family appears to be essentially unjust insofar as its loyalties are local and its use of resources self-interested. Modern political theorists ask how the inequities perpetuated by family can be mitigated. Contemporary theological accounts of family turn the question around. How would we have any hope for justice without family?

When Kathleen and James McGinnis issue their prophetic call to families, they make their connections between family and social justice through a sweeping critique of materialism, individualism, racism, sexism, violence, and militarism.[2] In other words, their approach does not present a model of family as much as the language and concerns of national politics and broad cultural reform. Their response to racism, for example, does not require any account of family. Their criticism is simply applied to how family should operate, as it could be applied to any other institution.[3] The McGinnis' challenge the bourgeois family, its closed posture toward the world, its consumptive practices, and its concerns for economic advancement and social respectability. They provide a guide for encouraging a stewardship of resources, practicing non-violence, and teaching multicultural attitudes at home. They claim that the world will be changed by family, but their immediate concern is a transformation of family rather than the world. Kathleen and James McGinnis turn the problems of predominant political structures in upon family.

In 1990, the McGinnis' *Parenting for Peace and Justice* (1981) was reprinted with a new preface and an additional chapter. The new material offers frank reflections about their own parenting from a perspective "Ten Years Later."[4] I should add, before going further, that the authors outline a commendable and ambitious program for parenting. Ten years later, when their pre-adolescents have become teenagers, they admit, admirably, both successes and failures. The shopping habits of their children is a good example. Their teenagers "continue to be comfortable with buying some of their clothes at second-hand stores."[5] However, the comfort of the McGinnis children is due, in large part, to peer approval. Among their friends, second-hand clothes can be both economical and cool. The tenor of their parents' sense of failure is that their sons and daughter do not stand out as leaders. In many ways, they are typical teenagers, not distinct in political mindset or ambition.

After reading the new preface of *Parenting for Peace and Justice*, I walked down the hall to discuss the book and matters of parenting with a colleague who holds our Chair of Catholic Social Teaching. His response was something like the following. "My wife and I read this book years ago, and we quickly realized that we could not pull that kind of thing off. We were operating at the level of trying to keep our boys from killing each other, and our solution to their fighting appeared when we were given a dog. When our kids would fight, the dog would become so upset that they would stop for her." I imagine that Kathleen and James McGinnis would see humor, if not dismay, in this bit of practical wisdom. They might be asking too much of family when most of us are trying to get through the day without anyone hurt. We ought not expect family to redeem or carry the moral weight of the world.

The previous chapter has proposed that the household economy functions as a part of a larger but still local network of reciprocity and social exchange. Family plays a vital part in neighborhood and community life, making for a rich and venturesome social world. The household cultivates a deep sense of belonging and personal identity. The McGinnis' interest in second-hand clothes, conflict resolution, and hospitality represents the grammar of the open home and its common neighborhood endeavors. The problem with their *Parenting for Peace and Justice* is not its sense of family, but its exaggerated expectations about what family can do. On a local level, networks of households can create a complex and interesting texture of social life, but it is not the role of family to transform the world. It is the social role of family to be dependent upon a larger social body (although depending upon pets for teaching peace is also an interesting idea that ought to be taken seriously). In theological terms, family is called to be part of the social adventure we call the church.

This chapter treats the recent history of Catholic social teaching, but its basic story line reflects the social role of family as it is understood more broadly. The social role of family has diminished in the last century or so, insofar as the modern economy and state have replaced functions formally within the purview of the household. Ironically, while the actual role of the home has been minimized, the proposed role of family has increased its moral burden. Recent concerns for family values, for example, have the effect of keeping the household isolated in its own independent sphere, while glorifying the virtues of the home (see Chapter 4). Theological considerations of family work differently, but they have a similar effect. By locating family on a global level, Kathleen and James McGinnis threaten to detach the household from its local habitat, and in the process, family is asked to stand above the very social world of which it is a part (in order to be the instrument of world transformation).

Likewise, accounts of transcendent nuptial union, such as those discussed in Chapters 2 and 3, have gained prominence as a way to position marriage and family at the core of social life. As a result, marriage is expected to be a self-contained whole, and social reciprocity or nuptial unity-in-difference begins to hinge almost entirely on gender. Family is reduced to the roles of husband/father and wife/mother. My intention is not to argue that gender roles and identity are unimportant (see Chapter 9). The problem with the personalist account of marriage is that it lacks social complexity.[6] The functional roles of the family itself, for instance, are reduced to a frugal two: father and mother. Surely, neighborhood life, work, food cooperatives, and networks of friends complete the internal operations of family and multiply its possible configurations. Families work well when we do not expect them to give us all we need, and local connections are internal to how the household works. The predominant theology of family, on the other hand, isolates it with the formidable and lonely task of being a whole communion.

Catholic social teaching

Family, in Catholic social teaching, is a mediating institution. In the time between Leo XIII's *On Christian Marriage* (1880) and John Paul II's *Letter to Families* (1994), many changes are evident in matters of sex, marriage, and the household, but all through the changes the institution of family continues to be seen as an organic body that mediates social life. This continuity fits with a constellation of developments, the most important of which, for our purposes, is a shift from conceiving of family as a conserving institution to identifying it as a reforming one. In theory, family moves from sustaining the social order to transforming it, from being a complement to economic and political institutions to offering an alternative social form. Family is expected to mediate a basic social communion that the dominant social and economic order tends to suppress.

A helpful analysis of these transitions is provided by Lisa Sowle Cahill.[7] She contrasts Pope Leo XIII's "external" understanding of marriage with the modern subjective turn. Cahill points out that Leo XIII sustains a "medieval vision," where " 'social policy was largely limited to the discussion of the *a priori duties* and responsibilities assigned to every social office and function in the community . . .' [T]he roles of married persons are defined 'outward' rather than in terms of the interpersonal bond itself."[8] Cahill marks the Second Vatican Council's *Gaudium et spes* (1965), as does John Paul II, as the point of transition. Vatican II is understood widely as the watershed dividing an external Augustinian theology of marriage from contemporary inter-subjective accounts. The contemporary account is preferred because it sets marriage on a foundation of inter-personal love.

The interpersonal turn makes the outward disposition of marriage ambiguous and its social character less distinct. According to Cahill, *Gaudium et spes* "moves the idea that marriage is a 'community of love' unequivocally to center stage," and by doing so, opens the way to make conjugal love prior to (as the basis for) the duties and functions of parenthood and family.[9] Citing the same paragraph of *Gaudium et spes* (no. 48), John Paul II offers a similar definition of marriage, as "the covenant of conjugal love freely and consciously chosen, whereby man and women accept the intimate community of life and love willed by God himself, which only in this light manifests its true meaning."[10] From this point of general agreement, disagreement emerges. Cahill and John Paul II agree that conjugal love is the context in which to broach questions about the good of procreation (while Leo XIII did not); yet, Cahill sees the turn toward love as offering latitude on questions of contraception, while John Paul II does not. Cahill also understands the new locus of conjugal love to necessitate, or at least make possible, reform in the matter of gender roles, while John Paul II is less encouraging. Further, John Paul II's theology on conjugal union, particularly his theme of complementarity, is used throughout the spectrum of contemporary theology, but in ways contrary to his own purposes (e.g., to buttress arguments for the ordination of women).[11] The unequivocal turn inward produces equivocal outward expressions.

Cahill is worried about another outward ambiguity, that the modern model of personal fulfillment and love "is inadequately attentive to the solidarity Christian values imply both for the couple and family and for the connection of the narrower relation to the wider society and religious communities."[12] The problem is obvious. When marriage is defined by inward relations rather than outward roles and duties, connections between interpersonal harmony and the social function of family become loose. Cahill is concerned that such a situation cuts marriage off "from social and kinship supports and purposes which augment the resources of the couple to sustain their relationship through times of difficulty."[13] John Paul II and activists like Kathleen and James McGinnis conceive of family as a basis of social reform, but Cahill rightly expresses concern that the inwardly defined union tends toward a closed account of family.

This tendency toward self-contained communion has its source, ironically, in a growing dependence upon family as a primary social agent. The increased focus on the home has its touch point in Vatican II's description of family as "domestic church."[14] "Domestic church" in the teaching of Vatican II "helped appro-priate the notion that the Christian couple and their children participate in an ongoing sacramental reality through which they are sanctified and invited to participate actively in the outward mission of the church, especially through service and hospitality."[15] *Lumen Gentium* (no. 11) speaks of domestic church in terms of the role of parents as "the first heralds of the faith with regard to their children," and through child rearing, encouraging religious vocations.[16] *Apostolicam actuositatem* (no. 11) refers to family as "a domestic sanctuary of the Church," that has the mission of being "the primary cell of society" through its prayer, worship, mutual affection, nurture of children, hospitality, practices of justice, and care for the poor. John Paul II in *Familiaris consortio* (no. 21) uses "domestic church" to highlight the role of family as "a specific revelation and realization of ecclesial communion," particularly in terms of the love that animates family's interpersonal relationships. The language of domestic church positions family as a site for the "reproduction of the Church."[17]

This personalist account of marriage reflects wider currents in ecclesiology, toward an understanding of the church as communion.[18] At first glance, "communion," especially in reference to the interpersonal affection of family, looks like an inwardly oriented institution that is focused on matters of its own common life. However, ecclesial communion is understood to be intrinsically ordered outward through the character of the gathered body as a sign of God's presence, patterned in the way of Jesus and the life of discipleship. The community is a sacrament, an outward and visible expression, that brings real change to the world. Likewise, the family's communion and its character as domestic church are used, in the main, to emphasize the family as "an agent of transformation of the social order, so that human well-being can more adequately be served within it."[19] The idea of a domestic church is used in an attempt to intensify the social role of the household by presenting family as a contrast-society in a culture of attenuated social relations.

Leo XIII

Pope Leo XIII explains in his *On Christian Marriage* (1880) that "God intended it [marriage] to be a most fruitful source of individual benefit and of public welfare."[20] He defines marriage through traditional Augustinian goods of procreation, fidelity, and sacrament (indissolubility).[21] Following this tradition, Leo XIII holds that marriage provides for social order. It provides for the propagation of the race, brings forth children for the church, and establishes good order in the home. The married state is a means for a couple to attain both natural happiness and supernatural holiness, "by their lightening each other's burdens through mutual help; by constant and faithful love; by having all their possessions in common; and by the heavenly grace which flows from the sacrament." Marriage, when characterized by its triad of goods, serves the state as well. "From such marriages as these, the State may rightly expect a race of citizens animated by a good spirit and filled with reverence and love for God, recognizing their duty to obey those who rule justly and lawfully, to love all, and to injure no one."[22]

At first blush, Pope Leo's account of marriage seems to parallel contemporary invocations of family values. Like more recent defenses of family, he assumes that monogamous marriage is a natural state, with a gender-based division of labor and with parental authority that reflects and sustains good government and the good order of society. Leo XIII assumes that family is a mediating institution of God's providential order, of which the nation-state is a mediating institution as well. According to Leo XIII's (Thomistic) logic, the family mediates goods of the state only when a state reflects divine governance; otherwise, family and state will be at odds. In other words, Leo XIII disavows the viability of both godless marriage and the godless state.[23] He presupposes a distinction between church and state but not a separation in the modern sense. Church and state work in harmony, with distinct roles, to a common end. Pope Leo's *On Christian Marriage* is written against secular states that usurp the church's authority in matters of marriage, undermine the nature of family, and challenge God's providential design. He holds that guidance by the church is necessary for the good order and flourishing of civic life.

While recent appeals to God and country might appear similar in reference to divine providence and national vitality, the Leonine project is distinguished by its organic character. Family is not an independent institution. Leo XIII conceives of all social life as an ordered whole, so that his references to the roles of family are not set in contrast to independent economic or political relations, but dependent upon them. In contrast to modern economic and con-tractual arrangements, Leo XIII's organic view is not reducible to the poles of individual and state or individual and society; rather, common life is characterized as a social body that is institutionally diffuse. The roles and functions of various distinct bodies within the wider social body are not reducible to a single form.[24] Fathers, mothers, children, husbands and wives are social agents in relation to (and in harmony with) other agents such as governing authorities and their subjects, clergy and lay, rich and poor, owners of capital, labor, and trade associations. The social body is constituted as diverse but overlapping hierarchies where relations are reciprocal but not identical, where the employer is due something quite different than he receives from labor and where he owes the laborer at least what the laborer owes his children and wife.[25]

The civilization of love

While Pope Leo conceived of the household in terms of harmony with the social order, more recent theology understands family as a contrasting social form. In John Paul II's *Letter to Families* for instance, he speaks of a civilization, or more precisely, he speaks of two civilizations.[26] It is tempting to underscore the significance of two civilizations with reference to Augustine's *De civitate dei*. One city finds its beginning and end in God, and another falls to pride in its own temporal limits, to its rejection of God and, as a consequence, to its fundamental rejection of human good. Like Augustine, John Paul II intends to show that what is for him the reigning civilization is no true commonwealth. However, the Pope's notion of a "civilization" differs from Augustine's "city" in a few important ways. John Paul II's idea of civilization offers a means to circumvent a detailed account of institutions associated with the city, whether Rome, London, or Washington, DC. Civilization, as John Paul II develops the concept, allows a shift away from Augustine's temporal structure and toward social forms that underlie human culture. Family, then, is defined less by its relations to other social institutions and more by its ideal form. The ideal is a communion of persons.

John Paul II speaks of not simply a civilization but a civilization of love. His framework of two civilizations provides a way to assert an organic social bond that is fundamental to persons and prior to the city and social institutions. His idea of civilization springs from his theological understanding of the person, who is not in any sense an isolated individual but always in communion with God and others (as "I" and "Thou"). The person is destined (oriented and disposed) to share in divine life and in human community (*Letter,* 7). Family is the origin of the person and "continues to be, as it were, [an] existential horizon, that fundamental community in which the whole network of social relations is grounded . . . Do we not often speak of the 'human family' when referring to all the people living in the world?" (*Letter,* 2).

The civilization of love finds its source in God and is the very possibility and a basic endowment of human life. He cites Gen. 1.26–7, "'Let us make humankind in our image, according to our likeness . . .' [I]n the image of God he created them; male and female he created them." Not only in reference to Genesis but also to God's Trinitarian love, Pope John Paul recalls that "the divine 'We' is the eternal pattern of the human 'we,' especially of that 'we' formed by the man and the woman created in the divine image and likeness" (*Letter,* 6).[27] He extends the divine image of our creation as "male and female," to fatherhood and motherhood: "Be fruitful and multiply." Human parenthood is creative in a way that is "rooted" in biological generation and "at the same time transcends it" (*Letter,* 9). Mothers and fathers produce offspring in a sense analogous to God's own creativity. In each case, the origin of life is love.[28] The consummate communion of persons is expressed through the nuptial complement of husband and wife who complete one another in mutual and "total" self-giving.

Accordingly, John Paul II shifts the meaning of civilization from its etymological relation to citizen (*civis*) to its theological grounding in our being human (*Letter,* 13). John Paul minimizes the civic or political dimensions of civilization in favor of connotations pertaining to human culture (*humanitatem*). Civilization, for John Paul, is defined by the personal relationships implied in *cultus*. Civilization belongs to the common achievements, endowments, and character of a people, and it also points to care and encouragement, to growth and flourishing in solidarity and friendship. Civilization cultivates human life. "Created in the image and likeness of God, man has received the world from the hands of the Creator, together with the task of shaping it in his own image and likeness. The fulfillment of this task gives rise to civilization, which in the final analysis is nothing else than the 'humanization of the world' (*mundi ad humanam speciem conversio*)" (*Letter,* 13).[29]

This shift away from the *polis* to culture is critical to John Paul II's strategy of social transformation. Consistent with Catholic social thought before and especially since Leo XIII, individual persons are defined not over against the social body (as in modern contractual government), but in terms of natural harmony, a shared life and common ends. With Leo XIII, this conception of social life is set in contrast to both socialism and liberalism. Socialism is rejected because, among other reasons, the state exceeds its rightful role by taking over the function of a variety of social agents, particularly the family. Socialism is mistaken when it denies that individual agents, in their use of private property, are necessary for the goods of each and all (*Rerum*, 4, 11). A similar case is made against liberalism; it undercuts intermediate social bonds and their natural reciprocity. On one hand, political liberalism conceives of the individual in isolation, and on the other, economic liberalism leaves the worker not only isolated but powerless and defenseless (*Rerum*, 3).[30]

John Paul II sustains this line of critique by moving from Pope Leo's institutional-organic harmony to an interpersonal-organic communion. Unlike Leo XIII, John Paul II does not reject the social contract in favor of an organic conception of the nation-state. When speaking in political terms, Pope John Paul uses the language of equality rather than complementarity and democracy rather than hierarchical ordering.[31] John Paul II's strategy is to counter contractual individualism and economic utilitarianism by defining the social bond as inter-subjective self-giving (rather than through presocial self-interest). Recall that Leo XIII, in contrast, speaks of outward duties. With John Paul II's shift, social life becomes fundamental (internal) to the person without Leo XIII's organic conception of political hierarchy, station, and function. An organic conception of family is sustained without reference to an organic social order.

The family contains the whole. John Paul II presents marriage as the emblematic community of persons.[32] This organic bond between male and female is always in the background as the basis for the coming-to-be of persons. The complementary "I" and "Thou" of husband and wife express our social nature and correspond to our "capacity to live in truth and love" (*Letter*, 11). Marriage expresses our essential communion through the movements of human knowledge (intellect) and freedom (the will). Truth and love, consciousness and freedom, are a single movement, where we know through the expression of our will to love, where we truly find ourselves in self-giving. "Love causes man to find fulfillment though the sincere gift of self. To love means to give and to receive something which can be neither bought nor sold, but only given freely and mutually" (*Letter,* 11). In the context of this foundational communion, gender becomes the basic category of identity and difference. The essential difference of male and female points to nuptial union as the loving of the "other" in a movement outside of oneself. Marriage is emblematic because it is self-completion through mutual self-giving: a unity-in-difference.

The most significant point for us is this. Marriage, along with parenthood, represents the basis of civilization (i.e., the humanization of the world); therefore, marital love is the conceptual basis of all authentic social contracts. In knowledge and freedom, marriage is established by the consent of willing love, so that family expresses the special human vocation to be a person completed in common life. As a contract, marriage is a promise and testament to the social nature of human life. As consent, it expresses the basis of human fulfillment, a conscious and free self-giving, not merely for purposes of social utility, but in order to "serve the truth in love" (*Letter,* 11). In giving myself to the "other," I find myself as a person, which is equivalent to saying that I find the "we," as we are moved by the primordial, Trinitarian "We." The image of God is expressed through the genealogy of every person, as each of us comes into the world through a union of man and woman. Regardless of its imperfections, this union is a participation in the creative love of God. The concrete form and meaning of family is the coming-to-be of a person for his or her own sake through life in communion. Family, in this regard, is "the center and the heart of the civilization of love" (*Letter,* 13).

Solidarity

John Paul II's other civilization or, more precisely, the anti-civilization, may appear in a variety of forms, but at the center of its logic is a rejection of the essential dignity of persons The other civilization threatens a "cultural uprooting" of family; that is to say, it undermines the genealogy of persons and the communion of persons which make family the "fundamental cell" of society and representative of the human family. In his *Letter to Families*, John Paul II isolates currents in contemporary civilization that are "linked to a scientific and technological progress which is often achieved in a

one-sided way, and thus appears purely positivistic" (*Letter,* 13).
Agnostic in theory and utilitarian in practice, this positivism denies
the essential (inner) dignity of human life, reducing common life to
"a civilization of production and of use, a civilization of 'things' and
not of 'persons,' a civilization in which persons are used in the same
way as things are used" (*Letter,* 13).[33] This other civilization of consumerism, commodified human beings, and death defines human
life externally and instrumentally, rejecting the inherent dignity of
the person as she exists for her own sake.

In contrast, family is tied, not to institutions that may represent
the anti-civilization, but to the civilization of love, which is formed
by the generic vocation of all persons. Family and the civilization
of love are related as seed to whole; that is, the pattern of family is
generative and representative of a larger pattern (*Familiaris,* 42).
Family is unique, for John Paul II, but unique as original (i.e.,
the original society), not distinct as one particular element of a
variegated whole relates, functionally, to other parts. John Paul II's
concept of "person" levels social relations to a non-specific set
of relations, at least initially, in order to provide a basic social alternative. His "person" is an alternative to the modern category of
individual who, at some theoretical moment, stands apart from the
social contract and concrete social relations. John Paul II's person is
found, from the start, in communion. Along with the meaning
of person, ideal of family is generated by a formal contrast to the
pre-social individual.

By beginning with a formal account of inter-subjectivity, John
Paul II is confronted with a typically modern problem of defining
and justifying social roles, duties, and unequal (yet reciprocal) relations. While Leo XIII refers to social harmony as a state of affairs
among institutions, John Paul II appeals to the virtue of solidarity as
personal attitude or virtue. Nevertheless, solidarity has a definite
outward character. It is not a "feeling of vague compassion [but] a
firm determination to commit oneself to the common good"
(*Sollicitudo,* 38). Leo XIII defines family as a "society" in terms of
its inner governance and function (i.e., husband/father as head, wife
as mother, and so on). The relation of family to the social body as a
whole is conceived in similar terms. The family has a unique place
in God's providential order, so that it is ordered to the state in a
particular way, with reciprocal rights and responsibilities. John Paul
II, on the other hand, proposes that "person" is a role (the human

vocation), and that family is the "first and vital cell of society" insofar as it is the origin of personhood (*Familiaris*, 42). The "social" is defined formally in contrast to modern isolation.

This subjective approach allows Pope John Paul to take advantage of the modern democratization of personhood, where social equality precedes apparent differences in status and ability. This modern advance can be seen particularly in the relationship of children to their parents and to the state, which offers children rights and protection over against their parents. John Paul II is concerned, as well, to assert the equal dignity of the elderly, handicapped, and unwanted infants. His emphasis on human dignity translates to the political language of individual rights and a preference, unlike Leo XIII and his predecessors, for democratic (or at least "participatory") government.[34] Unlike Leo, John Paul II acknowledges the secularization of governments and other institutions (e.g., trade unions). Because prevalent institutions are secular, John Paul II makes his theological proposals through individual persons as the primary social agents. Personhood is a vocation that precedes one's role as trade unionist, employer, legislator, laborer, neighbor, or citizen.

Following this logic, John Paul II's inter-subjective communion of persons corresponds to its outward, objective role. Social life is internal to the meaning of person, so that the social role of family is concretely present in the world through interpersonal linkages. John Paul turns Catholic social teaching toward what he calls the "subjectivity of society" and away from the priority of material structures and predominant institutional agents. In *Sollicitudo rei socialis* (35–40), John Paul II holds that the mutual interdependence of persons (*qua* persons) ought to be understood as a "system" that determines the character of economic, cultural, political and religious affairs.[35] He makes the moral element of economic and political structures primary, and holds that "structures of sin" are reducible to personal sins, "always linked to the concrete acts of individuals who introduce these structures, consolidate them and make them difficult to remove" (36). Through sin, these structures become vested with dispositions and actions opposed to God and neighbor, namely, "the all-consuming desire for profit . . . [and] the thirst for power with the intention of imposing one's will upon others" (37). John Paul II calls for solidarity as a counter disposition. Solidarity is a virtue which sees each human being as a person, recognizes the interdependence of all people, and acts on our coinciding responsibility to each other as we are bound essentially in a communion of persons.

The family's social role

The social role of family is sustained internally so that its outward vocation can be detached, if need be, from the dominant political order and materialist conceptions of economic life. The outward, objective vocation is found in the family's subjective structure. In effect, the relation between male and female, husband and wife, is where social roles are grounded, not first of all in social institutions, but in the person. John Paul II's outline of marriage and family delineates reciprocal gender roles and outward social duties largely consistent with what is received from Leo XIII. The wife is primarily mother and "body" or our sign of "embodiment," while a husband/father is primarily a wage-earner and "head" of the home. Without Pope Leo's institutional links, John Paul II's inward turn appears, at least at first glance, to be the foundation of the closed home.

As persons, women and men share equal dignity, but as women and men, they have distinct, yet overlapping, vocations. Fatherhood is directed toward work, and motherhood implies a special role in the home, which does not exclude access to a career or other opportunities, but does point to a woman's special dignity. The equal dignity of women, on one hand, "justifies women's access to public functions," and on the other, "requires that clear recognition be given to the value of their maternal and family role, by comparison with all other public roles and all other professions" (*Familiaris*, 23). John Paul II hopes to show that the role of motherhood is an essential aspect of a woman's dignity and that any androgynous or gender-neutral account of equality denies real equality and undercuts the particular vocations of women and men.

The special role of women is embodiment. In his theology of the body, John Paul II proposes that the female body not only has a different role but has a different taxonomy in relation to a woman's identity.[36] John Paul II says little about male embodiment. On the contrary, he is concerned to show that the woman's embodiment forms the context for the man's vocation, as Mary's cooperation with God's redemption gives shape not only to Joseph's life but to all humanity. He understands home and family as the definitive human dwelling place, and the woman's body as its most distinct sign. Fatherhood is oriented, in large part, to work outside the home and more cognitive tasks in the household, like guiding, giving counsel, and uniting work and home.[37]

When John Paul II moves (and moves quickly) from interpersonal communion in marriage to vocations defined by gender, he is accused of betraying his own personalist point of view. Lisa Sowle Cahill argues that John Paul II's personalism is "co-opted in the service of an impossible (and hence judgmental and discouraging) ideal, which, far from supporting true mutuality, continues to subordinate women and to narrow stereotypically the roles of both sexes."[38] The impossible ideal, it seems to me, is a consequence of the idea that marriage is a complete communion. It is impractical to hope that one person can be completed by another, or that one's spouse would be able to receive the "total" personality and texture of the other. We should hope that friends and co-workers will tease out and cultivate personal qualities and make demands that our husbands and wives cannot. Even if marriage is a primary source of one's identity, it is quite a different matter to assume that we can exhaust one another's "total" self.

The romantic ideal of mutual absorption threatens to make friendships and other social relations appear as optional or as intrusions. John Paul II's personalism, while not quite romantic, risks the same kind of isolation. More than unworkable, the prospect of complete complementarity is not very interesting in social terms. Gender-based identity and vocations are enriching, but when isolated in a two-person operation of husband and wife, gender makes for a narrow sense of personal agency and purpose. The self-contained picture of nuptial union cuts the household off from so-called "external" relationships between neighbors and kin that constitute family's complex and variegated internal forms. Our friends enrich our marriages and home in important and practical ways.

John Paul II resolves the problem of the "self-contained" home when he turns to the church as a particular community with a particular role in relation to the world. The church is gathered with the vocation of embodiment. "[T]here is discerned in the light of faith a new model of the unity of the human race . . . This supreme model of unity, which is a reflection of the intimate life of God, one God in three persons, is what we Christians mean by the word 'communion.' This specifically Christian communion, jealously preserved, extended and enriched with the Lord's help, is the soul of the church's vocation to be a 'sacrament' " (*Sollicitudo,* 40). The church is a sacrament, the visible, social presence of solidarity, which "leads her necessarily to extend her religious mission to the various fields in which men and women expend their efforts in search of the always relative happiness which is possible in this world, in line with their dignity as persons" (*Sollicitudo,* 41). The church's mission is humanity, and we Christians are called to bind ourselves to our neighbor in a practical way, especially the poor and even our enemies, with the love of God. When John Paul II calls family "the way of the Church," he locates household communion in a social body greater than itself.

Like Kathleen and James McGinnis, Pope John Paul specifies the social role of family through practices of discipleship and church. Family is called to hospitality, a preferential option for the poor, and stewardship of the human good; it is called to protect the dignity of human life from economic abuse of laborers and from cultural inhospitality to the elderly and young. The social task of family "also involves cooperating for a new international order, since it is only in worldwide solidarity that the enormous and dramatic issues of world justice, the freedom of peoples and the peace of humanity can be dealt with and solved" (*Familiaris,* 48). This vocation of family is not particular to the home, but we can imagine that households and neighborhoods will contribute to the social mission of the church in particular ways. The social role of family is to takes its place in an order of love, because the family *per se* does not have a direct relation to the world. The way of the church constitutes a social body in imitation of God's way of love in the world. In this sense, the church precedes, at least in form, all other authentic social bonds, and in this regard, I take exaggerated expectations of family's social vocation to be a distraction. Theologically, the way of family is to be transformed by the church.

Part Three

7

The Order of Love

Introduction

Lenny Skutnik is a name worth remembering. On a cold, snowy day in January 1982, Mr. Skutnik was trapped in a traffic jam with countless federal employees who, like him, were trying to get home before a winter storm hit Washington, DC. To everyone's horror, a passenger jet, departing from National Airport, crashed into Washington's Fourteenth Street Bridge, "sheared through five cars like a machete, ripped through 50 feet of rail and plunged nose first into the frozen Potomac River."[1] Most passengers were trapped in the plane, and a few were clinging to the jet's protruding tail and chunks of ice. By the time rescue efforts were underway, the survivors were nearly frozen to death. One woman, Priscilla Tirado, was unable to grasp a lifeline and began to slip underneath the ice. Lenny Skutnik felt helpless, he recalls. On the river bank with rescue teams and bystanders, he tore off his coat and boots, and jumped into the water. He risked his own life and saved Mrs. Tirado.

Skutnik was immediately hailed as an unlikely hero. One *Washington Post* writer noted that Lenny Skutnik had been undeterred by responsibilities at home to his wife and children. He had not been rendered passive by the threat to his own life or his lack of emergency training. He was "moved . . . to an act of spontaneous, uncalculated courage, devoid of phony machismo, that few of us have ever had the privilege to witness but that all of us, not only Mrs. Tirado, have cause to be grateful for."[2] Skutnik showed us "that an ordinary man, in the course of what might have been an ordinary day, can perform an extraordinary act, as unself-conscious an act as a person is capable of, an act that requires as much self-possession as a person is capable of."[3]

Mr. Skutnik did not want fame, money, or recognition. After the rescue, he was barraged by news reporters. He was invited to television talk shows, received awards, was honored in President Reagan's State of the Union Address, and was applauded by both houses of Congress. He was offered free rent from a local developer, and a new car from an auto retailer. With a salary of $14,000 per year, Skutnik took the rent but refused the car because, in his words, "we couldn't afford the car insurance and anyway we already had a car."[4] By all accounts, Lenny downplayed his hero status, and he seemed to look forward to a return to ordinary life. He claimed that he did only what anyone in his situation would do. In fairness, he was partly right. Lenny actually was the second person to jump into the water. The first was tethered to a rope that fell short of the victims, and more importantly, one of the passengers did not survive because he repeatedly passed the lifeline on to those with him in the icy river. These noble acts of others do not diminish Skutnik's role; they underline the point that ordinary people are capable of extraordinary self-giving.

Believe it or not, this chapter will argue that Lenny Skutnik's heroic act is not a paradigmatic form of love. Exemplary love is represented better through a comment from one of the many interviews given by his wife. She explains that Lenny is "the kind of man everybody in the neighborhood goes to when they have trouble."[5] In the neighborhood, there is opportunity for give and take, and this "give and take" allows relationships and our capacity for love to deepen over time. In time, we come to belong and to be bound to others. On a daily basis, we learn to give and receive our lives. If a biography of Mr. Skutnik were written, I imagine that it would tell the story of Lenny's ordinary life in order to make sense of his extraordinary act on January 13, 1982. The story of his life would demonstrate that his altruistic jump into the Potomac is fully consistent and derivative of his love for his children, wife, and friends. This is the argument of the chapter: that love in its basic and highest form is cultivated in ordinary friendships and duties of neighborhood and home. Love tends toward a fullness of mutual regard and care among a circle of friends. In line with the conclusion of the previous chapter, I will propose that love of the household and neighborhood is not complete, but moves beyond itself through its grounding and its end in the love of God. The love of the household is carried forward by the universal love that is the call of the church.

The Good Samaritan

The parable of the Good Samaritan (Luke 10.29–37) is introduced with a lawyer's question, "Who is my neighbor?" First, the lawyer puts a question to Jesus in order to test him, "What must I do to inherit eternal life?" Jesus turns it back to him. How do you read the law? The scholar of the law then answers, "You shall love the Lord, your God, with all your heart, with all your soul, with all your strength, and with all your mind, and your neighbor as yourself" (v. 27). Jesus agrees. "Do this and you will live," he tells the man. The lawyer wiggles a bit. He has set out to put Jesus to a test; instead, he answers his own question to Jesus' satisfaction. Wait a minute. Who is the judge of whom? Who is testing whom? In order to gain the upper hand, the lawyer intends to get an answer out of Jesus. Precisely what does the law require for righteousness? Who, precisely, is my neighbor? The neighbor, as received from Torah (Lev. 19.18), is a fellow Israelite.[6] That definition will be expanded by Jesus' story of the Good Samaritan, and the lawyer, once again, will find himself responding to his own question, this time, with an answer disagreeable to him.

According to the parable, a man falls victim to robbers while traveling the well-worn route between Jerusalem and Jericho. The man, who is by implication a Jew, lay half-dead. A priest and Levite, each in turn, pass by on the opposite side of the road, rather than (it can be inferred) risk violating Torah sanctions against contact with the dead. A Samaritan is moved by compassion. He bandages the man's wounds and takes him to an inn. The following day, he gives the innkeeper charge to care for the man and, to pay for the service, he offers his wages for two days and a promise to pay any additional costs on his return trip. After the parable, Jesus asks the lawyer, "Which of these three, do you think, was neighbor to the one who fell victim to the robbers?" The lawyer answers, "The one who showed him mercy." Parallel with Jesus' earlier command, "Do this and you shall live" (v. 28), he now tells the lawyer, "Go and do likewise" (v. 37). Jesus has turned the table on the lawyer once again.

A common interpretation of Jesus' parable proposes that the Good Samaritan is a paragon of neighbor-love because his love is "unilateral" rather than reciprocal and expressed toward a stranger rather than friend or kinfolk. The Samaritan is a neighbor to the man because he loves unconditionally and impartially. He "does not wait, anticipate, or demand a response in kind as a requirement for [his] attention and care," and his love goes beyond the boundaries imposed by "particular roles and practices" or specific duties toward one kind of person or another. "The text does not tell us whether a friendship arose between the Good Samaritan and the man he helped."[7] Unlike the priest and Levite, the Samaritan suspends his own interests and personal commitments. Unlike them, he attends to the needs of the victim regardless of the man's particular identity, state, or relation to him (i.e., whether he is a Jew or Samaritan, friend or enemy, rich or poor, clean or unclean). The love he showed toward the suffering man has a source that is entirely independent of its object. Nothing that the victim can do will change it.[8] In this way, the Samaritan fully expresses neighbor-love, inasmuch as his love is fundamentally unilateral and most purely demonstrated toward a stranger.

Gene Outka, in his *Agape: An Ethical Analysis*, makes a case for this unilateral love as the fundamental character of Christian love. "Agape is, in both its genesis and continuation, an active concern for the neighbor's well-being which is somehow independent of particular actions of the other."[9] The others are regarded for their own sake and for what they might need without expectation of return. In this way, neighbor-love flows in one direction, from the will of the lover to the good of the beloved. This love is heroic because the one who loves stands alone. Unlike friendship, this form of neighbor-love does not depend upon affection, especially not mutual affection. It is impartial and universal, and it is superior to reciprocal relationships because it is self-sustained and unaltered by the feeling and attraction of special relationships.[10] Agape, in Outka's view, is a regard for *every* person as human being.[11] This disinterested love is, at best, only supplemented by friendships, the parent–child bond, and other special relationships.[12] At worst, special relationships will cloud our judgment. They cultivate self-love through mutual benefit, and this kind of reciprocity, if fundamental, is set against true love.

Outka's account of agape is powerful and seems to ring true of saintly and divine love. This chapter will provide a counter-proposal, that mutual love is fundamental and that unilateral love is secondary: that Outka's unilateral notion of neighbor love is useful but derivative of love which forms communion. Unilateral love is sometimes the option that is open to us, but it is not basic or complete, because one person's expression of love is always open to be returned and completed in friendship and common life. In this regard, unilateral love is incomplete insofar as its context is limited to the solitary human being who can somehow generate love from within. This one-directional proposal runs aground on the meaning of love as a gift from God to which we are called to respond. More on this fundamental exchange of love will follow. At this point, it is useful to see how unilateral love limits our reading of the Good Samaritan.

The idea of unilateral love to a stranger narrows the parable in at least two ways. First, it misses the specific hostility between Jew and Samaritan and their strictures against contact with one another. In the immediately preceding chapter of Luke, for example, Jesus is not welcomed by a Samaritan town precisely because he was on pilgrimage as a Jew to Jerusalem (9.51–56). The lawyer, upon hearing Jesus' parable, is forced to conclude that his neighbor is "the one who showed mercy." With this conclusion, he is also saying, while avoiding actually saying the words, that the despised Samaritan is the neighbor. "Neighbor" implies a special relationship, that of fellow-countryman, so that the hard lesson of the Good Samaritan is not only the call to show compassion but also the expansion of God's peoplehood. This expansion is consistent with the Lukan journey of the gospel from its climax in Jerusalem outward to Rome. God's offer emanates from Jerusalem and goes to the ends of the earth (Acts 1.8). If the lawyer were to heed his own answer to the parable, he would have to call the Samaritan his brother.

Second, the priority of unilateral love misses the parable's shift in agency. Outka's ideal of love without return conceptualizes the neighbor or the one in need as a passive object. The parabolic twist of the Good Samaritan is that the neighbor is active, not only active but also representative of the One Who Shows Mercy. Consistent with the Lukan narrative, the outcast is set near to Christ; that is, the Samaritan is honored as a model for how we should live (cf. Luke 17.11–19). The lawyer asks about the neighbor whom he should love, but Jesus' answer comes through a story of a Samaritan/neighbor who loves. The lawyer is called to identify with the neighbor, with the neighbor's doing of love, and with the Merciful One whom the Samaritan represents. All at once, the neighbor is both a despised schismatic whom the lawyer should call neighbor and one who shows mercy to a victim who, from the Samaritan's point of view, is a despised Jew. An improbable but reciprocal love is at the heart of the parable of the Good Samaritan.

Underlying this unlikely exchange between Jew and Samaritan is a dynamic and expanding covenant, which, in Luke, is the very fulfillment of God's promise to Israel. Underlying the expanding covenant is a call to imitate Christ, who gathers those on the margins, the lost and the outsider (cf. Luke 4.15). The ever-widening promises of God bring a call to people like the lawyer to understand and join with this movement of God's grace.

The theme of God's far-reaching love is consistent throughout the Gospel of Luke. Jesus' rejection at Nazareth (Luke 4.16–30) and his call to Simon Peter, James, and John are illustrative (Luke 5.1–11).[13] In Nazareth, the people are initially amazed at Jesus' wisdom, but their amazement turns to anger when Jesus suggests that God's glad tidings may go to foreigners rather than to Israelites. His own people drive him out of town. The outcome is different in Luke 5.1–11. After catching nothing through the night, Simon Peter and his fellow fishermen lower their nets when Jesus commands. As a result, they raise an unmanageable load of fish. Simon Peter's response of amazement, "Depart from me, Lord, for I am a sinful man," provides an interesting parallel with Jesus' rejection at Nazareth. Peter has done nothing wrong and has no apparent cause for guilt or shame. However, rather than expressing gratitude for the bounty of fish, Peter attempts to send Jesus away. Peter's "Depart from me" fits with the pattern of the Gospel. His attempt to push Jesus away reveals the same challenge that Jesus sets before the people of Nazareth. After Jesus responds, "Do not be afraid; from now on you will be catching people" (v. 10, NRSV), Peter, along with James and John, leaves the bounty in order to follow Jesus.

In Luke 4.16–30 and 5.1–11, a call comes as a response to the abundance of grace. The encounter at Nazareth ends in rejection, while Peter's response leads to discipleship. Likewise, the three parables of the lost and found in Luke 15 (i.e., the lost sheep, lost coin, and lost son), culminate with amazement, in this case, with the anger of the good and faithful son. He is astonished at the bountiful treatment that his father heaps upon his prodigal brother. The father asks the good son to rejoice "because your brother was dead and has come to life again; he was lost and has been found" (15.32). The compassion and mercy of the Samaritan in the parable requires a similar decision from the lawyer: rejection or discipleship.

Neighbor-love is set within the wider Lukan context of God's exceeding grace and the expanding covenant people. In this way, the parable of the Good Samaritan proposes neighbor-love as a response to the love of God. The lawyer must contend with the challenge of the Samaritan, not as anonymous neighbor, but as bearer of their common (i.e., God's) way. The parable of the Samaritan is likely to offend the lawyer because he will have to learn the lesson of love from an outsider who loves a fellow Jew.

Reciprocity

Lawrence C. Becker, in his *Reciprocity*, argues that reciprocity is a fundamental virtue, required for social life and the moral excellence of individual persons.[14] Becker's presentation is important for us because he gives account of reciprocity as a virtue of the recipient rather than the giving-agent. A habit of response, the virtue of reciprocity is not by any means equivalent to love, but nevertheless provides a wide angle from which to view love. Reciprocity presumes a sense of mutuality, and offers a stark contrast to disinterested and unilateral conceptions of neighbor-love. The virtue of reciprocity not only frames relationships in terms of mutual benefit and self-concern, bringing together love of neighbor with love of self; it also excludes one-directional accounts of giving. Reciprocity frames "receiving" as an important social activity. From the recipient's perspective, giving is a starting-point that opens the way to give something in return (if only thanks). Reciprocity puts our agency in terms of response; in this sense, it is nearer to both our love of God and our call to common life with our neighbors. In theological terms, no love is without communion. God's Trinitarian love is communion, and even when we love our neighbor without return, we love him or her with the love we receive from and share with God. Love may be sacrificial, but selfless love is a contradiction in terms.

In developing reciprocity as a virtue, Becker argues that it is a habit of how we are *disposed* toward the good from others, the good for others, and the goods of life. Becker proposes that we ought to be disposed (1) to return good for good, (2) to *not* return evil for evil, (3) to resist evil received, and (4) to provide restitution for wrongs we have done.[15] Reciprocity is not, then, simply a method of exchange, where one good or evil is traded with another. It is not a way to make things even, and it is clearly distinguishable from a payback and revenge. Reciprocity is a disposition to do the good in terms of what and how we receive.

Reciprocity will override simple and terminal forms of exchange, when the good received exceeds our contractual limits and draws us to carry on further with each other.[16] Reciprocity offers a sense of moral and relational balance. We might find that the good received surpasses the voluntary limits that we have set through a contractual agreement. Imagine that my dentist goes beyond what is required of him as a dentist. Perhaps he calls in the evening to inquire about my recovery from a root canal procedure. His call will be outside the formal limits of his fee for services. I will receive his call in gratitude, and my guess is that I and my family will become "attached" to him either as dentist, friend, or both.

Reciprocity presses upon us whether or not we have chosen to receive or accept. It is well suited to the unexpected gifts of everyday life. According to Becker, "reciprocity fixes the outline of our non-voluntary social obligations – the obligations we acquire in the course of social life, but acquire without regard to our invitation, consent, or acceptance."[17] Reciprocity is suited to living in community. We have not chosen our parents, our siblings, our neighbors, our co-workers, and our fellow Christians; yet, whether we like them or not, we do not hesitate to call them our own. Reciprocity includes our response to the good and bad givens of life.

Although it is based in mutuality, reciprocity does not exclude gift-giving or receiving. It only requires that the meaning of the gift include not only the intentions of the giver but also the agency of the recipient. The recipient in Outka's unilateral account of love is passive by definition, and any reciprocation is supplemental. Reciprocity, in contrast, is the activity of the one who receives. "A gift may be given with no expectation of return; no desire for a return; a desire that there be *no* return."[18] As a recipient's disposition, reciprocity does not govern the good will of the benefactor. The gift-giver may intend to be selfless and altruistic, but the beneficence of the giver does not depend on precluding the agency of the recipient. The one who receives must know how to accept the gift. I can easily ruin a gift by giving one in return and announcing, "See there. Now we are even." I can undermine the graciousness of the giver by persisting with exaggerated declarations of unworthiness. "Please stop," the giver will have to say, "I did not give you the gift so that you would be indebted to me." The agency of the recipient is required for the gift to be given as gift rather than something to be earned, retroactively, or paid back.

Receiving a gift as gift is a form of reciprocation. If selflessness were required for gift-giving (and actually it is not), this giving away of self would fall harder on the side of the recipient. It is the recipient who allows herself to be filled by the doing of another, who is open to have the gift and activity of the giver take action in her life. It is the giver who, far from selfless, is the primary agent. So-called selflessness, as in the Gospels and the letters of Paul for example, is a matter of losing oneself and being made new by the grace of God. Denying oneself or dying to oneself is an activity of acceptance and imitation; Christ's new life with God becomes one's own. Receiving the gift is what it means to be poor and why it is vitally important in the Christian life to *receive* the poor as the *agents* of Christ (Matt. 25). Simple giving is the easy part. In doing for the poor, we must receive the poor as grace. In receiving them, we will be changed. So-called altruism, as giving purely without return, does more to undercut the agency of the recipient than to empower him or her. Altruism is an isolated focus on the giver's own purported selflessness. Receiving the gift, in contrast, entails the risk of being transformed by another.

As openness to another, reciprocity fosters a depth and subtlety of community. Sometimes we know that the best thing *to do,* the thing we ought *to do,* or the only thing that we can *do* is to accept, use, enjoy, or take delight in a gift. A person unable to receive a gift is not overburdened with reciprocity but deficient in it.[19] Such persons would be limited in their capacity for friendship inasmuch as they seek to deny the gratuity of their own coming-to-be in the company of others. Someone who fashions himself or herself to be self-made lacks the virtue of reciprocity. Theologically speaking, he or she would be unable to respond and share in the life of God. Again, the goal of reciprocity is not a payback. In receiving grace, we do not return something to God that God needs. God is not deficient in good.[20] Rather, the very meaning of grace is God's giving to us the capacity to respond to God and to share in divine life. In friendship with God, we will the good that God is. We love with the love of God, for God's sake, for our own, and for our neighbor's. We love our neighbor (and even our enemies) for our neighbor's own sake, as our neighbor's own good is the good will of God.[21] On a mundane level, reciprocity takes on an analogous quality. Not only do we offer mutual aid and good will to each other, but also we share each other through sharing our lives.

Reciprocity sustains the equilibrium of a social ecosystem. The first maxim of reciprocity is that "good received should be returned with good." Through a system of reciprocity, certainly, we will receive the things we need, from guidance and affection to the material necessities and extras, like the list of things I want for Christmas. Through reciprocity, human community is maintained in instrumental and material terms, but more importantly, exchanges of good for good "are typically a potent source of pleasure in themselves . . . independently of how highly the partici- pants prize the things that are exchanged. (We often mean it when we say it's the thought that counts.)"[22] Reciprocity sustains intrinsic goods of community. It cultivates a social context for further exchange, and it puts mutual willing of good at the center of social interaction.

In this regard, a repeated failure of reciprocity is a threat to common goods, and inversely, the disposition of reciprocity is required (obligatory) for common life. The obligation does not mean that we all ought to have scruples about writing "Thank You" cards and constant worries about what we owe to whom. As noted above, the virtue of reciprocity is not the orientation of being in debt. It is a disposition of return in terms of the good. As such, reciprocity is selective, not contractual or mechanical. It is set with- in the temporal character of common life. It is not *completed* by a transfer of common currency or by an even exchange; it is *opened* to the unfinished nature of social transaction, whether gift or trade. Like paddling a canoe, let us say, reciprocity is a matter of balance and equilibrium. Sometimes I must paddle alone; sometimes with my partner in the canoe, and sometimes I must sit and wait till my fellow-traveler sets us in the right direction. In each case, all of our oar strokes are made in relation to the movement and efforts of the other partner and in terms of where we are going together. As a virtue, then, reciprocity requires judgments about what is fitting and proportional.[23] It requires judgment about the difference between trivial and important matters, the distinction between a debt and the gift, and differences between one person in relation to us as (e.g., a co-worker) and another (e.g., a spouse). Reciprocity involves judg- ments about when and how we respond in terms of the kind of relationships being sustained and our obligation to foster common life.

The content of our life together will fill in (and in some ways alter) the formal features of Becker's account. Earlier, I suggested this kind of alteration through our receiving the poor as agents of Christ (Matt. 25.31–46). If the hungry and thirsty, sick and imprisoned, with their dirt, smell, and bad manners, are Christ, then receiving them in hospitality is not ultimately a matter of duty or selfless service, but a privilege and a matter of self-concern.[24] Dorothy Day notes that "if we hadn't got Christ's own words for it, [this idea] would seem like raving lunacy."[25] Christians are called to community with God such that the poor and homeless are not merely symbolic of Christ's presence, but are the very presence of Christ. "What you did to the least of these my brothers, you have done to me" (Matt. 25.40). Dorothy Day understands our presence to the poor in terms, not only of hospitality to Christ, but also of our setting right our human tendency to "put out" God and neighbor. As privilege and recompense, our love of neighbor gives us honor and sets us right. In this way, mutual good will does not simply maintain the status quo. With the content of Christian faithfulness, reciprocity is transformative.[26]

Mutuality

In the working of reciprocity, giving is completed when giver and recipient receive each other, so that the gift opens the way for common life. In the context of reciprocity, the gift is a matter of shared presence through time. Within this framework of the gift, we now turn to Christian love (agape) as communion and mutuality. Stephen Post, in his *A Theory of Agape*, offers this definition. "Agape is an affection of the heart, an attunement of the person's deepest center that issues in a faithful will to exist for God and others as well as for one's own fulfillment. It is sustained and reinforced in religious fellowship by reliable acts of reciprocation: at best, love forms a circle of mutual giving and receiving between God, self, and others."[27] We will consider Post's description of love in terms of altruistic regard for the needs of others, the love of God, and our call to love all neighbors and enemies, near and far.

Altruistic love is regard for the interests of another person. Modern philosophers and sociobiologists are inclined to set up an opposition between egoistic self-interest and altruistic regard for others. Truly loving acts are believed to be done at the expense of one's own welfare.[28] Others argue, in contrast, that altruistic concern ought to be directed toward oneself as well. We ought to care for a person as an anonymous human being, whether this human being is another or oneself.[29] In this framework, proper self-love counts one's own welfare neither above nor below the welfare of others. We treat ourselves with the same disinterested love. This second view coincides with the first (i.e., the opposition between self- and other-regard), insofar as each assumes a detachment from preferential regard for ourselves and for those near and dear to us like family and friends. Special regard for our children, for instance, is considered merely an extension of partiality for our own interests. Altruism is thought to be a superior form of love because it is invariable, not altered by the merits of the ones we love, their attractiveness, or potential benefits they might bring to us. Within the altruistic frame, proper love of self and of family and friends ought to be, at its core, this type of unconditional, impartial regard.

When altruism is made definitive, it sets our loving against the way that we are moved by love, the way that we are drawn near to our beloved. Consider the difference between altruistic regard and being in love. In love, we are drawn into a sphere of action where the other's good is good for us. We become delighted at making another person happy. For this reason, primary status is given, in Catholic social teaching, to the preferential option for the poor. The preferential option is not impartial. To be accurate, we should say that it does not operate with the moral taxonomy of partiality as opposed to disinterest, or self versus neighbor. The option for the poor is a call to common life, a call to see ourselves through the eyes of the poor and to receive our vision of common life in company with them. Preferential love is the bond of communion, and for this reason, everyday bonds of family and friendships are seen, in Catholic social teaching, as representative of wider possibilities for the bonds of human community. From beginning to end, we are persons in communion, from our creation in God's image to our redemption in the communion of saints. Theories of altruism, in contrast, set "the person *qua* human being" over against our natural desire for community.[30] Altruism, when made definitive, disengages our neighbor-love from our embodiment in community, from our very particular habitats and homes. Relationships between parent and child, brother and sister are considered a problem to be explained or justified, or in the least, they are seen as polluted with temptations of partiality and attachment. The pure context of love is thought to be found in episodic encounters with strangers.

Defining love in terms of fellowship and common fulfillment does not exclude the good of altruistic acts, but shows them to be incomplete and, at their best, to be nascent yearnings for communion. Sometimes, in extraordinary situations, we will love at the cost of our own well-being. However, even in these situations the so-called selfless giver is likely to express self-satisfaction or even joy in the act. Ought not Lenny Skutnik, who saved Mrs. Tirado from the Potomac, feel good about himself? After simple acts of kindness, it is appropriate to say, "I enjoyed doing that good thing." Our acts make us who we are, and what better to be than generous, loving, and courageous. We ought to love our goodness. If there is self-concern in giving all my money to the poor (and there is), then the contrast between self-concern and altruism does not mean very much. Both giving to the poor and taking advantage of their weakness may reflect self-concern. The difference is my conception of who I am and who I ought to be. I want to be the kind of person who loves for my neighbor's own good, and who understands and loves the good that transcends my limited self-interest. Using another as a mere instrument for what I desire is not, in the end, good for me.

Altruism is best defined by its limited probability of return (rather than a lack of self-concern). Extraordinary conditions may be such that our loving will be incomplete, and our motivations for neighbor-love will have to correspond to this eclipse of reciprocity. In exceptional cases, we must act outside of ourselves, as it were, without ordinary concerns for personal benefit and attachment to the ones for whom we care. We might have to love without the possibility of being drawn together. In extraordinary circumstances, we are called to an incomplete love as the best option available. We might have to give up our lives or suffer some indignity. The extraordinary nature of this love hardly makes it definitive. On the contrary, being moved by another, being moved by love and compassion, suggests that we are inclined to draw near to him or her. One self-giving act will probably draw us into more such acts, as we are moved to the love of fellowship and common flourishing. Feeding the poor remains truncated until we break bread *with them* at the table.

Altruism is an irregular and asymmetrical necessity of extra-ordinary situations, but conditions of common life might be such that this abbreviated form of neighbor-love will be understood as the ordinary option. When common life is fragmented, the best we might be able to do is give without response, to give anonymously without social means for the gift to bring us into communion. Altruistic disengagement will fit, for example, with an impersonal economic and political system where self-love is defined in terms of competing self-interests, where the rights of individuals are conceived over against common goods, where attachment and mutuality are associated with the private sphere of home, and where the so-called real structures of social and political life are based in *laissez-faire* competition, contractual individualism, and the notion of self-making.[31]

Such a context will perpetuate the assumption that mutuality and reciprocity – of the private sphere of family, neighborhood, church, and home – are just other forms of individual self-interest. Because self-interest is defined as competitive over against the interests of others, real regard for others (it will be assumed) will have to take shape apart from the private sphere and its reciprocal relationships, apart from attachments like those of family, neighborhood, and kin. Other-regard will be defined by categories that preclude substantive common life, because public life is determined by competition and contracts. Helping a stranger will be considered more pure than helping a friend. In effect, so-called selfless love will be given priority because it is separated from the attachments of home. Altruism will be astounding because it has no functional role in the purely self-interested public sphere. In such a context, love as com-munion will be seen as retrograde and parochial. Community itself will be seen as self-serving, and often self-styled communities will be nothing more than self-serving enclaves, insofar as they are organized voluntarily according to common lifestyles, consumption patterns, and recreational interests.[32]

Ironically, the non-voluntary family and similar commitments to neighborhood and community are radical in the modern context. It is altruism that is conservative. Because episodic and individual, altruism leaves the structures of social life as they are. When con-sidered definitive, love for strangers perpetuates our modern dis-placement from common life. It keeps focus on the self-sufficient acts of individual agents who act without reciprocation or personal need. It portrays saints and moral exemplars as those who refuse to take their place in the "give and take" of human community.[33] When family, on the other hand, is understood as pointing to the character of true love, it is a transforming institution. Love's basic habitat is the household economy, not necessarily the biological family, but primarily the household of God. From within the bonds of the open home, we can begin to conceive of what is implied in well-worn references to the "human family," and we can undertake altruistic acts as necessary but incomplete expressions of love in a fragmented world, always with the end of mutuality and communion in view.

The love of God

Reciprocity and mutual love are more difficult to justify when speaking about the love of God. A standard view of God's love for us is that it is unconditional, spontaneous, and not motivated by our goodness or attractiveness. For this reason, agape, inasmuch as it is God's love, does not admit mutual fellowship between God and humans.[34] God's unilateral love, then, becomes the prototype and a justification for the primacy of altruism: to love as God loves is to love without return. This common view begins, rightly, with the utter difference between divine and human love, but then it concludes, mistakenly, that we never really become active loving agents in relation to God. Mutuality is excluded, rightly, because we cannot be equal to God or share "give and take" with God in any meaningful sense. If love is defined as mutual, we certainly cannot love God, and God cannot be said to love human beings. God's love for us amounts to something analogous to the mutuality between a person and a cat.[35] God condescends. According to this view, we do not love God in return, although faith and obedience are in order. Our love is excluded, in the end, because the altruistic view provides inadequate accounts of God's Trinitarian communion and how our loving is changed when we are brought into the love of God.[36]

Divine and human love are incomparable. We humans are drawn to love others by the qualities discovered *in* what and whom we love, to the beauty of a performance or to what is lovable in another person. Even if we love another who is not noble or attractive, we might say that we love her despite certain flaws, or we love him because of how he makes us feel, or we love her because she is a child of God. In each case, we connect our love with its object. God's love, in contrast, has no external cause. While human love is moved by an object, God is the subject of divine love. God's love is not moved by or attracted to an object of love, but is the source of its being. God is not "moved by" but is the cause of love's movement. God is not "attracted by" but makes attractive. God's love, more specifically the sacrifice of Christ, gives righteousness to the unrighteous and redemption to the ungodly (Rom. 5.6). God is the very possibility of the lovable. "Indeed, rarely will anyone die for a righteous person – though perhaps for a good person someone might actually dare to die. But God proves his love for us in that while we still were sinners Christ died for us" (Rom. 5.7–8, NRSV).

From this point, it may seem to follow that God's unconditioned love is unilateral. The difference between divine and human love seems to indicate that humans can share love with each other but never make a return of love to God. God cannot be our object without ceasing to be God; therefore, for God's love to be meaningful as love, it seems necessary that it move only from God to God. It seems necessary to conclude that God shares divine love with us without self-concern and reward. Contrary to this conclusion, it is the very difference between God's love and ours that makes it possible for us to share the love of God, to respond in love, and to love our neighbor in a new way.[37] God's intra-Trinitarian love of Father, Son, and Spirit is a communion, which is expressed outward in the world through the biblical history of salvation. God's love is an invitation to common life. The incarnation and cross of Christ bear witness to God's willing of creation as an outward movement, without cause or necessity, and as an offer of return to God in love.[38]

"God's love has been poured into our hearts through the Holy Spirit that has been given to us" (Rom. 5.5), and that Spirit is the loving of Father and Son. "The Father's love for his natural Son in eternity is thus the origin of the Spirit, the motivation of creation, and the explanation of God's love for his adoptive children. The love of adoptive sons is but the prolongation of the Father's love for his eternal Son, and thus indigenously a trinitarian mystery."[39] God is subject of love, but that "subjectivity" is communion, and the end of God's "condescension" is that we would be brought into communion. "For this is what is involved in the gift of Jesus," Herbert McCabe explains, in the self-giving of the incarnation, which is Jesus' mission and way to the cross. "God loves Jesus and loves him from eternity as his co-equal Son, owing his existence indeed to God though not created, but . . . 'loved into existence.' It is into this eternal exchange of love between Jesus and the Father that we are taken up, this exchange of love that we call the Holy Spirit. And this means of course, that we are taken up into *equality*, the equality demanded and involved in love."[40]

The equality to which McCabe refers is not equality of status or measure but of a shared life, not an equality that is possessed by us but always a *given* equality, always contingent, let us say, on the eternal loving of God. The love of God is God's communion, and our mutuality is possible in a sharing of divine life. God's communion opens the world to God and makes it possible for us to inhabit the world as God's world, to inhabit God's world as free-willing and consciously loving human beings. God's self-communication in love, as communication, makes room for our agency of reception and response. We are made into lovers of God by God's unceasing love.

The self-abnegation of Jesus in the garden of Gethsemane and on the cross of Golgotha ought not be denied. As the passion narrative unfolds, Jesus suffers not only the anguish of being God-forsaken, but also the loss of human friendship. Both are critical to his sacrifice and to our redemption. Jesus is alone as he stands before Pilate, and he must die alone because the end to which his self-sacrificial love points is communion. He dies in alienation and is risen in unity with the Father, so that we may be united to God as well. The whole of the biblical narrative is the activity of a loving and jealous God, who grieves when humanity turns away. Divine wrath and forgiveness are directed to turn Israel faithfully back to God. Likewise, "divine suffering [both grief over human sin and Christ's sacrifice] is virtually incomprehensible unless a response from the beloved is sought after."[41] We are brought into friendship with God. This friendship and the meaning of love as communion do not exclude the possibility of our loving our neighbor without return or our suffering alone for the sake of neighbor-love. On the contrary, our sufferings in this regard, like our love, are taken in and are made comprehensible by the communion of God's love.

Family, friends, and distant neighbors

Mutuality implies a question about the order of love. If neighbor-love moves toward completion through communion, then should we love our family and friends more intensely than distant neighbors? If so, will the reciprocity of kin and friendship divert us from the call of the Good Samaritan? Will our love be used up by kin and closed to the stranger? Selfless and non-reciprocal love seems to offer a superior neighbor-love because it is impartial, not giving preference to family and friends, and it is immediately universal in scope. If impartial, our neighbor-love will continue to be a matter of nearness (i.e., we do not encounter everyone), but this "closeness" will be a matter of simple proximity, not mediated by biological ties, the roles of family, duties of friendship, or shared conceptions of the good. Mutuality, from this point of view, is tied too closely to home and diminishes neighbor-love. The following will argue the contrary, that love as communion, as it is bound to specific roles and reciprocity, points to a practical habitat where loving agents are formed and called out – called out of the singular-agent-focus of altruistic self-emptying.

In question twenty-six of the *Summa Theologiae*, Thomas Aquinas asks if the love of God by which we love (i.e., charity) has an order of priorities.[42] He concludes that it does. The love of God is friendship between God and us, so that our first love is to God. Insofar as the principal concern of any friendship is the "shared good on which it is based . . . it is God, primarily and above all, who is to be loved in charity, for him we love as the cause of eternal happiness . . ." (II.2, q. 26.2). For this reason – God is the common principle, source, and good of all things – we ought to love God above ourselves and ourselves more than our neighbors. "We love God as the fount of that good which forms the basis of charity, ourselves as sharing in it, and our neighbors as partners": first, God; second, ourselves on the basis of our participation in the divine good; third, our neighbors as those associated with us in this participation (q. 26.4). To be exact, our souls (in unity with God) are loved more than our neighbor's union with us, so that (1) the good of our neighbor's soul might require our bodily sacrifice, and (2) our duty toward our neighbors' bodily well-being will be contingent on specific ways we are bound to care for their good (q. 26.5). Particular relations like those to family, friends, civic community, and so on provide the order of love toward neighbors. We ought to love one neighbor (particularly kin) with more intensity than others.

When giving order to neighbor-love, Aquinas speaks of two principles of order. One is our neighbor's nearness to God as the fount of good, and the other is the nearness of our neighbor to us (q. 26.6). In reference to the first, we ought to want the good for everyone, even our enemies, insofar as all people share in the love of God. In this sense, we should love everyone equally. However, all people do not have an equal degree of goodness, and because of their special nearness to God we ought to love saintly people more. As a matter of justice, we ought to desire for loving and godly people the kind of love fitting their "more perfect" sharing in the divine good. In reference to the second principle, proximity to us rather than to God makes for greater intensity of love. "A man loves those closest to him and wills them good more intensely than those who are better and for whom he wills a greater good" (q. 26.7). In other words, we love our sisters, brothers, and close friends more powerfully. They have "a hold on us" whether or not they are extraordinary people. This "nearness to us" comes in various degrees of intensity. For instance, kinfolk ought to be loved more than friends because "the bond of natural origin is something prior and more fixed" than other forms of relation (q. 26.8), and parents are bound to love their children with more intensity than their own parents "because parents love their children as being part of themselves" (q. 26.9).

Further qualifications should be made. Thomas' two principles of order (i.e., nearness to God and to us) do not make for a simple scheme that could be diagramed with even lines, concentric circles, or a pyramid of relations.[43] The order of love is practically complex and dependent upon the particular kinds of relationships we have and the differing bases upon which people share life-goods. "Nearness to us" is no simple matter, but a series of overlapping connections. For example, Thomas thinks of partiality toward kin and household in terms of material well-being. If a person were to give alms to the poor without first feeding her own family, she would be breaking the precepts of neighbor-love (II.2, q. 32.5). However, even this ordering is not a simple set of concentric circles or diminishing responsibilities as one moves outward. The precepts of alms-giving are ordered from the needs of the recipient as well. If a would-be recipient were starving while one's own kin were simply not sated, priority certainly goes to the hungry stranger rather than kin. This ordering on the basis of urgent need corresponds to a natural ordering of creation. The things of creation are set out by God, first of all, for common use, according to our bond as human beings (II.2, q. 66.7).

Aquinas' rule of discernment is this: "[I]n comparing one love with another, we must follow the comparison of one such union with another" (II.2, q. 26.8). The good upon which friendship is based determines the priority of that "love" in its own practical sphere. Friendship between citizens might be based in common goods of trade and good governance, between neighbors in the goods of raising and educating children, between co-workers on the internal and instrumental goods of the common work, between members of congregations in faithful living, fraternal correction, and mutual care, and between other kinds of friends in the flourishing of artistic performance, the cultivation of a craft, the good of team play or "the good of the game," and so on. Each of these friendships is ordered to the other kinds of friendship. The main point of this order is that we share more kinds of goods with those to whom we are closest, that is, with those with whom we spend time and share a place. So with my daughter, I share not only DNA and the wisdom of my years, but the love of basketball, visits to our town's nursing home, work in the yard and home repair, cooking dinner, pleasure in figuring out math problems, friendships with neighbors, and the like. Love is ordered to the complexity of practical life.

Stephen Pope, in his *The Evolution of Altruism and the Ordering of Love*, argues that Thomas' efforts to provide for the ordering of love is superior to recent accounts of love that, by and large, neglect the question of order altogether. Pope's chief concern, here, is the corresponding neglect (among theologians) of questions about human beings as part of nature, in favor of the historically and culturally formed "self."[44] To argue his point, Pope will attend to Thomas' theories of natural appetency, the sensitive appetite, and the particularities of natural human loving in terms of our intellect and free will. Thomas arrives at an ordering of natural love that is sustained in the order of charity, in our active participation in the love of God. We may not be convinced by Thomas' claims about reproductive biology, for instance, whereby one's father ought to be loved more than one's mother because the father is a principle of origin "in a higher way than the mother, who supplies the passive or material element" (II.2, q. 26.11). Pope argues that we ought to take our methodological cues (rather than ancient science) from Thomas and attend to "current scientific and empirical information and theories regarding natural human sociality."[45]

Pope gives an appraisal of modern theories of love, and offers a pertinent critique of personalist focus on communion of "I" and "Thou" (see Chapters 3 and 6). According to Pope, personalist accounts of love do well to undercut individualist theories of love by appealing to the existential constitution of the self through interpersonal relations. I discover myself in relationship to others. In this way, personalism understands the self not as static and self-contained but as dynamic and relational. Pope argues that the problem with the personalist theory of love is that its context is too narrow. "Indeed, at times, the perceived sphere of human interaction is narrowed down to an 'I–Thou' conversation between two adults found on the set of an existentialist play . . . [T]he personalist understanding of love can be fairly criticized as a kind of *égoisme à deux* that narrowly collapses moral concern into immediate interpersonal relations."[46] It is no mistake that, for personalists, a romantic ideal of marriage tends to be representative of all interpersonal relations.[47] The interpersonal framework of marriage, its two-in-one flesh, seems amenable to the dyadic intensity of the existential "I–Thou." In everyday life, practical matters of home and work are, thankfully, too pressing and diverse for the ideal. Married life does not allow us to gaze long into each other's eyes – thankfully, because the "two in one" may readily become an attenuated egoism of two.

I have argued in previous chapters that the inter-subjective orientation of modern accounts tends toward abstraction, not only from the natural settings of human inclinations and desires (Pope's main concern), but also from the multiplicity of concrete relations that form our subjectivity and shape our loves. Love, it is assumed, simply springs out of us by the force of will into a generic relational space. I emphasized in Chapters 2 and 3 that this relational space is, more often than not, nowhere in particular, but an otherworldly "place." According to Stephen Pope, "emphasis on freedom and on the dyadic context of intersubjective relationships tends to exclude natural dependencies and responsibilities existing prior to free choices, for example, the claims made by aging parents on their grown children or on siblings by one another. It is sometimes suggested that humans are individuals first who then consciously and deliberately choose to enter into relationships and social ties."[48]

Pope observes that many of our relationships are established and sustained by consent, but they are not equal, and they are given to us prior to our free choices, such as relations between siblings and between parents and children. Other relationships follow from related choices, as contingent givens. For instance, a student might choose to attend Mount Saint Mary's College, but he or she gets stuck with me as a Moral Theology teacher. In deciding to matriculate, students enter a set of roles and relationships that are beyond their control. Likewise, we often choose our neighborhood, but we do not choose our neighbors. Even in the consent of marriage, we do not have full knowledge of what we will give and what we will be given when we say "I do." We choose without prior knowledge of circumstances (sickness or health, poverty or wealth).

We might choose to be a husband or wife, but the role precedes us, as do the roles of parent and child, brother and sister, teacher and student, neighbor and friend. Without detracting from their particular contributions, students enter a classroom, whether for the first time in kindergarten or the nth time in secondary school, with a place to fill. The students' roles and responsibilities are structured in relation to the role of the teacher and to the common social purposes of education. Likewise, parents and children live into prior roles. Parents have the duty to love their children in socially or "publicly" defined ways, offering nurture, discipline, material care, and protection. Children are required to give none of these inasmuch as they are children. They are required not to love but to obey. It would be considered abusive if I were to punish my son for not nurturing me or providing material goods, but I ought to discipline him if he does not obey my right and reasonable demand, and, for example, disobeys my instructions to not punch his brother. From his point of view (particularly as a three-year-old), his violence is justified. His obedience, in the end, does not hinge on reasonable consent. He must learn first the internal logic of being a brother and friend.

Through its prior roles and duties, the practical order of love widens the context of love. Our personal identities and life in community are expanded by specific relationships, roles, and duties, and by particular forms of reciprocity, all based on a variety of shared goods and ends. In this regard, the practical relationships, especially of the open household, constitute a complex time and place where love is discovered and formed, where love precedes us and where we learn to live into it. God's love, in distinction from human love, is known to us inasmuch as divine love for us is coextensive with God's activity of creation (out of nothing), and as we inhabit the world as God's creatures in the image of God. God's love implies a distinct relation. In contrast, personalist love, when it depends upon a generic inter-subjectivity (the "I" and "Thou"), perpetuates the modern idea that love is a distinct realm of activity with a reality prior to the roles through which it is expressed. Put differently, romantic isolation sustains the modern notion of a discrete self that stands apart from the natural and social givens of everyday life.[49] The personalist framework is vulnerable to modern romanticism about love that encourages a flight toward an unattainable, "other-worldly" ideal.

The same flight from practical roles and duties characterizes theories that privilege disinterested, altruistic love. Altruistic accounts promise to be impartial and universal over against the ways that we form attachments and come to discover who we are through the quotidian matters of life. Despite these goals, the ideal of selfless love still cannot get around the problem that our time and energy continues to be spent with people we know and trust. We know our friends as friends precisely because we share time and place and the activities of life. Disinterested, impartial love asks for, at least, an internal disengagement from those whom we love intensely. Altruism asks us to love over against the people with whom we share life, those who have become part of who we are and have taught us how to love. In effect, so-called selfless love demands a contradiction between our impartial internal affections toward all and our specific responsibilities to the people with whom we are bound.[50]

Love as communion shifts the problem. Love is no longer set against attachment. It is defined by the intensity of everyday connections and our common endeavors. Like accounts of altruism, proposals for love as fellowship recognize the limits of those with whom we can share our lives, but this love as communion frames the problem differently. The problem becomes not communion as such but the limits of our concrete communities. The problem is the simple fact that we humans are a fragmented race. We are human beings but not yet humanity: we are not yet a human people.[51]

Created as human family, we groan with creation until we are gathered again as adopted children of God (Rom. 8.23). In this regard, the church has a reciprocal relation to the world, a role to play in the continuing story of God's relationship to creation. It is the role of Christian communion to provide a fruitful way to live as we work toward the ideal of God's universal love.

Christian community is constituted by both the fracture of the cross and a foretaste of the resurrection. We are formed by the call to common life as a sign of God's good end when all people will be gathered as one fully human community. The church is by no means identical with that end; therefore the church is distinguished from the kingdom, on the one hand, and Jesus is identified with the kingdom, on the other. The biblical narrative and the historical presence of Israel and the church are not the story of human development as such, but the history of a people gathered as a sacrament of human history.[52] Israel is "called out" to be God's people, and the Spirit is given to the church, so that they might be a sign. The church as a sign of the kingdom and the sacramental life of the church are "an articulation of the deep meaning of human life," a sign of the future in "making present" the risen Christ as the meaning, the good news, and revolutionary destiny of the world.[53] The church is summoned to be a people of forgiveness and peace, to be a people who inhabit the story of Jesus in a fragmented world.[54] The church is gathered to be an embodied interpretation of human life through the cross and resurrection, through hospitality, reconciliation, and "a love that would overcome the powers of this world, not through coercion and force, but through the power of this one man's death."[55]

Conclusion

Recall Stephen Post's definition of love: "Agape is an affection of the heart, an attunement of the person's deepest center that issues in a faithful will to exist for God and others as well as for one's own fulfillment. It is sustained and reinforced in religious fellowship by reliable acts of reciprocation: at best, love forms a circle of mutual giving and receiving between God, self, and others."[56] From this definition and from the arguments of this chapter, it follows that love is not located in an individual's selfless will, "in" an individual at all, or in an abstract principle of the "I" and "Thou." The love of God in the world is carried on by community over time. Post likens agape to an ecosystem, a particular kind of organic body that is enlivened by the gift of God's grace, so that certain boundaries are necessary. Love, ultimately, knows no strangers. The circle of God's love is porous, precisely because of the kind of ecosystem it is called to be. As a sign of God's self-giving, of cross and resurrection, the community of faith is called to show partiality to the stranger and to the alienated and poor. To love, the church is called to bear the story of God from generation to generation, and for this reason and in this expansive sense, family is the way of the church. To love with the love of God, we are called to live as community, as an embodied interpretation, through time, of the world as the household of God.

8

The Happy Home

Introduction

I dedicate this chapter to Bridget, my wife, but not for the sentimental reasons expressed in the usual dedications to a wife or husband. I suppose that I could say that I love her deeply. I could express gratitude for her friendship and give honor to her talents and gifts. I could say that she has made this book possible. I could, but I will not. I will dedicate this chapter to Bridget because otherwise people will talk. Friends and colleagues might read the book out of duty. I know that her mother and sisters will, and they will talk. After reading my assault on sexual desire and romantic love, and after my skepticism about the nuptial "I and Thou," they will wonder if I love her with any passion. They will speculate among themselves, but never ask her directly. Do I have any romantic feelings for her at all? They will wonder if she should be pitied on my account. I will leave that question unanswered, but in this chapter, I will offer a proposal about the makings of a happy home. In jest, I worry that my wife's family and friends will talk, precisely so that they will talk. Hopefully, they will flip through the book looking for this page like school children with an anatomy text. I want them to begin with this chapter. In seriousness, I know that a likely criticism of the book, up to this point, is that I have given no place for love as passion. This chapter is the place.

Love as an emotional force and movement of desire is a basic means for moderns to make deep personal connections. Love as passion impels us to "fall" for another, and through falling in love, we are moved outside of ourselves and are bound in community with our beloved. A common theological approach attempts to argue for the lifelong commitment of marriage on the basis of this romantic connection (e.g., Genovesi in Chapter 2, and Hildebrand, Greeley and Durkin in Chapter 3). This approach is mistaken, it seems to me, because it hopes to stabilize marriage through what is known to be a fragile bond. Historically and conceptually, romantic love is defined over against the endurance of marriage. In this regard, the common approach is mistaken, but it is also uninteresting. The language and grammar of love as passion are so dominant in modern culture that there is little reason to argue for it, unless the theologian's intention is merely to be with the times.

Two people meet, and they fall in love. Their love sticks, so that they see marriage as the logical and inevitable next step. This story continues to be the predominant narrative of marital connection. It is a given, and I will not argue for it here. Neither will I argue for the idea that marriage fosters a special kind of intimacy and inter-personal identity. Arguments for the distinctive connections of romantic love and marriage are trivial because too common in our times. Instead, I will offer suggestions for the appropriate place of romance in marriage. More often than not, falling in love puts us in marriage, but it is not a foundation. In line with previous dis-cussions of the order of love and the open home, I will locate love as passion within shared activities of household management and the rich endeavors of a company of friends. Romantic love works, I will propose, when we do not depend on it to do any relational work.

The love of common endeavors

Love is central to the history of modern marriage and family. In contrast to external constraints of earlier times, marriages are negotiated and established by means of affective regard and the draw of passion. It is axiomatic that feelings of desire and love form the reason, context and glue for the loving relationship. Romantic love (as noted in Chapter 3) is defined over against utilitarian rationality and pragmatic concerns; yet, while not calculated or useful, love is marked by the values of the market and emotional investment strategies. Hard work is required to sustain spontaneous attraction and natural affection. Without glossing over this contra-diction, we can make some sense of it by pointing out that relation-ships require work but they are not useful in themselves. Within the romantic framework, we ought to invest in love, but not con-sider love for purposes of personal advantage, patronage, or social benefit.

Relationships exist for themselves, for their inner sense of connection. We do not get anything except that we have a "relation-ship."[1] The self-referential character of having a relationship corre-sponds to the curious idea of having a "lover." Lover, if considered a primary description, has no practical context other than the perpetuation of the relationship itself through passion. Without intending to be redundant, I might say that my wife is my lover. If I were to do so, I would be contrasting a functional meaning of my wife with a passionate meaning of lover. Such a contrast does not sit well with romantic views of marriage. My wife and I cooperate in home economics, in tasks such as managing finances and taking active roles in our community. She and I might carry on these practical matters quite well without being "lovers." If such were the case, our marriage might be considered loveless and hollow. If, on the other hand, we were quite inept at practical cooperation but were full of passion, then many romantics would consider our relationship wonderfully alive even if in practical disarray.

Having a relationship is often considered natural, especially if we accept our partners for "who they really are." Managing a house-hold, on the other hand, implies reciprocal duties and requires an array of skills, from cooperation in common work to housecleaning (see Chapter 1). "Relationships" are represented by dinner for two, face-to-face, enjoying intimate moments and long conversations. The household, by contrast, orients a couple to matters of raising children, leaky faucets, and the politics of the neighborhood association. In the household, long conversations tend to become task-oriented. Relationships are focused on events pertaining to practical life, like a successful day of potty training or what to do about the noisy neighbors. Romantic love and "having a relation-ship" are oriented as a flight from home, as couples imagine renew-ing their bond through weekend trips to Bermuda, or dropping the kids off for a weekend at grandmother's.

Corresponding to the contrast (from Chapter 5) between the consumptive, closed family and the productive, open household, this chapter will propose that "internal" family love attains depth through an outward orientation, through common endeavors, and "productive" relationships, through an ordering of roles and reciprocal duties. Household "productivity" and affective relation-ships would have to emerge from a context other than market capitalism and contractual individualism, that is, from gift-giving, reciprocity, and community of the household economy. Modern love's flight from the home fits with a narrative of the modern family, which is represented by the trope (in Chapter 4) of the ideal suburban household. Like romantic love between "lovers," the love of the suburban family is self-contained, priceless, and anti-utilitarian. Ironically, such affection is likely to be very costly. The suburban home, with its thin economy of autonomy and self-reliance, is oriented toward the dominant market economy and toward contractual relations. In this context, it makes sense to be married and to "have" a family simply for the purpose of expressing affection and "having" love. This self-referential love (or family for family's sake) represents attenuated affections of the home, suited to an attenuated understanding of the household economy and more likely than not to be characterized by weakened filial bonds. As counter-intuitive as it may seem, it may be that love and affection attain their depth through common work and through a common vocation.

In their study of the contemporary household, Mihaly Csikszentmihalyi and Eugene Rochberg-Halton offer some sur-prising conclusions about shared affection within the home.[2] The bulk of their *The Meaning of Things: Domestic Symbols and the Self* is devoted to a sociology of households objects, but the authors include a record of interviews pertaining to what they call "emo-tional integration" and to the affective qualities of happy families. The authors distinguish what they refer to as warm and cool homes by the self-assessment of family members. Families whose members agreed in their positive assessment of shared affection were con-sidered warm over against families who shared cool attitudes toward each other. Csikszentmihalyi and Rochberg-Halton con-clude, interestingly enough, that positive affection is fostered by productive relationships and a sense of social responsibility.

Csikszentmihalyi and Rochberg-Halton begin their interviews, appropriately, with an unrealistic question: "If you had the time and money to do *anything* you wanted, what would you do?" The question fits well with an inquiry about a family's emotional bond, since modern romantic love seeks a liminal place outside the struc-tures of everyday life. The bond of love as passion, in other words, is located on a threshold outside household time and space. Like typical tales of romance, virtually all responses to the unrealistic question imagined some form of travel, "the favorite destinations being Hawaii, California, Colorado, 'around the world,' and

Europe."[3] Csikszentmihalyi and Rochberg-Halton liken the liminal dream of travel to a pilgrimage or quest. The respondents imagined themselves on a journey to a place where the true self is confirmed, and the meaning of everyday life transformed. The desire for a meaningful pilgrimage did not distinguish warm from cool households; rather the distinction lay in whether the quest was conceived as an escape or as a productive endeavor. Cool homes were escapist. Their members were inclined to seek travel only as form of consumption and pleasure. A good example is one father's hope for exotic encounters on some faraway coastline. Warm families, in contrast, were productive. They emphasized goals for personal growth and improving the well-being of others.[4]

While cool fathers focused on pleasure, responses from fathers of warm homes imagined travel as an important learning experience for children, or they mentioned other goals for themselves unrelated to travel, like taking time to develop their musical talents, to read, or to study history. A boy from a warm home put fixing his friend's poor eyesight on the top of his wish list, while cool home children conjured up only high-tech versions of Pinocchio's Pleasure Island. Mothers from cool homes, in contrast to cool fathers and children, tended to be anxiously productive. Csikszentmihalyi and Rochberg-Halton attribute their hyper-productivity to the cultural burdens of motherhood combined with a general lack of cooperation within their families. They found that mothers of warm homes were less defensive and more open to idle dreaming precisely because productive concerns were secure. Csikszentmihalyi and Rochberg-Halton conclude "that when the members of a family share positive emotions about their home, they develop aspirations that lead beyond immediate gratification to some productive outcome."[5]

Csikszentmihalyi and Rochberg-Halton's line of questions moves from emotions to aspirations, but they want to avoid post hoc conclusions that would give the temporal sequence a relationship of cause and effect, from positive regard to a productive orientation. Neither would they assert that goal-oriented households are necessarily harmonious and loving. Their point is that positive affection and productive agency are correlated. Emotionally integrated families *think* of enjoyment in terms of goals that are consistent with activities of the household, such as raising children, developing personal talents and skills, and serving the community. Cool households, by contrast, conceptualize pleasure and happiness as an escape from the quotidian matters of home. Happiness in cool families is elusive because set outside the social economy of family and neighborhood. Csikszentmihalyi and Rochberg-Halton are convinced that highlighting cooperation and common endeavors within the household will enhance positive affection. We could say that love is cultivated through activities that are not focused on love, but on common, goal-directed purposes.

The distinction between escapist and productive orientations is consistent with Csikszentmihalyi's Aristotelian distinction between pleasure and enjoyment.[6] Hedonistic pleasure, he proposes, "refers to a value derived from satisfaction that is an end in itself; it is the consummation of a feeling and not the meaning or purpose of that feeling that makes the difference."[7] Pleasure makes a person feel good without reference to one's own or another's goals. "Enjoyment," Csikszentmihalyi explains, "results from the purpose aimed at by the activity and intrinsically involves the integration of pleasurable feeling within one's context of goals. Enjoyment, then, is a purposeful feeling inseparable from the interaction and not merely a subjective, individual sensation. It implies self-control, the development of skills in the pursuit of voluntary as opposed to spontaneous goals."[8] Csikszentmihalyi and Rochberg-Halton's warm families express their positive relations in terms of purposeful enjoyment rather than mere pleasure. Happiness and emotional integration are experienced through cultivating personal and common growth as a craft.

While a craft provides a context for enjoyment and pleasure, pleasure alone is mere consumption. Csikszentmihalyi notes that pleasures are important to our quality of life insofar as they conserve or restore equilibrium. Eating, sleeping or a vacation to Acapulco will replenish us and return us to a good state. Pleasures, though, are not sufficient for happiness because they require no venture of one's abilities or efforts. Pleasures are not carried forward by the agent, and as a result, the agent is not carried forward by them. Pleasures are likely to be engrossing or captivating for a time, but they are evanescent. While likely to be satisfying or even exhilarating, they will leave our lives stagnant. They leave us where we were before.[9]

Enjoyment, in contrast, is superior because it is a quality of purposeful activity that moves us forward in life, extends our abilities and awareness, and constitutes a complex (or we could say deep or substantive) self. Enjoyment requires engagement in performance and meaningful activity, and will foster a kind of selflessness or forgetfulness of self that opens us to possibilities we thought beyond our grasp.[10] I have experienced a kind of "zone" of heightened awareness and performance while playing basketball, running, and writing, and when working and playing in the company of friends. Apart from an extraordinary "zone," each of these activities has offered ordinary enjoyment, engagement and an extension and discovery of self, through the intrinsic goods of their performance. Csikszentmihalyi mentions tennis games, good books, and engaging conversation, but we could also add being a pianist, carpenter, spouse, or parent. Being a mother or a wife, sister and friend refers to a daily grind, or perhaps we should say daily groove or habit, that makes demands and offers growth.

Being a husband, father, neighbor, and son refer not to affective connections as much as to a set of roles and practices that require an attainment of skills, proximate ends, and overriding purposes, as well as attendant experiences of affection and pleasure. These roles have intrinsic ends. They are not identical but complement each other, so that the intrinsic good of one role is discovered in relation to the others. Husband is not simply set in relation to wife, but father to wife, mother to son, daughter to brother, and so on. The network is complex and offers a depth of enjoyment and work. Being a parent, for instance, brings a host of unanticipated challenges and joys. One learns patience and love in new ways, in relation to helpless infants, irrational two-year-olds, and teenagers who have become adults. Parents learn how to be present to their children regardless of sentimental attachments. I cannot remember how many times, when an adolescent, that I told my mother that I hated her; yet, she continued to be a mother to me as though I had been professing my love. I think that she took a good bit of pleasure in calmly pointing out that my feelings were irrelevant. Hate her or not, I was her son, and I would do as I was told.

Being a mother or son is like a craft. Now that I am a parent I realize that I have to work at acquiring the skills of being a good parent, and that there is joy in doing what is right for our children, regardless of if we or they like it at the time. A weighty part of parenthood is teaching children the craft of being good brothers and sisters, sons and daughters. Each has a role, set of duties, and fit with the whole. We continually have to remind our oldest child that she is not a parent. She likes to scold her brothers with our words. We remind her that she should not be doing our job, and that she cannot be a sister and a parent at the same time. In fact, being a sister and eldest sibling is not an easy task. It requires a host of skills that will shape our daughter's identity and her whole life. We are formed by her as well. Our family would not be the same without her.

The roles of family precede us. They are passed on to us, and like apprentices to a craft, we are trained in the skills of their performance. Although our roles and duties come before us, each of us fits into roles that are part of a particular network and carve out a place that is unique to us. Our Abigail is not a generic older sister, but a sister and daughter who shapes the family and her role in a particular way, surely not to be repeated by anyone. Partly because of her, I am the kind of father I am; I have come to be a father in relation to her. Likewise, her brothers and mother are marked in a unique way by her presence as well. Everyone in the family plays a part by sustaining a network of reciprocity that not only forms us but is also formed by us. The meaning of family is larger than us, particularly as it plays a part in the life of the church. In expansive networks of family, we are able to take part in purposeful activities that extend our character and bring both enjoyment and pleasure.

Csikszentmihalyi and Rochberg-Halton find, much to their surprise, that warm homes extend their productive orientation beyond the household. The warm household is open; it is not an enclave. For example, the authors find that members of emotionally integrated homes, in comparison to cool ones, are significantly more involved in the endeavors of their neighborhoods and communities. Along these lines, Csikszentmihalyi and Rochberg-Halton inquire about role models, assuming that "people become acculturated to their society in part by selecting to pay attention to certain 'significant others' whose behavior and values they internalize."[11] Warm family members were more inclined to name public figures rather than their own family members or friends. A more striking difference between warm and cool was evident in reasons why public figures were admired. Cool family members were attracted to public personalities, like Michael Jordan or evangelist Billy Graham, precisely because of their "warm" personalities. Warm families considered role models desirable for their expertise and creativity, like Yo-Yo Ma or Jimmy Carter, or perhaps Michael

Jordan or Billy Graham, but for their talents rather than personal attractiveness. Csikszentmihalyi and Rochberg-Halton conclude that emotionally integrated families "are close, the relationship among their members is warm, yet they are the ones that foster productive goals, active involvement in social action, and public models and values."[12]

When considering the internal workings of family, Csikszentmihalyi and Rochberg-Halton find, again to their surprise, that personality patterns within warm homes are complementary rather than identical. In their study, spouses were apt to have different propensities toward order and discipline, nurture and sociability. While Csikszentmihalyi and Rochberg-Halton did not expect this to be the case, complementary differences make sense when people are working together for common ends. Each person fits into a role that fits with the good functioning of the whole, and in this way, individuals become part of endeavors that extend them beyond their individual capabilities. More opportunities for growth and enjoyment are actualized. In this regard, Csikszentmihalyi and Rochberg-Halton found that even formative relationships were not identical. "It does not seem that children simply acquire parental traits through modeling or imitation. Rather, a certain set of parental personality dimensions calls forth a complementary set of traits in the children. The father's sense of order and discipline does not impel the children to be equally ordered and disciplined but might give them enough of a feeling of security to be warm and nurturant."[13]

The authors, though, found no one-to-one correlation between trait A in a parent and trait B in a child. Relationships in the warm home are less rigid and more diffuse. Productive and affectionate homes are inclined toward functional complexity. Csikszentmihalyi and Rochberg-Halton propose that in warm, outwardly oriented families "whatever effects shape the child's personality are mediated by the total network of family relationships, especially by the meanings attributed to actions, objects, and the home as a whole."[14] A conception of one's family as a "total network" would itself be beneficial insofar as each member would then be able to place him or herself in a context of meaning larger than individual relations. The "productive" rather than "escapist" home is open insofar as it forms its members in the skills and wisdom of common endeavors. In this sense, family life can be conceived within an overarching framework of vocation.

What about romance?

The household structure of roles and practical purposes need not exclude times of romance and connections of passion. Attraction, desire, and the rush of "falling in love" are simply placed within a broader context of practices, goods, and ends. In the home, feelings of love are located within the narrative of relationships, or a network of relationships, that are characterized by Csikszentmihalyi's conception of enjoyment, by growth and by a complexity of personal identity and common life. Enjoyment comes through activities that have internal goods and ends, such as playing tennis, carpentry, or raising children and managing a home. It is hard to imagine a craft that would include more moments of high pleasure, more personal struggles and frustrations, more need for cooperation and mutual care, and more movement beyond one's previously known capacities and skills than child rearing and supporting family through a lifetime of endeavors. It is hard to imagine that the flow of love would not be suited to such an engaging adventure. This flow of love, as movement, is characterized by change and growth. In this regard, romantic love would not be excluded but recognized as limited. It is indeed narrow in focus (on one person only) and lacks complexity. Romance offers only a short spectrum of experiences and emotion, and it tends to resist growth and change.

Romantic love constitutes only a subplot (albeit an important one) in the story of a home. It is a good and wonderful experience to be in love: to think about our beloved during every moment of the day, to seek constantly to be near him or her, and to hang on every word and glance. The wonderment of romance has its place: long candlelight dinners for two, walks along the beach, and nights out on the town. Romantic love is criticized, in Chapter 3, for its tendency to make spontaneous emotion and exotic adventures definitive for the grammar of love and to consider relationships that extend into the routines of everyday life as somehow static and lifeless. While the romantic will look down upon marriage as routine and dull, a person's life is far more static and repetitious if he or she is limited to a romantic script. When limited to the romantic plot line, a person falls in love with another, exhausts the experience, and then begins the whole pattern over again with a new lover, and then another and another. Perhaps the romantic will even take the new lover back to the usual romantic places and use previously successful techniques. The romantic lover winds up his or her love-spring, lets it loose, and winds it up again for the next person. In effect, the romantic lover cannot bear the future, change, or transformation. Note, for instance, that lovers continually seek a return to the beginning, to the first moment of attraction and desire, to the renewal of their anniversary, even to the places (clubs or vacation spots) where they were first seized by passion. Like Csikszentmihalyi's pleasure, romantic love, once spent, leaves us back where we already had been. Romantic love can be a wonderful thing, but it tends to limit growth. In this sense, it is simply immature.

Calling romance immature is not an aspersion as much as a qualifier that puts it at an early stage of development. Romantic love is fitting when it is transformed and leads to something else. "Falling in love" and "being swept off one's feet" are curious ideas. They indicate a sense of abandonment, a giving over and giving up of personal agency. Falling in love implies a passive being moved by another. On the one hand, this "being moved" is a necessary part of being attracted to another person. When we love, we are drawn to the good that is in another. The passive verb is important. The attractiveness or good in the beloved works upon us, and we are moved. By being moved, we should expect to be changed by sharing our lives, deeply, with the other person. On the other hand, love is our active embrace. We seek what is attractive and good. To this degree, falling in love is an intentional stepping out, a venture into the arms of another. We are able to be drawn to another because love is in us. We act with love. We open ourselves outward in the hope that we will be transformed. We love for our own good.

The love that is in us and expressed through our actions will correspond to the love that attracts us, moves us, and draws us near. Put differently, how I am able to love will correspond to the love by which I am able to be moved. If I am capable of loving only in terms of satisfying my desire for pleasure (in Csikszentmihalyi's use of the term), then I will be attracted to a person only for the pleasures that he or she offers, such as physical attractiveness, a sense of humor, or sexual availability. Physical attractiveness, sensual pleasures, and humor are good, but if pursued only in the context of pleasure, they will be used rather than enjoyed by the lover, who will not be open to the "something more" of the beloved or the "moving forward" of love. If we are immature in our own movement toward the goods of life, we will be attracted to other people for superficial reasons as well. Young adults, for instance, who expect to establish their identity by struggling against practical dictates of school and home, will be attracted to each other for the same reactionary reasons. They will seek an enclave of relationships oriented to pleasure or to reacting against their practical life at school and home.

When love is not set over against practical life, our attraction to others will include matters that fit with practical skills, with the beloved's character, and his or her capacity for enjoyment and "moving forward" in friendship and love. If I understand goods of life in terms only of the market economy and contractual individualism, my feelings will have no practical home. My love is limited to ephemeral moments of romance, and my feelings will always be impractical and unsuited to what I conceive of as work. If, on the other hand, I locate my identity in the productive goods of the household and in the vocation of family, I will see the attractiveness of qualities that suit the roles of mother and father, wife and husband, brother and sister, neighbor and friend. A person's profession and practical skills will be attractive, as well as his or her ability to contribute to common life and to cooperate within the household and neighborhood. Being attracted to a nurse because he is a nurse, for instance, is far less superficial than judging him by current fashion, his hair, or whether or not he puts out an air of coolness at parties. The day-to-day care that he gives, as a nurse, will continually shape who he is, and unlike the party-scene, the skills of nursing will transfer to skills of intimacy and interpersonal care. Likewise, he might be attractive because he is active in his community, coaches baseball, has good friends, and treats his siblings and parents well. None of these aspects of his identity are somehow less romantic than other reasons for one's attraction to him, but they are superior and far less arbitrary than idle pleasures because they promise a way to move more deeply into common life.

There is an irony here. When romance is the linchpin of a relationship or a marriage, then the couple, after the first wave of passion is gone, will have to work a great deal in order to conjure up passion and spontaneity. The romance is likely to die because one or both partners will become tired of working to restore what is supposed to be spontaneous passion. When marriage and life in the household are not dependent upon romance, the couple is free to be spontaneous and passionate. The couple is free for passion because romance is something extra, a delight rather than a requisite for the very existence of their life together. When a couple has a practical bond, they are free to be less clingy. They will not fear diverting their attention from the romantic gaze. Because sentiment is not the whole of their bond, they will be more open to other intimate friend-ships. Other friendships will be considered an asset rather than a threat.

The affection of the household is characterized by respect, fond-ness, familiarity, and mutual care. The love of the open home is a kind of "taking for granted." Love of home is an interdependence and trust found through cooperation and a common identity. The "we" of the household is more quotidian than romantic or emo-tional. The irony is that romantic relationships tie passion and spontaneity to strenuous labors in a way that productive and role-oriented marriages do not. When a wife's intimacy with her husband is founded on common practical ends and a shared vocation, she is bound by a different affective regard, and she may be surprised now and then when passion stirs up. Romantic desire may arise, or it may not. Happiness does not hinge on it. Precisely because it is inessential, romantic love will be experienced not as labor but as gift.

Gazing into another's eyes and enjoying romantic days of caring just about each other is fitting if it is not the whole story. The wider narrative context is provided by the household, where a couple undertakes the adventure of common endeavors. They pass through unpredictable stages and events: rearing infants and arguing with teenagers, sponsoring neighborhood clean up days and coaching football, scraping by with little income, enjoying times of plenty, cultivating friendships, sharing trouble, watching and feeling each other's bodies sag and age, struggling through hurts and failures, asking for forgiveness, helping each other develop personal talents, and renewing a youthful romance now and again just for the fun of it. Marriage in the household is an adventure that the modern romantic has little skills or courage to bear. Marriage and family, in this context, make possible an intimate knowledge of others, abiding trust, and willful affection. The open household is a story of discovery and a training ground for coming outside of oneself and "moving forward" in love. The household is a venture open to people coming in and changing things, to various stages of life, per-sonal projects, failures, and improvement, and mutual sacrifices.

The household is an undertaking that may be a fertile context for nearness of heart and a place of common endeavors not suited to the fainthearted romantic. The home provides the possibility of friendship among those who work and journey together.

Friendship

Romance is hardly mentioned in contemporary theological accounts of marriage, but much is made of love. Discussions of marital love are relatively new, and a good number of theologians regard the Catholic tradition's only recent, tardy consideration of conjugal love with some embarrassment and frustration. At any rate, all contemporary writers (as far as I know) count the Church's long, loveless tradition on marriage as something to advance beyond.[15] Germain Grisez provides a good example. Like others, he marks Vatican II's Pastoral Constitution on the Church in the Modern World, *Gaudium et spes*, as the decisive document. *Gaudium et spes* identifies conjugal love as an intrinsic good of marriage over against the earlier tradition, traceable to Augustine, that marriage is only an instrumental good providing for the procreation of children and "a remedy for concupiscence."[16] For much of its history, theology and canon law have been concerned to provide an external definition of marriage, to determine what makes someone a valid husband or wife rather than a good one. Recent accounts define marriage according to its internal or interpersonal character, as an expression of love that, in the words of *Gaudium et spes*, "leads the partners to a free and mutual giving of self, experienced in tenderness and action, and permeates their whole lives."[17]

Marriages of old were not supposed to be or expected to be loveless; rather, marriage was not considered, as it is today, as "a" or "the" representative expression of love. This distinction between old and new inclines some toward hyperbole. Consider this example. A man married a woman out of a vendetta, "wanting to subject her to a life of cruelty and thus pay back her family for all the injuries they had inflicted on him and his family. But by the old [Augustinian] rules this would be a valid marriage since he intended to have children, be sexually faithful, and live with her until death. Obviously something was missing – he did not love the woman."[18] The author is certainly correct that this marriage would be valid, in the same way that many abusive marriages are legally valid today.

His overstatement comes when he implies that the church had nothing more to say.

According to standards external to marriage, the man's vendetta would have been considered a corruption of marriage, and the man lacking the virtues of justice and charity.[19] The man shows his privation of justice by not giving his wife what she deserves. His vendetta seeks punishment merely for the sake of revenge, without the good of the guilty party in view. Even if we were to grant that she deserved punishment, the man's thirst for revenge remains disordered inasmuch as his retribution is not directed to the woman's good. He is merely vindictive. Put simply, the man's vengeance controls him, so that he is incapable of wanting good things for his wife. Unable to desire the good for another, he is incapable of neighbor-love, and among other things, he is not a good husband.

These criteria of love and justice are determined outside marriage but apply within. The same holds when contemporary theologians and married couples turn to the question of conjugal love. We find the language and practices of love set deeply within the tradition, but not particularly in marriage. Our rich tradition of inquiry about neighbor-love is the basis for contemporary understandings of companionship between husband and wife. Augustine, for instance, may be infamous for his disparaging attitude toward sex and his lukewarm defense of marriage, but there is strong affinity between his discussions of love and recent accounts of conjugal union. Like modern theologians, Augustine sets his elaboration of love mainly in terms of friendship. Unlike more recent accounts, his view of companionship is set, not within a self-sufficient "I–Thou," but among a company of friends.

Augustine, as noted above, holds that marriage is not a good sought for its own sake, "such as wisdom, health, and friendship," but a good that is "necessary for something else, such as learning, food, drink, sleep, [and . . .] sexual intercourse."[20] In "On the Good of Marriage," he justifies marriage in response to those who would reject it entirely, by showing its relation to the goods of procreation (which creates a natural unity and affinity of the human race), permanence of union (signifying the unity of all in God), and sexual fidelity (including the marriage debt). In other words, marriage may not be an end in itself but it serves the goods of the human family and the church. Given this instrumental view of marriage, it strikes many as odd when Augustine also speaks of marriage as a bond of fellowship not wholly contingent on the good of procreation ("On the Good of Marriage," ch. 7), as a true good and not simply a lesser evil (ch. 8), and a "natural companionship between the two sexes" where "the order of charity" flourishes (ch. 3).[21] Is Augustine contradicting himself, claiming in these instances that conjugal love is an end in itself, that marriage is an essential rather than instrumental good?

The contradiction between marriage's essential and instrumental goods is eased if we assume, first, that Augustine writes "On the Good of Marriage" in order to justify marriage, and, second, that he does not expect marriage to be a representative context for love. On the one hand, Augustine seeks to defend marriage as a good over against its denigration by ascetics.[22] On the other, he prefers celibacy, the spiritual union of marriage over against the corporeal, and the spiritual desire for children rather than the carnal.[23] Like other ancients, he locates the good of fellowship primarily in associations between men.[24] If this is the case, then Augustine would not expect to convince many, nor be convinced himself, by justifying marriage as exemplary of fraternal love. Affection and companionship might be expected as essential qualities, but they would not constitute reasons for the marriage. Augustine defends sexual intercourse in marriage, but he sets conjugal union in the pattern of "spiritual" friendship. In "On the Good of Marriage," he admits that the rationale for entering marriage (and justifying sexual intercourse) does not provide a full account of all that marriage is.[25] This something more is not much of a concern for him. For representative examples of love, union, and common life, he looks instead to the company of friends.

Augustine follows the classical idea of friendship as he received it from reading Cicero's *De Amicitia,* while adding theological qualifications.[26] Friendship is founded on likeness and agreement, accompanied by mutual regard and affection. Friends will be able to see themselves more clearly and truly through the eyes of a good friend. This clarity comes to be when true friendship is given its form by what is good, when friends are mutually attractive because of their goodness (i.e., their virtue). Friendship is good will toward one another and willing good for one another. With their eyes on the good, friends are bound outwardly, beyond individual gratification and self-satisfaction, beyond mere usefulness and pleasure, beyond desires for wealth, honor, and fame. Friends make us better people, but sharing their troubles could make us worse in matters of wealth and fortune. Friends avoid pretense and useless flattery. They correct one another in cases of wrong-doing, and they suffer each other's troubles. Friends seek each other's good for the sake of good. In other words, good friendships are open to risk, growth, and the goodness of other friends.

In Cicero's *De Amicitia*, friendship is what could be called a public or social station. The good friend is a man of means, power, civic leadership, and service.[27] A man who is known as a good friend is nothing other than a man who is known to be good. His goodness is known through his loyalty and upright character, through his wisdom, fairness, and generosity, and through sharing the afflictions suffered by his friends. In the Roman world, being a good friend characterizes one's place in civic life. Having a good friend is to be cherished, but being a good friend is an honored position. The good friend would not have just one other friend, as a good painter would not be considered good because of a single painting. The good painter is known through a life time of painting well. The master painter is a paragon of the art. Likewise, the good friend reaches and represents high standards of character in a society of friends.

Friendship is practiced, in Cicero's world and in Augustine's own life, among this community of friends. Friendships are set within a complex set of friendships of various kinds and differing levels of reciprocity, among equals and unequals, young and old, old friends and new.[28] A friendship may have a dyadic character, but even a single friendship does not have a dyadic context. We could say that friends need other good friends and lesser friends for whom to will the good together. Friendship, because it is good, is oriented to the wider common good.

In Augustine's hands, true friendship comes to be founded on the outpouring of the Holy Spirit, upon the good who is God. Struggling in the *Confessions* with the loss of a dear friend, Augustine's thoughts turn to God. "Blessed is he who loves you, and loves his friend in you and his enemy for your sake. He alone loses no one dear to him, to whom all are dear in the One who is never lost. And who is this but our God . . ."[29] God sustains friendship and increases it through grace, so that both the natural virtues and the natural delights of friendship (as in Cicero's account) are exceeded. Augustine's friends love one another, correct one another, share each other's troubles, and work for each other's good, which means that they bring each other closer to God. Good friends are bound by a supernatural good in this life, and they will share, in heavenly perfection, the enjoyment of God in friendship.

God's love gives friendship the widest possible scope. As the Romans direct the virtues of friendship to the civic good, Augustine orients our friendships to common life in God. The unity found among an intimate circle of friends is Augustine's image of universal charity. The unity expressed in the church's sacramental practices and "the discipline of actual love in community" offer key means for understanding and experiencing the love of God.[30] In a homily on 1 John, Augustine encourages his listeners to "obtain from God the gift to love one another." He entreats his audience to "love all men even your enemies, not because they are your brethren, but that they may be your brethren . . . Wheresoever you love a brother, you love a friend. Now is he with you, now is he knit to you in unity, yea catholic unity. If you are living right, you love a brother made out of an enemy."[31] Augustine's notion of friendship begins with an intimate circle and widens to characterize the unity and charity of the church.

A family of friends

Similar connections between friendship, neighbor-love, and the church are important to contemporary theology. Michael Lawler, a prominent writer on marriage and director of Creighton University's Center for Marriage and Family, sets his account of marriage within the framework of friendship, which then gives way to accounts of neighbor-love, conjugal communion, and God's love for the church.[32] Lawler's discussion starts with the observation that we all need other people. "Without other human persons in our lives, without emotional intimacy, intellectual stimulation, personal and social connectedness, we will never achieve full humanity."[33] Lawler uses Aristotle's distinction between friendships of usefulness, of pleasure, and of the good in order to point to the kind of friendship that is not based *simply* on self-gratification. Friendship of the good is based on both the good of another person and the good that is this other person. "This person's goodness may be, of course, both pleasurable and useful to me, but in the third friendship it is not pleasure or usefulness but the *person* that I love."[34]

Appealing to the Greco-Roman tradition, Lawler points to the social nature of friendship and its essential relationship to the virtues. In this regard, he departs from a formal "I–Thou" that puts conjugal love merely in terms of interpersonal exchange. In friendship, it also matters whether or not we are cultivating the skills and habits to be good to and for one another. Friendship is social by definition because it is sharing the practical activities of life and doing so over time. Affection, intimacy, trust, and mutual respect are shallow if instantaneous; they must be practiced day to day, year to year, decade upon decade. Shared time fosters the continuity and depth of common life. Good friends endure. Friendship requires continuing effort, but the work is not merely a means to an end. It is a moving forward and growth, as the cultivation of a craft where the means and ends of the good work coalesce. The good work of friendship is the nature of good friendship itself. A friend is honest, loyal, and respectful. Friends are near through times of weakness and failure, through mutual correction and understanding, through common support, acceptance, and expectations for good. Friends bind themselves to each other and to each other's good.

This basic outline characterizes a multitude of good friendships, but the compatibility and reciprocity between particular friends, Lawler explains, are specific to an individual pair. Within the broad range of good friendships, Patrick's friendship with Linda is different than his friendship with Kevin, and Linda and Kevin have a somewhat different way of relating to each other. Each of us is "good in a few things . . . [and] deficient in many," so that we are attracted to others with whom we share the good, but we also admire them for goods they sustain that are different from our own.[35] It follows, from Lawler's point, that a single friendship flourishes within a complementary network of friendships, or a company of friends. Patrick, for instance, has become friends with Linda in the context of his friendship with Kevin. In subtle ways, Kevin helps hold them together. Friendships are rich because they are specific and not repeatable. Kevin is drawn to Linda, and Linda to Patrick in ways particular to each of them. Some friendships are better and more complete than others, but none is entirely complete. Each one of us enjoys and struggles with different aspects of common life with each friend. With some we play; with others we work. With some we seek advice; with others we test out ideas. With some we grow in patience; with others we grow in courage.

Here, we should make a distinction between open and closed friendships. Although Lawler cites Aristotle and Cicero, he distinguishes himself from this ancient tradition by beginning with how we need other people. Both Aristotle and Cicero are more careful. They want to protect true friendship from the desires and usefulness that come with practical needs. For them, self-sufficiency is the basis of good friendships.[36] Aristotle and Cicero insist that wealth and honor cannot be the basis of friendship, because advantage and good standing are the currency with which these men operate. Self-sufficiency and virtue are the basis of friendship, so that mutual service and good will between friends will not be reduced to the external goods of position and honor, and so that the sharing of burdens and troubles in friendship will not be confused with the weaknesses and needs of inferior people. For Cicero, true friendship is the aspiration of an elite cadre insofar as virtue and social standing are limited to the same.[37]

The Greco-Roman tradition assumes that friendship is a privilege of the privileged, of an elite class of adult males who are free citizens of wealth and political responsibility. Not only that, when civic goods shape the outward orientation of friendship, the city (i.e., the *polis)* sets the boundary lines. Part of what it means to be a good friend in Athens is to be an Athenian; that is, virtues of friendship serve the good of free males of one city over against another, and the virtuous man in one city might be an outlaw in another. When Aristotle calls the human being a political animal, he provides not only a social conception of human life but one bound to the *polis* as well. The Greco-Roman tradition develops an open conception of friendship (outward to the good), but with a closed conception of the social body, closed in terms of who might count as a friend (the free citizen) and what might be reckoned as good.

Lawler's starting-point, in comparison, gives our friendships an open posture, particularly in terms of the church's interpretation of human needs and the social body. We are deceived if we fashion ourselves as self-made and self-sufficient. In order to be faithful to God's incarnation, we need to learn poverty of spirit (Matt. 5.3) and to find ourselves and God through community with the poor, the prisoner, the stranger, the sick and infirm (Matt. 25.31–46). Faithful Christian living sets the open Greco-Roman friendship within the boundless context of God's household, within the universal scope of the city of God. God's self-giving constitutes the social body, so that boundary lines of friendship and virtue come to us not through self-sufficiency but through openness to God.

God's love rather than good human standing brings us in, and for this reason, the common life of the church is founded not on the virtue of its members but through forgiveness.[38] Forgiveness is a practice of a broken community. Common life is constituted by gathering together, by reconciliation and transformation. In contrast to the city-state, the bond of friendship is established through the gospel's reversal of order. The lowly are lifted up, and the proud are scattered (Luke 1.51). Christ empties himself, takes the form of a slave (Phil. 2.7), and suffers indignity at human hands, obedient unto death. For this he is exalted. Jesus gathers a band of disciples who are an odd, bungling bunch and ill-suited to their station. Peter, for instance, is remembered as much for his denials as for his faith; yet, he holds the keys to the kingdom as a dubious representative of the ways of heaven (Matt. 16.19). The cross, in a word, is the mark of our redemption in friendship with God.

It is this politics of God's household that opens the family as a "location" of social transformation, as put forward in Chapter 6 in the words of James and Kathleen McGinnis, Lisa Sowle Cahill, and John Paul II. Friendships, and marriage as friendship, are outwardly oriented, as ancient friendships were oriented to the good. In addition, they are understood to be temporally incomplete, inasmuch as the social body, God's church, exceeds the limits of human self-making and the structures and virtues of the earthly city. The family is structured beyond its mediation of the nation-state and the market economy, beyond the conserving institution of "family values" or the autonomy of family (see Chapter 4). Insofar as the suburban home represents a closed, self-sufficient social form, and the aspirations of an upwardly mobile middle class, suburban love and harmony will be the domain of a social and interpersonal elite. The advantaged will set themselves apart.

From a theological angle, we can say, in contrast, that good friendships and loving marriages are always incomplete, and are dependent on a wider company of friends. Practically speaking, marriages ought not be considered self-sufficient, and couples should not be expected to give each other everything (or even a high percentage) of what each needs. A marriage works when husband

and wife have common as well as separate yet overlapping circles of friends, when friendships broaden their roles and duties, and when a couple is not burdened with the notion of completing (or exhausting) the identity of the other. When marriages are conceived as friendships, there is a tendency to think in terms of a complete pair, a whole community, or a perfect fit, like a puzzle with only two pieces. In this context, my total self would be discovered through my spouse, a single other, because we are a complementary whole. This understanding of the dyadic self imposes not only idealistic expectations for the beloved, but also a heroic conception of one's own identity. Once more, the dyadic self lacks complexity (like the puzzle with two pieces). No wonder the closed, suburban marriage is thought to be a bore. The incomplete marriage, in contrast, is set within a complex web of complementary roles and functions within a complex and broken social body rather than the self-sustained *polis*, social elite, or interpersonally heroic.

Now and then, I walk down the street with my son to look through the wide windows of the volunteer fire department. Fire trucks make him happy. We have been to family events at the firehouse on many occasions, and all of us have a good time. Looking through the windows at the men in their circle of folding chairs, or women running a game of bingo, or children running about, I often wonder how many marriages the fire department has saved. From what I have witnessed, I expect that the main benefits of being a volunteer are friendships and the opportunity to be part of the "productive" fire department household. Friendships, there, are cultivated through meaningful work and community service. Families are brought out of themselves. Their activities are directed to the good of the firehouse and community. In the process, friendships will allow fathers to be fathers together, for wives to be wives with each other, for parents to scold and praise each other's children, for kids to act like brothers and sisters, and, most of all, for families to be good families and marriages to be good marriages without having to be good at being complete or ideal spouses and family.

By no means do I intend to idealize the volunteer fire department or the notion of a company of friends. The point is that, within the context of common work and community, a husband can be something more than a husband, a friend and volunteer, while set within the context of being a husband to his wife. A mother can be more than a mother, a project manager, while still being a mother to her children. Note that the dominant market economy sets parenthood over against work. The two spheres compete for time and commitment. The fire department, on the other hand, is a neighborhood economy. Its open friendships broaden the load of family relationships, so that marriage and parenthood need not be the purview of an interpersonal elite. A company of friendships is fertile ground for being more than we would be alone.

It is a common experience that, among the good company of friends, one or two are not so easy to get along with; yet somehow they get along and move forward. One or more friends might be eccentric or not so congenial. Some might lack the maturity of the other friends. Nevertheless, the company of friends is sustained as good company. The eccentric ones are included, not despite their dysfunctions but because of their good. Sure Brian is irritating, but there is more to him than that. He knows how to get things done; he works hard, and he sticks with us. He claims us as his friends, and his continuing presence with us is good. I might admit that I do not manage well with him alone, but he is a friend nonetheless. The Greek idea of friendship assumes a seamless unity between self-sufficient friends, but the Christian idea, I dare to say, is structured to accommodate dysfunction. Good friendships are made good by the reciprocity of a wider circle, always seeking the richness of life with others in God's good company.

When a conversation among friends turns to the relationship of a particular married couple, inevitably someone will wonder out loud, "I don't think that I could be married to either one of them," or "I don't know how she tolerates him." An obvious response is: you are not married to either of them so you have not learned how to be. Marriages are not perfect, but they do not have to be complete in order to be good marriages. People have to know how to work things out. On a deeper level, we should add that most marriages would probably not work if the two were isolated. Few of us would be chosen by many to share the proverbial deserted island. If we wonder, "I do not know how she gets along with him," the fact of the matter might be that she probably could not if the two were left alone without friendships and support. If we consider this lack of wholeness, not as a failure, but as part of the social character of the household, then we will be open to a network of households and friendships that enrich our marriages and cultivate the talents and skills of being loving husbands, mothers, sisters and sons.

9

Order, Gender, and Function

Introduction

The New Cana Manual, a guide for Christian marriage published in 1957, offers a list of masculine and feminine traits gleaned from social scientific studies of the day. *New Cana* explains the differences between men and women in order to enhance marital relationships and to deepen our understanding of conjugal love. The list is not intended to be exact, but open to "individual differences and infinite mixtures."[1] Nonetheless, it is specific enough to be useful.

Masculine	*Feminine*
Physically stronger	Physically weaker
More realistic	More idealistic
Logical	Intuitive
More emotionally stable	More emotionally volatile
Objective	Subjective
More factual	More fanciful
Slower judgment	Quick judgment
Literal	Tangential
Seeks love	Wants love
Self-assured	Less self-assured
Holistic thinking	Grasps details
Less adaptable	More adaptable
Less possessive	More possessive

Along with this list, *The New Cana Manual* notes that men need achievement and recognition, while women need affection, attention, and appreciation. Men are aggressive, courageous, and efficient; women are tender, sympathetic, and sensitive. Men want to rule, and women want to give themselves to someone.[2]

Whether the *New Cana* list appears absurd or accurate, it suggests that arguments about household order are inextricable from questions about the ordering of gender. In the context of the *Manual*, the list supports the leadership of the realistic and efficient husband over his idealistic and sensitive homemaker. This ordering of home is a problem, not because general gender divisions are identified, but because these gender qualities are identified with a clear sense of social function. Masculinity and femininity make a difference to what men and women do, but it is not always clear what that difference might be. In other words, gender impinges upon our identities and common endeavors, but being male or female is not equivalent to identity or function. Being a man deeply affects my role as parent, but my own siblings agree that my style and attitudes of parenting are obviously like that of my mother. Likewise, I teach as a man, but my differences from particular women on the faculty do not seem contingent on my masculinity. Our differences in social class (as slight as they may be), personality, and training seem to play a far greater role. The problem, then, with the *New Cana* list is not necessarily the traits, but the use of the list to establish a simple role division at home.

The purpose of this chapter is to offer a different social taxonomy for ordering the household. The modern conception of political equality establishes fairness between men and women through detachment from home. Women, like men, are given opportunities in the public sphere of work and social governance. However promising this notion of equality might be, it offers little room for gender identity and difference. Contractual individualism and its ideal of the closed home give status to women as individuals in the public sphere, while gender differences are set within their personal relationships and, possibly, the private sphere of home. The problem with this contractual equality is that gender and sex ought to make no social difference; yet, the point of asserting equality hinges on the claim that gender does, in fact, matter to who we are. I will argue that a "thicker" conception of social life can highlight gender differences while distinguishing gender from role and function.

While theological considerations of marriage gravitate toward the imagery of body/wife and head/husband (Eph. 5), I will suggest that this binary set of roles is diffused within the New Testament's mixed metaphors of the body.[3] I will do so with the apostle Paul's metaphor of the social body in view: "the body is not a single part, but many" (1 Cor. 12.4). The relation between gender and social function in the New Testament is not consistent. This inconsistency is an asset, not a liability. I will propose that accentuating gender can bring complexity to the social body if gender and social function are considered overlapping but not identical categories. In reference to contractual individualism and the closed home, I will argue that the problem of gender inequality is not gender difference, but attenuated social contexts like the so-called public sphere and the closed, nuclear home. Neighborhood reciprocity and the social economy of the household are far less manageable than the "traditional" middle-class divide between husband and wife allows. A complex relationship between gender and function is not only possible, but necessary to sustain a significant depth of common endeavor and a richness of social life.

Social station

The New Cana Manual offers a list of gender differences that, for the sake of argument, I would like to accept. Certainly, several of the characteristics are as outdated as the black-and-white reruns of "Leave It to Beaver," where Ward Cleaver slowly makes his way to Wally and Beaver's room to give them stern correction and dispassionate guidance. Today for instance, almost fifty years after the *Manual* was published, "holistic thinking," which is on the *New Cana*'s male side, is more likely to be coordinated with intuition, subjectivity, and adaptability, which are all feminine traits on the list. Some gender distinctions in the list might still be accepted. In particular, differences in physical strength, male aggressiveness, female nurturance and receptivity are emphasized by recent studies in physiology and socio-biology.[4] Women bear children. While the social significance of childbearing is often overstated, it seems careless to assume that our bodies make no social difference at all.

The advantage, for argument's sake, of accepting the *New Cana* list is not found in the particulars, but in the very idea of having a set of general differences that provide social complements. What kind of difference does gender make? Modern theologians and philosophers, from the writers of *The New Cana Manual* to John Paul II to feminists like Julia Kristeva and Lucy Irigaray, will agree that gender distinctions do not establish basic inequality.[5] Different is equal. This assertion of equality means that women, as women, have equal standing in relation to law, culture, and work. This idea of equality is minimal, but necessary, given the history of male rule over women as women. Equality is a protection and an open-ended provision of opportunity for women to be defined beyond the traditional imposition of an inferior social status.

Recent appeals to sexual difference are also proposed as an advance for women. Ancient philosophers considered men as complete or potentially complete human beings. Women were inferior. In essence and form, they were not fully self-sufficient or autonomous social agents. This tradition is partly sustained in the thought of Thomas Aquinas, who assumes that sex differences are necessary for procreation but not to social life, which is conceived as a company of men.[6] Modern theologians break with the past by envisioning gender differences as social counterparts. Human beings, created as male and female, are thought to be completed through complementary difference.

Difference is believed to enhance and elevate the social role of women. Theologically, the idea of a "man" implies a lack that gives way to the notion of a "woman," and vice versa. The creation of human beings, in Gen. 1.27, in the image of God as "male and female" is read as separate from (but not in contrast to) the "Be fruitful and multiply" of Gen. 1.28. Men and women are non-identical equals who share the dignity of God's image and are incomplete when set apart. Creation as male and female has come to represent the basic social nature of the human being, who is not self-sufficient and independent but made with a need and yearning for communion.

The distinction of gender, then, makes a difference to how human beings and human community are formed and sustained. When a thin egalitarianism minimizes difference, accounts of the household tend to sustain only attenuated proposals for common life. One example is William Johnson Everett's *Blessed be the Bond*, where he characterizes modern marriage as an egalitarian bond over against hierarchical and reciprocal arrangements.[7] His point in contrasting egalitarian from reciprocal or hierarchical forms is to highlight the character of marriage as a free association based on emotional attachments of love. Love precedes and then establishes the contours of practical life. On the basis of egalitarian affection, Everett will call for a reform of home and the workplace, so that parenting and household tasks can be shared.[8]

All seems well, but underlying Everett's conception of love and attraction is a mere equality of sameness. Like attracts like. Love, as a result, establishes a "simple" contractual bond. Love through sameness is "simple" because the foundational connections of social life lack functional complexity and depend, instead, upon a modern conception of the pre-social individual.[9] Everett provides no way to account for social differentiation. Household tasks and career opportunities amount to a formal exchange. We just split things down the middle and call it even. Fitting with this contractual conception of the social body, Everett reproduces a romantic ideal of love. His conception of love begins with the discrete (pre-social) individual; love, then, is assumed to produce the social bond from within. Oddly, Everett expects his account of egalitarian marriage to transform the very forms of contractual individualism that produce it. He perpetuates the logic of the closed nuclear home.

In the context of contractual individualism and the closed home, gender difference is either everything or nothing. Either male and female identities are basic social differences, or they are not considered valid distinctions at all. This "either–or" is the dilemma of liberal feminism.[10] When feminism accepts contractual individualism as its point of departure, then either women are defined by a difference that has no place in the public sphere (and they are confined to the private role of home), or women are defined by the contractual politics that conceives of the individual as a genderless man.[11] Contractual theory has no place for women as women. Its historical conception of the individual is decidedly male, particularly in its post-industrial conception of the "head of the household" and its model of fraternal rule.[12] Everett attempts to overcome gender inequality; however, he reproduces the modern political rejection of the social role of women *as women*. He reproduces a dilemma specific to contractual politics.

If we accept even *New Cana*'s divide between male and female, the dilemma of equality and difference might be resolved when set within a different social economy. In a complex system of reciprocity, there may be less pressure to identify gender precisely with social station. In fact, the necessity might lie on the side of mixing gender with other forms of social difference. For example, in a government of *New Cana*'s "more realistic" and "less adaptable" males, most would agree that a strong dose of "more idealistic" and "more adaptable" legislators (women) would give much needed balance and a fresh perspective in matters of the common-weal. Likewise, gender difference could be used to fit parenting with notions of childhood development. Teenagers may benefit from rearing by *New Cana*'s less possessive, more emotionally stable father. Perhaps, families with teenagers will be best served by stay-at-home dads. Given the *New Cana* list, men may be better suited to housekeeping in general. Their physical strength would be put to better use than in the office, meeting, or sales floor, and their desire for achievement, recognition, and rule would transform the languishing modern family. In other words, when gender differences are understood as complements, such as "logical" versus "intuitive," a diffusion of these differences *within* social station and function are required for a sense of complexity and social flourishing.

The *New Cana* list provides an interesting case because it implies social simplicity. In the context of the *Manual* as a whole, the list would not give easy access to roles such as the stay-at-home father and women law-makers. We are inclined to blame the list, but the rigidity of roles and gender is the fault of the *Manual*'s underlying political and economic assumptions. The list of traits implies that the home is a private, affective sphere where intuition, attachment, and subjectivity reign and that the public sphere depends only on dispassionate justice and objective fact. The home is feminine and idealistic, while the world runs on masculine realism. In other words, the gender divide is structured as the fundamental social divide between the public world of governance and the private world of the closed nuclear home.

When the household is a productive social institution, the social world becomes more complex and personal identity richer. The so-called public and private are no longer distinguished as social and objective on one hand, and personal and subjective on the other. The simplicity of the *New Cana* list is undone. When the household is conceived as a social network, order and governance are no longer equated with disinterested law or impersonal contracts. Reciprocity, gift-giving, and patronage make social relations more elaborate: baroque rather than bureaucratic. The *New Cana* list represents a gendered account of the social relations only when sex difference is made equivalent to the structure of social life, when the feminine and masculine represent separate spheres. When gender overlaps with other forms of reciprocity and role differentiation, masculinity and femininity will not be reductive, but part of a rich taxonomy of function, equality, and personal identity.

Ordering the household

Consider the following four ways of ordering the home. The four ways, as presented here, are artificial, particularly because these households are described as if networks of kinfolk, neighbors, and friends were not relevant to their internal organization. For that reason, the four cases ought not be taken as representative types. They serve the limited purpose of shifting a taxonomy of family away from such categories as nuclear or traditional home to closed and open, to families that function with a contractual model as opposed to neighborhood reciprocity and the social economy of home.

Case 1: dual careers

A married couple is raising two children ages four and two, and each works full-time. One has a career in sales, and the other a career in accounting. They have an equitable marriage. Their incomes are comparable, and they divide the tasks and time of childcare and household management. Both children spend the work day hours with a childcare provider, which means that the sharing of tasks between mother and father amount to the hours before and after traveling to work, about 7:00–8:30am and 6:00pm to bedtime.

Case 2: the "traditional" look

A husband and wife, with three children, a six-year-old, a four-year-old, and a five-month-old, divide household management according to what could be called traditional gender roles (a post-industrial middle-class tradition). The man earns a teaching salary, and he pursues an academic career within the limits of his responsibilities as husband and father. His schooling and career have been cause for various moves, from Boston to Berlin to a little town in Ohio. The woman is college-educated as well. For several months, while her husband was in school, he cared for their oldest child, who was an infant at the time. She worked as a supervisor in early childhood development. Since then, she has been at home full-time.

Case 3: working class

This couple would be inclined toward the "traditional" home represented by case 2, but they certainly would be happy with the dual
career track of case 1. Each works full-time for wages, one at a
grocery store and the other on a production line. Because childcare
for their two pre-school children is not affordable, the husband and
wife arrange their shifts so that they minimize the need for baby-
sitters. One works first shift and the other second. Between them,
they log in more hours at home than the couple from case 1, but
much less "free-time" and less time with each other.

Case 4: home daddy

This case could be considered the opposite of case 2 because it is
presents a gender reversal, but its ordering of the household follows
the same pattern. The husband manages the household full-time,
caring for the couple's two children, and the wife works in the
advertising department of a newspaper. Their arrangement emerged
after the birth of the second child. They had used childcare services
for the first child, but the woman decided, with the coming of the
second, that she would stay at home. As it turned out, the flexibility
of the man's job and his temperament were more amenable. He
began to cut back on his time as a way to help work out her new
adjustments, and then the two realized that it made more sense for
him to stay at home. With some emotional adjustments of his own,
the husband accepted his new role.

In terms of simple equality, case 1, the dual career, and case 3,
working-class couple, are superior to couples 2 and 4. The four
cases are described only in outline, so that we do not know if the
husbands in the equal homes (1 and 3) actually share the domestic
load. Nor do we know the level of engagement by husbands 2 and 4.
Assuming only the outlines, cases 1 and 3 are equivalent inasmuch
as husbands and wives share identical responsibilities and work
loads. However, the two cases are certainly not alike in terms of
desirability or their practical operation. Few would choose the
working-class couple's staggered shifts, while the dual-career couple
represents a comfortable, socially and economically advanced situation.

Insofar as case 1 is attractive, it is interesting that, for the dual-career couple, equality is achieved (rather than merely accepted) not so much by sharing time and tasks at home, but by minimizing them. I should add, at this point, that the real-life couple behind case 1 is able to afford a weekly cleaning service, and they are able to pay a babysitter so that they have an evening out at least once a week. Their contrast with the home-bound, working-class couple is striking. Desirable equality for the dual-career couple is achieved by a common withdrawal from the constraints of home and equal access, not merely to work, but the kind of careers that provide social and economic advantages. First, equality is established outside the home; then roles within are equalized by ensuring joint detachment from them.

If case 1 is superior in terms of simple equality, it represents a more shallow level of reciprocity and cooperation. Many may balk at this claim. They will cite various logistical problems that require planning and cooperation, such as getting the kids to daycare, finding time to wash clothes, and the haste with which dinner must be prepared. Proponents of case 1 will indicate that the traditional division of labor between housekeeper and wage-earner allows a clear separation that makes cooperation unnecessary. The accusation is likely to be true for the closed, nuclear ideal, which, ironically, is more like case 1's dual-career equality than a division of tasks within an open household. Like case 1, the traditional division of labor within the closed, suburban family is structured outside the home. The mother/housekeeper toils in isolation while (or so that) a husband's public identity is sustained through a job or career. Case 1 simply opens the world of work to the wife as well, and leaves the home in an asocial private sphere. Both the dual-career couple in case 1 and the traditional division of labor are formed by the same shallow conception of social life. The two cases are structured from the outside, where the market economy and contractual politics define the "social" or "public" sphere.

The cases look different if we assume that the household is a social economy, if the so-called public sphere is recognized as thinly social and if the neighborhood and home are recognized for their deep-rooted social character. The household represents more strenuous and more ambitious social work. Case 2 is titled, "the 'traditional' look," because appearances can be deceptive. Many consider the role of housekeeper traditional when performed by the wife of case 2, while the "home daddy" of case 4 is thought to be breaking new ground. The functional pattern within each household is the same, even though the public role of men and the private role of women is reversed. From the public or workplace side of the public–private split, the (1) dual career, (3) working class, and (4) husband housekeeper would be considered similar insofar as each crosses the traditional gender line: women enter the public sphere. From the side of the household economy, (2) the housewife, (3) the working-class couple, and (4) the home daddy are similar. These cases (2, 3, and 4) are similar if these households are open, if they are oriented outward rather than closed as suburban enclaves. Case 1 seems to stand alone as a practical flight from home.

The full-time management of home does not require traditional gender determinations (as in case 2). The dual-career parents might draw clearer gender lines, probably not in relation to work outside the home, but perhaps in terms of typically male activities and personality traits, on one hand, and female interests and behavior, on the other. Boys in the dual-career home might be required to be rough and tough, while girls are encouraged to dress up in order to be attractive to men. The stay-at-home mother of case 2, on the other hand, might encourage her daughters to pursue careers and to have a high level of independence from men as men. There is no reason to equate staying-at-home with an inferior position or a less active social role. Housekeeping will be considered inferior if the dominant contractual sphere is made definitive for what it means to enter social life. When wage-earning and career are given social priority, the parent who works outside the home will be expected to rule it (see Chapter 4). If, in contrast, privilege is given to the household as a social sphere, then wage-earning and external work will not be given higher value or equated with management of the home. The family member who manages an open home is likely to be functionally dominant.

The structural differences between the contractual home and the household economy are sometimes subtle. Our dual-career parents are likely to expend more resources on child rearing, and they might, in fact, log in more hours of intentional "quality" time.[13] It could be that the stay-at-home mom and the stay-at-home dad are more project- or work-oriented at home. In the open home, parent–child relationships might be more diffuse, mediated through a "productive" orientation to the home and through playgroups, family friends, and community activism. The closed household is more likely to emphasize the parent–child relationship, as it has few other functions. The open household, on the other hand, is more likely to build networks of support. A parent will seek to locate his or her parenting within a network of parents, if for no other purpose than to overcome isolation and to counteract our cultural tendencies toward the closed family. The open home is socially complex insofar as it directs itself away from the child-centered home.

Parents who spend their days at home are likely to have little or no anxiety about the parent–child bond. Children are practical givens. They have a way of attaching themselves to their mothers and fathers like barnacles on a rock. Connections are physically and personally deep. Standing still to wash the dishes or fold laundry, a parent will have an infant or toddler attached on the hip or leg. They do not need to get to know each other better through quality time at an amusement park. When such is the case, parental efforts are likely to be directed outward so that children do not dominate the realm of home. Parents will be oriented outward in order to counterbalance the dangers of loneliness, intellectual atrophy, and "going slightly bonkers" as adults in a puerile world.[14] Parents in the dual-career home may work hard to enter into the child's world and to create a child-friendly environment. In the open home, parents are more interested in how children get along with each other, without active parental intervention. They will be more interested in teaching their children to behave and contribute in productive settings, such as helping out at the community center, looking after younger siblings, learning skills of conversation with elderly neighbors, and learning to dust the furniture. The open home puts children to work. Parents who manage a home full-time will be concerned to create parent–child friendly environments, where, in the same setting, adults are able to relate as adults and children as children. When the household is your social location, it must be something more than "kid's world."

It is possible to fill in the details of cases 2, 3, and 4 so that they represent something more than the closed household. Case 1, in contrast, cannot be reinterpreted because there is no one at home to manage it as a place. For the "traditional" look, working-class couple, and home daddy, the household can become a location of community exchange and interdependence. The housekeeper might sustain a tradition different than the suburban, nuclear home.

Household management, in agricultural communities and working-class urban neighborhoods for example, has been important for sustaining household productivity and informal networks of economic exchange.[15] According to Christopher Lasch, housekeeping for the rising middle class of the late nineteenth and early twentieth century was focused not on child rearing but on community work. The housewife's practical task was intensely social.[16] The housekeeper's role may include unpaid work at a food co-op or soup kitchen, trading garden vegetables with the neighbors, and cultivating a permeable border been community and home.

The open home provides greater social complexity and richer personal identity. The world of wage-earning and career, in contrast, tends to simplify social interaction in order to minimize conflict and to enhance market efficiency. The workplace tends to be characterized by simple hierarchies, clearly defined role designations, stratified titles and income, and standard criteria for judging merit. Many companies will simply rank jobs and employees according to a series of levels, which determine benefits and value. The institution will be uniform and stable. A worker will be defined (within the system) by his or her job inasmuch as the business institutionalizes efficient structures of authority and accountability. Many people enter the so-called "public" realm of work by sitting alone in their offices or laboring in clearly defined roles among two or three others. The lines and limits of interaction are clear. When wage-earners go home to the neighborhood, social life gets messy, and claims upon a person become less manageable and more profound. Insofar as the open home is functionally complex and inefficient, it makes us, especially women, dependent and vulnerable. In the face of the risks, the simplicity of contractual arrangements appear attractive.

Complex equality and reciprocity

The home-bound character of cases 2, 3, and 4 makes determinations about equality much more difficult. There is no objective or standard means to compare a bad day at home with a bad day at the office. There is no currency with which to evaluate various activities of the household and neighborhood, and then to standardize their relation to frustration at work or an hourly wage. Instead, husband and wife depend upon judgments intrinsic to the household economy as a social space that is organized and sustained through reciprocity and gift-exchange. Gift-exchange finds its equilibrium through its extension over time.

Marriage can be called a mutual endeavor, 50–50 let's say, but it is seldom equal at any particular time. Over the course of ten, twenty, or thirty years, equality requires an elaborate set of judgments rather than simple or instantaneous fairness. Personality differences, divergences in ability, and even tacit disagreements come into play and make the system work. One spouse likes to be busy, for example, and the other needs more time for relaxation. This couple will work out their cooperation differently than other couples:

> Husband: "Honey, I am tired of doing most of the work around here."
> Wife: "No darling, you are tired of doing work. You actually like to do most of the work around here. I try, but I usually cannot get you to sit still. Please, just sit down with me and relax."
> Husband: "Oh."

Negotiation and cooperation are continual and multifaceted judgments. Equilibrium might be established through relationships between neighbors and friends. Ironically, the workplace and the public sphere are characterized by practical inequities that tend to be more static and more clearly justified because they are established by merit and office. In the household, personality and preferences matter. The human resources and personnel, if those terms can be used by analogy, continually shape the system according to their changing needs, development, and opportunities. People grow up and grow old together.

If the household is open, then unpaid work, bartering, reciprocal exchange, and gift-giving will be given priority. If in good working order, one unequal exchange (as in the giving of a gift) will be exceeded by another. One imbalance will be offset by another. In an economy of gift-exchange (see Chapter 5), the temporal character of reciprocity is intrinsic to the social bond and the continuity of a person's place in community. Likewise, in the open household, reciprocity is set within a narrative of past and present imbalances. If, for the benefit of others, a person carries the burdens of a difficult job or if she is struggling through a difficult time at home, she is due. There ought to be no selfless love in family. Within the flow of household reciprocity, there is no way to determine even exchange, but it is clear that the imbalance cannot remain static if common life is to continue. Sharing a home is a mutually beneficial endeavor.

As an aside, we ought to distinguish the character of reciprocity between adults from reciprocity between adults and children. Imbalances between adults and children ought to remain, and remain weighted on the side of adult responsibility insofar as children are being guided and nurtured into maturity. A father owes an infant intimate care and love; the infant owes the father nothing. A mother owes a seven-year-old nurture and guidance, the seven-year-old owes the mother respect and obedience. She will not punish him for not hugging her, but the mother ought to correct disrespectful behavior, if for no other reason than to teach the child to treat other people well. Relationships between adults and children will change, but an asymmetry between parent and even an adult child may not. These matters of family have a multitude of different possibilities depending upon the course of life and the mix of relationships and personalities.

Suffice it to say, prescriptively, that adults of the household and community are responsible, as active adult members, for a different level of reciprocity than children. Children are educated, nurtured, and loved in ways that they ought not be expected to return. When children grow and have children of their own, the weight of responsibility will be on their side for the sake of their children. Parent–child reciprocity is especially diffuse. My return of nurture and care goes primarily to my children rather than to my parents; yet, they are somehow served by it. I do something for my parents when they see that I have become a good parent myself. The temporally delayed character of this parent–child reciprocity is not so much a contrast to reciprocity in general but protracted intensification of it.

If the household achieves a level of social differentiation, it will be characterized by overlapping dependencies and hierarchies. This idea of functional hierarchies is put forward, here, as both a descriptive and a normative claim. In the workplace, the one who makes the most money or invests the most makes the managerial and financial decisions. In the household, it is likely that the one who earns the most money is not the one who manages finances or the household. The husband in case 2 (the traditional look) earns a salary, but his wife takes charge of the financial decisions. She is responsible, by and large, for organizing the various tasks and time of the household. His teaching job impinges upon household time, and his career structures their calendar; yet, he does not make independent decisions about work-time or schedule. The household is bound by his work, and he is bound by the dictates of the home. Tasks are divided in various informal ways. Add children to the mix, and roles and authority become even more complex.

Authority and responsibility are not uniform in the household economy. Even young children and infants impinge upon community and family networks. Our eldest daughter, for example, has an inclination to care for and to control her younger brothers. They chase each other around, and sometimes they form coalitions against her. These systems are distinct but not quite separate from our relationships to our children. Add neighbors and friends, young and old, and the overlapping functions multiply. In the neighborhood, parents relate to their children not only as individual parent to individual child, but also as a group of parents to children. In our town, for example, all adults are parents de facto. Any unsupervised child is under the eye and open to correction by any adult. Likewise, I have a sense that authority in typically male-dominated households is undermined by coalitions of women in the community. Wage-earning husbands enter the household as individuals, but they encounter, in their wives, representatives of a network external to, and far more formidable than authority in a particular home.

The key point, particularly in relation to the "traditional" look of case 2, is that the simple hierarchy of "public" work over against "private" home is undercut, not in sentimental ways, but in terms of power and control. In the open home, the privileges of the market economy and contractual individualism are displaced, so that thin equality will not function in the same way. In order to make this point clear, the case of the dual-career/contractual home has been set over against the "traditional" look of the housekeeper (whether mother or home-dad). There certainly are many other variations, including part-time work, other dual-income arrangements, and wage-earning at home. One important case not treated is the single parent home, which is likely to be highly open and connected to networks of kin and neighborhood support. The fundamental contrast between this kind of home and another pertains, not to traditional gender roles or to one particular way of dividing labor versus another, but to where the social ground of everyday life is located. The ordering of the open home requires that priority be given to the neighborhood as the time and place of social production. In the household economy, equality is complex because reciprocity is based on such matters as personality, need, particular configurations of roles, and relationships outside the home.

Gender and function

If our embodiment as men and women is affirmed, gender will make a difference. Attempts to erase gender differences lead, in the words of Lisa Sowle Cahill, to a "'new dualism' in which physical forms and differences have no correspondence with cognitive or affective characteristics."[17] According to Cahill, this dualism encourages self-deception, asserting that there are no significant sexual (physical) differences between men and women and that our bodies make little difference to who we are. Apart from the illusory character of the dualism, it impoverishes personal identity and diminishes possibilities for gender-based social intricacies. When a woman gathers with other women as women, social life is enhanced insofar as she also gathers with others in kinship groups, on the baseball field, in community activities, and through endeavors of common work. She carries her different associations with her from one location to another, and in this sense, being a woman ought to make a difference.

Gender differences need not be established as "natural" distinctions *over against* cultural formations. The natural is not a pre-social essence over against historically formed conceptions of social life. The search for the natural *over against* the social is merely a different kind of disembodiment, where the "social" is distinguished from an abstract, ahistorical nature. In day-to-day living, the natural comes to us as the social; that is, our bodies point to our social nature. Our community-bound interpretations of the body are part of what it means to be "embodied." Human beings do not stand outside of time and space. On the contrary, to be embodied means to inhabit a particular place. Taking the body seriously requires that we ask questions about social life. In terms of gender, important questions pertain to kinds of social formations that sustain the flourishing of men as men and women as women.

The market in sex and love, discussed in Chapters 2 and 3, produces gender distinctions that are shaped by an economy of passion and unfulfilled desire. Under the guise of equal access, sexual inequalities are perpetuated. Sexual availability, for instance, often characterizes what it means to be female, and sexual opportunism is the nomenclature of being male. Women's bodies, far more than men's, are commodified, and women are encouraged to enhance their sexual currency through commodities like cosmetics and clothes. The social economy of the household, in contrast, will produce different categories of gender distinction and a different framework for our embodiment. Bearing children, for example, distinguishes a mother's identity and situates her differently in relation to the home. The challenge of the open household is to take the procreative goods of sex seriously without reducing gender differences to a simple division of roles.

In form, gender differences are analogous to functional ones. Within the home, it is convenient to equate the two, to claim that gender differences are functional differences and vice versa. It is tempting to claim that a woman's reproductive role prescribes not only qualities like nurturance but also a specific social role like homemaker. The household, some will claim, is the location where gender differences are clearly functional ones. This identity between function and gender is orderly and clear, but too efficient. Gender becomes similar to a good job description that limits personal tasks according to a corporation's prior systemic needs. The job description is a contractual attempt to control common endeavors. The employment contract manages by excluding variations and by restricting what count as idiosyncratic contributions. Such management helps to make cooperation immune to changes in personnel. Likewise, identifying gender with function makes being a man or woman into a clear role but, in the process, reduces the subtleties of social life. In the modern world, the gender divide has produced the attenuated nuclear home, forcing men and women into limited roles and monochromatic spheres of life.

Theologically, these issues of identifying gender and function have been debated and worked out in reference to New Testament interpretation. If the open household is characterized by reciprocal roles and overlapping functions, Paul's image of community is the place to begin (1 Cor. 12). In Paul's conception of the social body, distinctions such as eyes, hands, head, and feet are constituted by gifts of the Spirit, such as wisdom, knowledge, healing, and prophecy. Distinctions are constitutive because the body has many non-identical parts. The gifts lack equivalence, "The eye cannot say to the hand, 'I do not need you'" (1 Cor. 12.21). Consistent with role reversals elsewhere, Paul points out that "the parts of the body that seem weaker are all the more necessary, and those parts of the body that we consider less honorable we surround with great honor . . ." (vv. 22–23). The social body is constituted as a reciprocity of members in the economy of Christ's body, where the lowly are lifted up, and all are made new through sharing the life of God's Spirit.

Common life, rather than gifts of the Spirit *per se*, provides the rationale for ordering the body. On the basis of the corporate good, Paul, in 1 Corinthians, argues that the gift of tongue-speaking is inferior. "For one who speaks in a tongue does not speak to human beings but to God, for no one listens; he utters mysteries in spirit. On the other hand, one who prophesies does speak to human beings, for their building up, encouragement, and solace. Whoever speaks in tongues builds himself up . . . One who prophesies is greater . . ." (1 Cor. 14.2–5). Insofar as gifts are concerned, tongue-speaking may be a high honor. Inasmuch as gifts are distinguished within common life, speaking in tongues is inferior. It short circuits reciprocity and interdependence. Unlike wisdom and prophecy, tongues offer only unintelligible sound drifting off into the air without meaningful hearing and reciprocation.

Before the discussion of gifts in 1 Cor. 12, Paul addresses the question of women who pray and prophesy in the assembly (1 Cor. 11). Paul's proposal in this section fits with his understanding of gifts in community, even though he adds a qualification pertaining to gender and custom. Paul insists that a woman, even one who prophesies, should cover her head in the assembly, as is the custom. Men ought not cover their heads. For Paul, the distinction pertains to the order of creation, "A man . . . should not cover his head, because he is the image and glory of God, but woman is the glory of man" (1 Cor. 11.7). The gender distinction does not undercut or cancel out the gift of prophecy among women. It merely coincides, so that prophecy among women takes on a different look, let's say. The prophetess, with covered head, communicates two distinct orderings, one of the Spirit's gifts and the other of creation. Gender and gift overlap but are not identical.

There is also an overlapping use of the body metaphor. The body is multifaceted in 1 Cor. 12, when Paul refers to gifts of the Spirit. In reference to distinctions between men and women in 1 Cor. 11, the body metaphor is simplified. The husband is the head (v. 3), and it is implied that the wife is the body. Elsewhere, particularly Eph. 5.21–33, the reciprocity between head/husband and body/wife is made explicit. The body is reduced to two parts; the husband is the wife's head, and she is his body. In 1 Cor. 11, the simplified metaphor is diffused by the logic of "many parts" in 1 Cor. 12. The gender divide between head/body is not discarded, but it is displaced through the gifts of prayer and prophecy. Women have a role in prophecy, and they speak in the assembly as women and as prophets.

Other New Testament passages pertaining to the role of women are more uniform when taken alone. They tend to fall either on the side of gender divisions (head/body) or gifts of the Spirit (the body's many parts). While uniform in the particular, on the whole, these passages make the New Testament more varied. On the one hand, we find household codes, such as Col. 3.18—4.1, where the rule of the ancient *paterfamilias* is set firmly in place. These household codes locate social relations not in the context of worship or Christ's body, but precisely in the household. Common life is ordered by the functions of husband and wife, parent and child, and master and slave, and all are put under the rule of the father. On the other hand, some texts use or imply the hierarchy of male over female only to overturn it, presenting a christological reordering of the world and the redemption of the lowly. Still, in other passages, we find references to women where the role of wife over against husband does not function.

Paul's Corinthian correspondence sends these kinds of "mixed signals."[18] Paul advises virgins and widows, in 1 Cor. 7.25–39, not to marry precisely in order to avoid entanglements that come with the station of a wife in relation to her husband. This advice in 1 Cor. 7 is consistent with Paul's concerns about women who pray and prophesy in 1 Cor. 11. Both sections can be read consistently with Paul's seemingly contradictory command for wives to be silent in 1 Cor. 14.34–36, if it is assumed that Paul sees a distinction between married and unmarried women.[19] According to this interpretation, married women are limited to being wives, and unmarried women are free to exercise a variety of gifts in community and to do so prominently, as women. Although this division of roles between married and unmarried women brings these three sections together

(1 Cor. 7, 11, 14), it does not hold for the remainder of Paul's letters. Paul calls Prisca, wife of Aquila, his co-worker in Christ (Rom. 16.3). Prisca is always mentioned before Aquila in the New Testament, and Paul makes reference to her and her husband's house in 1 Cor. 16.19, that is, not merely to the house of Aquila as *paterfamilias* but to Prisca and Aquila's household.[20]

Jesus' relation to women adds to the ambiguity, as his contact with women lends itself to the gospel's reversal of power and order. In Luke and Acts for example, the outpouring of the Spirit "brings with it a pervasive reversal of fortunes for the powerful and the oppressed."[21] The poor are lifted up; the powerful are brought low, and the rich man seeks the aid of the poor (Luke 16.24). The prodigal is welcomed into his father's house while the good son is admonished for his resentment. The good shepherd leaves the flock and tends to the lost. Finally, in Acts, Peter has a vision of the unclean as clean, and the Gentiles are grafted into the covenant. In this context, women are portrayed as "fully rounded characters essential to the unfolding of salvation history, characters whose personal response to God counts for everything."[22] According to Richard Hays, "the significant role given by Luke to women is not based on some a priori conviction about the inherent equality of the sexes; rather it is another sign of eschatological reversal, of God's setting the world right by deposing the powerful and lifting up the lowly."[23]

When all is said, the New Testament cannot be read seamlessly in matters of gender and function. The two are not the same, and often conflict with one another. On the whole, the Gospels and letters give women a place beyond the social constraints of the day. Women (like Gentiles and slaves) enter the community in their own right, not on the basis of their relation to men: "[In Christ] there is no male and female" (Gal. 3.28). Even if we were to give priority to the simplified "head and body" and to the "male and female" of the household codes, it would be difficult to draw functional conclusions. What precisely does a man do if he is the head of the body? While 1 Peter 3.1–6, 1 Tim. 2.9–15 and Titus 2.3–5 are straightforward in their subordination of wives to husbands, the practical working out of that subordination is not obvious. It is not obvious, for instance, that women are more nurturing, better at doing the laundry or managing a home, less suited for manual labor, or lacking in talents for work outside the home. The Bible makes no such claims. The code in Eph. 5.21–33 complicates matters further. The patriarchal structure is turned on its head through the metaphor of Christ's headship.[24] The headship of the husband is set in terms of Christ's headship of the church, so that the priority of the male-head translates to a priority of service and love, to a male priority of being subject (lowered lower) within a relationship of mutual subjection.

The "mixed signals" of the New Testament ought not be considered a problem as much as a set of clues to the complexity of the social body. The household codes give us a picture of reciprocity in the ancient home, especially in the way that the New Testament codes break with their contemporary (ancient) usage by addressing the duties of wives, adult children, and slaves, not only the husband-father-master.[25] The agency of the *paterfamilias* is relocated from the politics of the city to the mutual subjection of Christian community. In this sense, distinctions in the New Testament between man and woman, husband and wife are important, but they are not identical with functional distinctions. The very nature of the body metaphor leaves function largely as an open question that depends upon the network of gifts. The household codes, in other words, do not stand on their own merit. They are read properly when their simplicity is undone by the social body's many parts.

Good order in common life does not mean functional simplicity or rigidity, but proper placement in a non-identical exchange of gifts. Paul, in 1 Corinthians, is dealing with the place of tongue-speaking in relation to the gifts of wisdom, healing, discernment, and prophecy. The precise list of gifts is far less important for us than their ordering in terms of the good of the body. Thus speaking in tongues, in Corinth, is judged inferior. It is not clear that the church in Philippi, for example, would have been contending with the question of tongue-speaking at all or the same set of gifts, but the logic of ordering does transfer (Phil. 2.1–17). Likewise, we, in modern times, are faced with a different configuration of functions and gifts. Women are not ordered to men as auxiliary agents, but as equals who are nevertheless different. Although our household ordering is different, the theological logic of order and reciprocity can be sustained: gifts are judged by their place within a network and by the good of the body as a whole. Apparent inconsistencies within the New Testament on the matter of men and women ought not be ordered neatly. Gender and the functioning of "many parts" are not identical, but overlapping distinctions that increase rather than diminish the roles and functional variations in common life. Highlighting the goods of gender differences implies that stay-at-home fathers and mother-legislators are not merely options, but a necessity for an interesting and full social body, for the complexity of personal identity and social space.

Family Miscellany

Introduction

"A Cambodian newspaper tells the story of a man who, lacking gas money, leaves his 9-year-old nephew as collateral."[1] After filling his motorcycle with gas, the man discovered that he was without his wallet. He had to retrieve it, and to guarantee his return, he asked his nephew to descend from the back of his motorcycle. It is now two years later, and the gas station owner says that she "is raising the boy as her grandson." I heard this story on my drive to work one morning. The car radio was set to a news station that begins each cycle of reports with something amusing or curious. Listeners hear of human foibles such as the young thieves who broke into a university student union in order to make false ID cards, but left their negatives in the machine. The Cambodian story was told in a similar context. It was the morning's quirky story.

The Cambodian story was retold several times that day, and I filled in more detail each time. Even now, I imagine the moments after the man's departure. Grandmother and the boy are looking blankly at the dust as it settles on an empty road. She invites him in to sit down out of the sun. She goes about her business, and they share vacant looks now and again. As the hours pass, she admits to herself that the boy needs to eat. And then he needs a place to sleep and something to eat the next morning. And if he is waiting there at the gas station, he might as well help with the work. And he will need to run off to play with other children. The story is indeed curious. How many meals will they eat at the same table before they stop hoping that it will be their last together? In how many days does the stranger become a grandson? How long does it take for room and board and helping out at the gas station to become familial love?

This ostensibly odd story is actually close to home. If we were to visit grandmother and grandson without knowledge of their first acquaintance, would we notice anything out of the ordinary? The "naturalness" of their day-to-day life might be confused easily with consanguinity. Indeed, blood ties provide the natural course of family, but families are put together regularly in peculiar and unanticipated ways. This integration of the "irregular" into the ordinary is an undercurrent through the preceding chapters on the open home. A natural progress of marriage and family provides the structure of the book as a whole; however, criticisms of the goals and successes of the upwardly mobile, independent home are central as well. Where the insular, nuclear family appears customary, the open household seems irregular. The very categories of the open and closed households frame questions of family so that classifications like nuclear or extended, traditional or non-traditional, natural or adoptive are not definitive. While the structure of the book pre-supposes a course of consanguinity – we meet, marry, and raise our children – this chapter highlights the adoptive character of family. The Cambodian woman offers a model of family insofar as her habits of hospitality make the home.

The chapter title, "Family Miscellany," refers not only to the varied character of family, but also to the assorted make-up of the chapter. The chapter is divided into a range of contemporary issues of family, like same-sex unions and the widespread practice of "living together." The series of topics is unified by attention to the relationships and contrasts between market formations of sex and love and the economy of the open home. Certainly, a whole environment of cultural practices contributes to recent develop-ments and debates about the formation of family. For instance, gay marriage in the U.S. is tied up in constitutional and legislative issues that cannot be reduced to considerations in this chapter. The con-trast in economies is invoked here, not to exclude other factors, but to emphasize the constructed and socially reproductive character of the home.

The body of the chapter begins with adoption and ends in dying at home. This frame outlines an irregular life cycle that is natural to the open home. For instance, home hospice care for the dying puts a practical strain on members of a household, and it often brings family dysfunction to the surface. For the dying, hospice care is likely to accentuate elements of personal disjunction brought on by suffering, illness, and disability. One is displaced within one's own home or within the home of a sibling or child. The dying process is likely to render a person incapable of common tasks, which results in a loss of autonomy and independence. In a world where people desire a quick and easy death, there is nothing romantic about dying at home. Likewise, adoption forms relationships against the stream of romantic desire, which promises us assurance that our loves "are meant to be." In adoption, birth parents, birth siblings, adopted children, and adoptive parents must cope with an unequivocal "what if." Families are made by means of what might be considered (by the members themselves) as circumstances of failure – a failure to have children, to raise children, or to be loveable and worthy. This is where we will begin our discussion of marital and familial unity, with a reversal of models – with the "imperfect" family.

Adoption

At a few points in the New Testament, St. Paul refers to "a spirit of adoption" (Rom. 8.15) and our adoption as children of God (Gal. 4.5). In these contexts, adoption satisfies a deep yearning for wholeness and nearness to God – the inward groaning and the labor pains that we share with all of creation (Rom. 8.22–23). Adoption means life because it is life shared with God who draws near in Christ and Spirit. We are claimed as God's own; we are ransomed, saved from bondage to our ways of self-destruction, and united with God. On this theological horizon, it is appropriate for adoption to have a prominent place in discussions of Christian family. But it does not. Adoption is overshadowed by analogies that link procreation, parental care, and our Creator's love. Going against the stream, some authors do argue that adoptive parents live out the love of God in a representative way, insofar as Christian love, not biological kinship, form the bonds of Christian community.[2] Like other ways of imitating the love of God, adoption reveals human frailty at the moment grace appears. Adoption, like the divine love we share now, brings our yearning for human unity to the surface.

Adoptive families and birth parents live with questions about "what could have been." For recent generations, these questions have been allowed to come to the fore. By the mid-twentieth century, practices of closed adoption were structured so that adoptive families would mimic natural ones. At this time, children, for the middle class, were no longer productive members of a working household, but investments in interpersonal love and economic mobility. In order to protect the bond of child and adoptive parents, relationships between birth parents and child were concealed "in the best interests of the child," who was retroactively born, by law and custom, into an adoptive family.[3] This "as if natural" quality of adoption began to shift in the 1960s and 1970s with rapid changes in sexual practices, the legalization of abortion, a rise in appreciation of ethnicity and pluralism, criticisms of "traditional" family, and a boom in popular psychology and self-help literature.[4] In recent decades, adoptive families have been loosened from secrecy and accepted as kinship systems in their own right. Adopting and being adopted have become legitimate identity markers and stories that can be told (although birth parenting and relinquishing usually are not).[5]

Nonetheless, during these same decades of growing acceptance of adoption, the currency on genetic inheritance and reproductive freedom has become inflated. Reproductive technology and attendant practices – *in vitro* fertilization, surrogate motherhood, genetic testing, abortion, and genetic therapy, and the ability to ensure sex determination – promise to make nature a choice. At the very moment that adoptive networks are finding a place, they are being unseated by a "dominant genealogical essentialism."[6] Abortion is often preferred over the pain of carrying a child that would-be birth parents would not be able to raise. Invasive fertility treatments remain, even after repeated failures, the most accessible option for childless couples.[7] "Adapted" family networks have become common amid conventional patterns of divorce and remarriage, step-parenting, children shared by two households, and combined families. The household has become increasingly disconnected from straight generational lines, and this disconnection has opened the way for a variety of family forms. This diversity, however, does not include an increase in practices of adoption. Adoptions in the U.S. have decreased from about 175,000 in 1970 to 118,529 in 1990, and the later figure includes a high number of adoptions by step-fathers.[8] When unmarried women in the U.S. carry through with their pregnancies, fewer and fewer are giving their children up for adoption, from 9 per cent in 1973 to 2 per cent in 1988.[9] This is certainly a good sign, but relinquishing and adopting infants continues to be understood in terms of a lack of choice – a lack of resources or will on the one hand and of fertility on the other.

Because adoption is often considered a last and least desirable option, it may offer the best place to begin to think about family. In theological terms, Stephen Post (author of *A Theory of Agape* discussed in Chapter 7) notes that adoption puts practices of Christian communion in clear relief. First, he acknowledges the deep connections between spousal union, procreation, and raising children. But he argues that adoptive networks also should have an honored place. Post points out that relinquishing an infant, in medieval Christianity, "was associated with self-giving love, was resonant with the worship of a God who sacrificed his own child for others, and was therefore deeply meaningful for the relinquishing parents."[10] From the adoptive side, he proposes that Christian community, bound as it is by practices of reciprocity, mutual correction, and care, "challenges the increasingly prevalent cultural assumption that the only real kinship is based on birth, biology, and blood . . . [E]ven if blood is thicker than water, it is not thicker than *agape*."[11]

In our time of reproductive choice and "genealogical essentialism," adoptive networks are unavoidably open, insofar as questions of identity and parental relationships resist closure. Birth mothers make difficult decisions, and they usually understand their choices in terms of grim (and sometimes retrospectively mistaken) necessity rather than what is desired. Many birth mothers experience ongoing grief and regret, which become especially pronounced on their children's birthdays.[12] They share this experience of birthdays with adopted children who, even as adults, might be unable to resist the nagging sense that they can prove themselves to their birth mothers.[13] For their part, adoptive parents might enter the adoptive process with their own regrets, and they, in raising adopted children, have to negotiate the "double bind" of making a child their own while admitting to themselves and to the child that she has other parents.[14] A climate of genealogical essentialism comes to bear on them, and adoptive parents might experience a marked sense of having to prove themselves as parents. Sustained conflicts between adoptive parent and child, whether mundane or inordinate, are likely to be blamed (at least for a moment) on a lack of consanguinity.[15] Adoptive networks, although made by conscious decision, are characterized by questions (although not necessarily regrets) about "what might have been."

Despite these struggles of adoptive networks and partly because of them, giving children for adoption and adoptive parenting are exemplary. When adoptive families are expected to mimic natural ones, closed adoption – that is, the anonymity of the birth mother, confidential birth records, and a preference for matching ethnicity of adoptive parent and child – is necessary. In contrast, open adoption acknowledges that a family lacks natural self-sufficiency. As noted above, Post argues that giving a child to adoptive parents ought to be understood, not just as a way out of a predicament or simply as a better option than abortion, but also as a gift to the adoptive parents, given with the compassion, hope, and generosity of gift-giving. Likewise, adoptive parents show exemplary hospitality and love. Children, for their part, are faced with the challenges of understanding the loves and losses, sorrows and joys of which they have become the center point. In these ways, adoption presents a representative (because not idyllic) expression of familial love. Its problems and imperfections are instructive. Adoptive networks situate family in a decidedly contingent social frame.

Practices of adoption make clear that family life depends on the giving of gifts. The birth mother sustains an infant's life, and gives her child to another. Adoptive parents give their love, their shared lives, and their home. Adopted children live out and give assent to the gift – a living "yes" to adoptive parents and sometimes to birth parents as well – a consent to "what has been done" over against "what could have been." This act of receiving and accepting by the adopted child is at the heart of living as family. One gift is contingent, not on its direct return or payback, but on its completion in what is given to another. Although stated in these elevated terms of "the gift," there is nothing romantic about giving a child to adoption, or impatiently hoping to have an opportunity to adopt a child, or working through one's place in relationship to adoptive and birth parents, or waiting year after year, holding on to a fragile hope that one will see a relinquished child again.

The expectations and gifts, the joys and unfulfilled hopes of relinquishment and adoption, highlight the social character of the open household. Adoptive networks clearly shift the bonds of family from blood ties to the practical matters of living well together, mutual presence and the subtleties of day-to-day life. The tensions of adopting, being adopted, and giving children for adoption underline deep connections between bearing and raising children, but they also underscore the fact that our place and belonging in family is cultivated in the same way, adopted or not. We make a home through wanting what is good for another and living this desire out, day by day, through times of harmony and discord, and misunderstandings and reconciliation.

According to an extensive study of adoptive families, adoption has no negative correlation to the well-being of an adopted child or the welfare of family.[16] It is the practices of household life that make a difference. The Search Institute's *Growing Up Adopted: A Portrait of Adolescents and Their Families* found that adoption, according to reports by adopted children, is not a central issue in their sense of identity and their personal development. It does not complicate their adolescence. "Adopted children are as deeply attached to their adoptive parents as their non-adopted siblings; adoptive families have considerably lower rates of divorce and separation than do biological families . . . [and] adopted children have slightly higher psychological health when compared with national norms for all adolescents."[17] Adoptive families must deal with the contingent character of family. Persons in the adoptive network receive each other from the outside and undertake to build a home. In this way, the set of practices that sustain adoptive networks may represent what is needed for all families to cultivate friendships and to pursue the shared endeavors of the happy home (cf. Chapter 8).

Sacrament

Chapter 8, "The Happy Home," makes reference to the tradition of understanding marriage as a sacrament. The middle sections of that chapter introduce Augustine's ends of marriage (unity, procreation, and steadfast fidelity) and develop Michael Lawler's account of marriage as friendship and a sharing in the love of God. This earlier treatment proposes that a married couple's relationship is not a self-sufficient union, but flourishes when part of a widening circle of friends and is completed in the friendship of God.

Following the theme of adoption, we should consider how some single-parent households provide interesting models of the open family. If a married couple raising children is the paradigm for the nuclear family, how might an obviously different kind of household illuminate features of this representative case? Few parents desire, from the start, to raise children alone. The economic standing and stability of most single households is not good, and typically the prospects for children are less promising than in two-parent homes.[18] Like adoption, single parenting is likely to follow unexpected circumstances, such as unplanned pregnancy or the dissolution of the relationship between mother and father.

There is, in effect, a break in the life-plan of the romantic and closed home. Single-parent households are liable to have an incomplete and dependent character. In working through practical matters of raising children, single parents might be more inclined to cultivate a network of relationships – uncles and grandmothers, natural and adopted – that sustain a fuller sense of kinship and an open home. The capacity of kin, a parish community, and a neighborhood to sustain single-parent families provides a test case for its shared practices of marriage and family. If single-parent households cannot be sustained, then something is wrong with a community's practices of marriage and home.

This part of the chapter on marriage as a sacrament will follow these themes of the contingent, social character of adopted family. It will reintroduce the topic of marriage as a sacrament in order to consider the union of marriage and family as gifts. As a sacrament, marriage has the character of being both made and given – made by the will to love each other and given by the love of God. The sacramental gift of marriage is evinced through the faithful endurance of partners, "for richer and for poorer, in sickness and in health." We have faith that when husband and wife endure hardships and share joys they will discover their marriage as a grace. In our voluntaristic age, however, the grace of family may be hard to recognize. Marriages are made and unmade frequently. Couples start new families, separate them, and make them new again by combining parts of old ones. Like the adopted child, spouses are likely to find the grace of marriage when they consent to "what has been done" while faced always with the question of "what could have been."

Again, we turn to Michael Lawler's summary of the tradition. Marriage, by design, "is a partnership of love for the whole of life, ordered equally to the well-being of spouses and to the generation and nurture of children."[19] Citing the Justinian code (sixth century), Lawler emphasizes that "marriage is a union of man and a woman, and a communion of the whole of life."[20] He also notes the ambiguity of the phrase, "the whole of life." Marriage is a union for "as long as life lasts" and through which a couple shares everything that they have, both spiritual and material.[21] Like bread becoming Christ's body in the Eucharist or baptismal water as a sign of grace, the "stuff" of marital love becomes a sign of God's love for the world and is transformed by it – elevated by God who shares the love that binds Father, Son, and Spirit.

If marriage is a grace, a couple's will to unite in marriage is vital, but they do not make their relationship simply by force of will. This fact creates a difficulty for understanding marriage as a sacrament. In the Catholic Church, the sacrament of marriage is available to all baptized persons when they acknowledge and agree to the Church's intention for their marriage, that is, when they accept its indissolubility, fidelity, and place as a witness to God's steadfast love.[22] This requirement of mere acquiescence puts the vows of marriage in a precarious setting. Many will receive the sacrament without the "active faith" or "active baptismal commitment" required to live out the partnership of marriage for the whole of life.[23] It seems that "the idea that all who have been water-baptized [i.e. have experienced the ceremony but lack an active faith] are ready to live the faith commitment of sacramental marriage denigrates the importance of this baptismal vocation."[24] It may seem better to make an active faith (rather than the mere ceremony of baptism) requisite to receiving the grace. Otherwise, the sacrament appears to lack efficacy.

This concern to connect an active faith and the sacrament of marriage is genuine and indisputable, but it presents a problem as well. Save the nuptial "I do," marriage and family life are sustained as much by consent – by a kind of resignation – as by choice. The reality of family life is that we may look back and think that we could have made a better choice. We may not have the husband or wife we imagined that we would have when we looked in his or her face and said "I do." We may choose to have children, but in the natural course of things, we may have children that we would not have chosen to have. Family life is largely about acceptance rather than choice; not withdrawal (or passive resignation), but the "yes" of the adopted child (noted above) who consents to what "the taking on" of family has made of him.

Consenting to our place in a family means that we hope that in accepting the demands upon us and the relationships into which we are drawn, we will find the depths of friendship that we desire – or that through consenting to family we will learn to desire relationships that give us genuine and lasting hope. Again (as with adoption), this assent should not be romanticized, for "submission" to family can easily be misunderstood as a reason to endure domestic abuse, or to justify inequities between men and women. Admittedly, the lines of giving and losing oneself are not always clear. Acquiescence means that we accept that we will be changed. We risk ourselves. Some transformations may be acute, as when we learn to manage our anger and to watch our harsh words. Other changes may be more prosaic, like taking time to garden or demanding attendance at a family meal. Some changes will alter the course of our careers. Sometimes we will take subtle steps along a different way. I received such subtle advice last Sunday when I was party to a conversation about child-rearing. I need to be more verbally expressive to our children; I need to tell them that I love them more.

If marriage in the church is a grace, then marriage and family life will be sustained despite our ambiguous choices and our lack of interpersonal expertise. The principal hazard of romantic personalism is its promise that marriage and family life will be self-sustaining joys. In contrast, the preceding chapters have turned to an extended and more complex setting for family life in neighborhood networks and an informal, and in a sense unmanageable, but rich, household economy. Have marriages failed when we learn to compensate for what they lack? Are families compromised when they fare better as part of a wider company of friends? This acceptance of being incomplete is at the heart of consenting to marriage as a sacrament. We will be fulfilled together from the outside, over time, and in the day-to-day working out of common life. And we hope that in the end we will be surprised with the love that we share, that we already have what we cannot live without.

The sacrament of marriage, like the love of God that it conveys, puts us in the place of the prodigal son (Luke 15.11–32). Like the young man with his inheritance, we might take our riches and set off to a distant land, where we live the high life but find ourselves empty and alone. We may not deserve much for our squandered opportunities – and we may expect little more, but grace begins to fill us when we turn our lives toward the household of God. Marriage as a sacrament finds its home in the kinship of God's love, which is lived when accepted as grace. This active acquiescence can be seen in the structure of Jesus' Sermon on the Mount, for instance. It begins with inverted blessings, like "Blessed are the poor in spirit, for theirs is the kingdom of heaven" (Matt. 5.3), and it sets out a conciliatory way.

Matthew 5—7 is not a program for the good marriage, but a way of life for disciples (and Israel as a whole) who are called to be the salt of the earth and light of the world (Matt. 5.13–16).[25] However, the possibilities for marriage and family can be inferred. Reconcile with your brother or sister – or husband or wife – before you lay your gifts on the altar (5.23–24). Settle your differences. Do not look with lust at a woman or man (5.27–30). Here, it should be noted that "looking with lust" is not an internal state but a relational act (and in our world a thriving industry) that, like adultery, divides rather than unites. Lust, like greed and dishonesty, is a habit that divides others between who they are in their own right and how we can use them.

In the middle of these disciplines of Matthew 5 stands the teaching on divorce (5.31–32). It is a mistake to understand this teaching in isolation. Jesus denies the legitimacy of divorce except in cases when the marriage is already illicit or broken.[26] But the teachings in the Sermon as a whole require much more than a resistance to disunity. We are called to reconcile what appears hopelessly divided. Discipline your words, and be bound to them. "Let your 'Yes' mean 'Yes', and your 'No' mean 'No'" (5.37). We should add: be faithful with ordinary matters of family and home. Do not retaliate against wrongs done (5.38–41), but go beyond your duty to serve others. Love your enemies (5.43–48) and show hospitality to your adversaries, especially when you share a bed.

The disciplines of the Christian life (and by inference the household as well) are not a private or personal code, but a way for gathering and sustaining a people who witness to God's love. The interpersonal skills of Christian marriage and family are carried by these practices of discipleship. Other practices should be added as well, such as sharing material resources, table fellowship, mutual correction, forgiveness (Matt. 18.15–35), and the works of mercy (Matt. 25.31–46). We should not forget that Matthew's Gospel is deeply concerned with the gestures of prayer (6.1–18) and conceives of the kingdom, not as a wedding or marriage, but as the wedding feast (9.15; 22.1–14). The wedding is the occasion for the gracious hospitality of the host and the gathering of uninvited guests. In following this way of God's hospitality, we acquiesce to God's way of grace in the sacrament of marriage.[27]

Living together

In the U.S., many engaged couples are appalled when they learn of
the liturgical guidelines for a Catholic wedding. The wedding is
supposed to be their day, but the liturgy shifts the focus off them
and on to the tasks of worship. When they are preparing for a
"traditional-church wedding," most couples imagine a solemn procession of bridesmaids meeting their corresponding groomsmen
who wait with the groom at the altar. The bride is supposed to
follow, accompanied by her father, who meets the groom and hands
the bride over to him. Along with this anachronistic exchange of the
woman, the slow and elegant procession points to the newly made
union of two. The magic of the moment is especially pronounced
when complemented by the custom that would-be bride and groom
should not see each other on the wedding day until he lifts her veil at
the altar. This romantic image is shattered when a pastor informs
the couple that the procession will fit the pattern of Sunday worship,
led by the processional cross and Bible which will be held high
before them. Bride and groom may be dismayed further by the
suggestion that together they greet worshippers when they arrive at
the church door. [28]

This struggle between the minister of the sacrament and the
couple is common. Bride and groom ask for institutional/ecclesiasti-
cal assistance in formalizing their private union, while the pastor
proposes that they play a role in the regular worship practices of the
church. They are likely to experience a sense of being displaced by
ordinary worship practices and set into a procrustean mold of institutional marriage. Added to this experience, they sense that religious
asceticism is being imposed upon them as well. For instance, grace-
ful dresses and stately tuxedos have no particular function in the
liturgy. The rigidity of the church's institutional practices seems to
be setting limits on what the couple desires for their special day.

This struggle over the wedding liturgy reveals tensions within
modern marriage. On the one hand, our imagined partners are
celebrating their relationship through the sacrament. On the other
hand, they are doing so by committing themselves to "a whole
framework of life, which sustains the love of the partners," but also
carries with it a vision of community, the common good, and
(specifically through the sacrament of marriage) God's enduring
love for the world.[29] This section on living together and the three

sections that follow deal with these tensions between a couple's isolated or pure relationship and institutional (social and public) frameworks for sex and love in the home.

Clarification of an "institutional" framework as opposed to a "pure" relationship is in order. The pure relationship is a term used by Anthony Giddens to refer to the kind of romantic relationships discussed in Chapter 3 – to relationships founded in what Niklas Luhmann calls "love as passion." According to Giddens, the pure relationship "refers to a situation where a social relationship is entered into for its own sake, for what can be derived by each person from a sustained association with another; and which is continued only in so far as it is thought by both parties to deliver enough satisfactions for each individual to stay with it."[30] A commitment to another in the context of institutional marriage is different. In marriage, a couple commits to an established social form that is independent of their specific relationship. They enter a set of social practices that shapes their relationship and their roles in social life. They have duties to society as well as each other. The basic structure of marriage precedes them, and they accept that they will have to bend to it, that their attitudes and habits will be shaped by this given structure of life. Marriage in the church is framed by its place as a sign of God's grace and by the journey of discipleship.

Living together – that is, cohabitation apart from the given structure of marriage – is now standard practice in the Western world.[31] Most who marry pass through a stage of living together beforehand.[32] But most that live together do not plan to marry. Cohabitation has become a conventional alternative for couples who want to sustain the "pure" character of their relationships and to avoid institutional constraints. Living together allows individuals to pair up in a situation that approximates freedoms of the single life. Living together, then, is usually understood in contrast not to singleness but to marriage. Its prevalence suggests that it may be a common model for understanding marriage nonetheless. Widely held conceptions of romantic relationships and living together effect popular conceptions of marriage. The point is simple, but it has significant implications for our couple's difficulties with the liturgy of marriage and marriage itself. A couple may recognize that the wedding ceremony is not confirming their relationship, as much as it is introducing institutional pressures for restructuring their shared life.

Relatively unrestrained and short-lived arrangements of living together are consistent with prevailing social currents, especially with contractual impermanence and the restlessness of the market. In current practice, cohabitation is not a state of life as much as a transitional stage. According to one study, "forty percent of all cohabiting couples either marry or stop living together within a year, and only one-third are still cohabiting after two years."[33] When living together was noticed as a trend in the 1960s and 1970s, most social theorists predicted that cohabitation would provide a testing ground for a relationship, that couples who moved on to marriage would enjoy more stable relationships. However, "evidence to date suggests the opposite: couples who cohabit before marriage seem to end their marriages at significantly higher rates than couples who never lived together before the wedding."[34] Likewise, theories of marital choice expected that a trial stage of living together would lead to more fulfilling marriages. Again, recent studies suggest the contrary. In matters such as conflict resolution and cooperation, those living together report a "poorer relationship quality . . . Cohabitors report more fights or violence than do marrieds, and they also report lower levels of fairness in and happiness with their relationship."[35]

The price for freedom from formal constraints of marriage is a lower commitment in enduring relationships. And the cost of informal ties is usually carried by women and their children. "Although [a] decline in commitment in relationships is usually explained in terms of women's increased economic independence . . . taking the male point of view makes this explanation less plausible."[36] Along with the rise in cohabitation, out-of-wedlock births are increasing, and "when taken together with the low levels of financial and social support children receive from their absent fathers, it [cohabitation] is clearly a story of men's declining involvement with the children they are fathering."[37] From the male point of view, living together offers freedom from marriage and the traditional "good provider role."[38] The opposite is the case for women. Women become both primary caretaker and provider, which means that most cohabiting households with children are essentially single-parent homes.[39]

Here, I should make reference to the example of single-parent households, which introduced the preceding treatment of marriage as a sacrament. The single-parent household is a useful illustration for the open household because it shifts the image of the home from the haven of the pure and isolated relationship to practical matters like raising children and making ends meet. Single parenting is far from the romantic ideal. Statistically, single mothers and their children are poorer and have fewer opportunities. Practically, family and household become a terribly heavy burden when carried by one adult. For this reason (as noted above) the well-being of single-parent households may be the test case for the practices of kinship and neighborhood networks. A test case for family is how well an interdependent network of families (a family of families) sustains those outside the closed, nuclear home. Living together, without intention to marry, represents the opposite image. It presents an attempt to sustain a couple's relationship by freeing it from social constraints and networks of families. Ironically, it is usually the relationship that is not sustained.

Those who study practices of living together make a distinction between couples who consider cohabitation a step toward marriage and those who see it as an alternative.[40] The premarital stage is more like marriage than living together as an alternative, when judged in terms of stability, relationship quality, and care for children.[41] However, this distinction does not mean that there is little difference between marriage and premarital cohabitation. A higher divorce rate among previously cohabiting couples indicates that the character of actual marriage is different from the preliminary stage. Decades ago, social scientists assumed that premarital cohabitation would improve marriage because individuals would have more information about compatibility with a potential spouse.[42] The assumption has proven to be false. Currently, the standard view is that "couples who cohabit do so at least in part because they have less commitment to the institution of marriage than do couples who marry directly," that they are likely to lack personal characteristics (or virtues) required to sustain long-term relationships, and that they "are relatively approving of divorce as a solution to marital problems."[43] In effect, the social and interpersonal conditions that make premarital living together a viable option, along with the experience of cohabitation itself, undermine marriage.[44]

Living together represents our modern predilection to think about love apart from formal and institutional intrusion. It also represents our diminishing ability to sustain interpersonal commitments. Ironically, those who are committed to interpersonal marriage *as an institution* are reported to have more fulfilling and enduring relationships – not because people with already wonderful relationships get married, but because a commitment to enduring, faithful marriage cultivates the possibility of bringing shared life to a wonderful end.

Sexual indeterminacy

As I write in February 2004, gay and lesbian marriages are at the center of political and legislative struggles in the U.S., particularly the states of Massachusetts and California. The Supreme Judicial Court of Massachusetts has ruled in favor of marriage for same-sex couples and against sustaining a separate category called civil unions. In California, the Superior Court will be called upon to judge the actions of the mayor of San Francisco who is violating state law by granting gay marriages.

It is not clear how and when these legal battles will conclude. The author of the majority opinion in the Massachusetts court, Chief Justice Margaret H. Marshall, explains that marriage is, essentially, a permanent and exclusive commitment of one individual to another, and that nothing about the commitment rules out couples of the same sex.[45] However, many are calling for state and federal constitutional amendments to define marriage as the union of a man and a woman. This legislative "backlash" is already a national pattern. A recent study of same-sex partnership laws (enacted between 1990 and 2001) has found "that a large number of localities offering domestic partnerships within a state actually encourage state legislatures to take action to preclude such partnerships from being translated into any form paralleling heterosexual marriage."[46] With a likely legislative reaction against same-sex marriage, a conclusion to the conflict is uncertain, but it is clear that pressure from both sides is not going away.

My intention in this section on "sexual indeterminacy" is to shift the center of the debate, and to sustain focus on the institutional character of sex and love. Given the divisiveness of the issues surrounding homosexuality, it is easy to construe the conflict simply in terms of whether or not same-sex oriented persons should have the right to marry. I am proposing that this characterization is superficial, and that on a deeper level an economy of sexual indeterminacy is the critical feature of the same-sex marriage controversy. I do not want to discount those who defend marriage as a faithful union between heterosexuals or those who seek to enter steadfast,

same-sex unions. But each side of the debate, particularly in theology, puts forward its arguments with little recognition that we, in
the West, live in an age that is already post-marital. We are fighting
over marriage in a public arena where the institution of marriage no
longer shapes desire and no longer gives form to love.

I dare assert, even further, that public recognition of homosexual
unions is emerging in a time that is also post-sexual-orientation.
Market desire has freed us for a multitude of sexualities, including
homosexuality. But the independent life of "sexuality" also requires
freedom from natural constraints – from the limits of sexual orientation, whether hetero- or homosexual – from the idea of an invariable desire for a fixed object. Those who argue that same-sex unions
are justified only in terms of a stable homosexual orientation will
stand in the way of sexual progress. This independent sexuality is
required of market desire, but it has a parallel in contractual freedom. In other words, contractual choice makes sexual "orientation" irrelevant to the decision of the Massachusetts court.
Marriage in the court is considered a private contract recognized by
the state. Sexual practices are restricted by law (e.g., prostitution or
child pornography), but they are irrelevant to marriage.

Because of its rapid developments in the late twentieth century,
the social and political life of homosexuality – as a sexuality – is particularly vulnerable to the market. Same-sex desire has become a
commodity or style that is detached from homosexuality oriented
persons and freed for a market of heterosexual consumption. In
The Body in Late-Capitalism USA, Donald M. Lowe describes the
emergence of "polysexuality," rather than homo- or heterosexuality. According to Lowe, a multitude of sexualities are possible and
available through mass consumption of "the sexual lifestyle."[47] A
sexual lifestyle, in Lowe's parlance, is a pattern of consumption
through sexualized commodities and *of* sex as a commodity. The
lifestyle is detachable from stable sexual identities and orientations.
In this context, homosexuality has become a trope. Coming out as
gay, in broad social terms (not necessarily as individuals), has co-
incided with the emergence of sexual lifestyles and a "gay" market.
Homosexuality has become a leading representative of sexual
lifestyles, which are sustained "beyond the boundaries of the
family."[48]

On this point, Lowe makes reference to Dennis Altman's *The
Homosexualization of America, The Americanization of the Homo-*

sexual.[49] Writing in 1982, Altman could have predicted David Beckham's image as the metrosexual or the identity of young urban "heteroflexibles." As a metrosexual, a heterosexual consumes elements of a homosexual lifestyle. A heterosexual male becomes more marketable among females when he is introduced to new possibilities of style and consumption. A cadre of gay men are his guides in "Queer Eye For the Straight Guy."[50] In the heteroflexible, young men and women are refusing the label "homosexual" but are taking on what they characterize as "gayish" identities and behaviors.[51] They are not homosexual, but not strictly heterosexual. Along these lines, Altman (in 1982) notes that homosexuality in the market is hardly opposed to heterosexuality, but simply part of the same development of modern, capitalist and contractual sexuality. His thesis is that homosexuality enters public life through a market that has already been sexualized.[52] Further, he explains that "homosexuality" will be both paradigm and social scapegoat. Because the social place of the gay community is carried by the emerging market, it will be the focus of despair for those who mourn the loss of social stability.[53]

Homosexuality is not a decisive issue that will determine the viability of marriage as an institution. The idea of marriage as private and contractual is already firmly in place. To this degree, practices of cohabitation among heterosexuals present a far greater challenge to marriage as a set of social and sexual habits. People who marry will struggle with the transience of the "pure relationship" and the restlessness of modern desire whether or not same-sex marriage or civil unions are made legal. In fact, same-sex unions are hardly the cause, but are more vulnerable to the economic and cultural practices that make marriage and household life difficult to sustain.[54]

The "issue" of homosexuality is skewed by the mistaken claim by advocates and opponents that same-sex marriage is a "hinge" or "threshold" issue. Gay and lesbian unions are neither paradigms nor fundamental problems. Opponents of same-sex marriage may win in state legislatures and on a constitutional level. If they do, however, they will have changed nothing about the social and sexual habits that challenge marriage. In broad social terms, marriage will continue to be shaped by extra-marital practices of sex and love. Advocates of same-sex marriage want public recognition and institutional support for same-sex unions. But if they succeed, they win a private and contractual sense of marriage that is too anemic to be sustained. Certainly legal rights will be gained, such as the right to include a partner on one's family health insurance. These rights are attained through partnership and civil union laws. The Massachusetts court, however, has decided that partnership laws are discriminatory. In order to decide for same-sex marriage, the court levels marriage to the status of partnership. It defines marriage as what it has already judged as unsatisfactory – as a contractual partnership or civil union that is private but acknowledged by the state.

Pushing the issue of same-sex marriage to the margin is not evasive. On the contrary, it is a step toward facing more fundamental social and institutional questions about sex and love. By displacing same-sex unions from the center, advocates and opponents can establish common ground in terms of the dignity of persons with a homosexual orientation.[55] In the modern West, much of the history of gay people is a story of suppression as a sexual and social threat.[56] Still today, more often than not, heterosexual unease in the presence of homosexual persons, especially if in a group, is justified as a natural response. Too often, violence against gay men and lesbians is defended – or the aggressor's culpability is mitigated – as visceral, as simply an inordinate response to a common natural unease. Opponents of same-sex marriage ought to share skepticism about how the market carries forward this discomfort with the homosexual. A sitcom like *Will and Grace* seems to be creating a hospitable public place for gay people, but it actually sustains sexual restlessness and connects heterosexuality and homosexuality through their dysfunction.

In *Will and Grace*, Grace, *the* heterosexual woman, is able to hold on to a hyper-romantic sense of marriage because her husband is usually absent. He enters the plot, now and then, in the framework of a date. After a brief encounter the two must part, and their relationship is set within a continual state of regression. Grace constantly works through the initial stages of dating. With her man she is filled with excitement and hope, but in his absence she obsesses, waiting for his call and wondering if he loves her. Around heterosexual men, Grace is an insufferable and giddy adolescent. Her female complement, Karen, is an oversexed alcoholic and a flirting would-be lesbian (or bisexual), who has had sex (in the framework of the narrative) only with her obese and boorish but rich husband.

She is attached to his money. Will, *the* homosexual, simply cannot find love. He is perpetually frustrated, but his homosexual complement, Jack, is always satisfied as the promiscuous, pubescent, and shallow gay man.

Granted, as a sitcom *Will and Grace* is supposed to present human foibles. But in the context of market sexuality, it allows representations of homosexuality to be consumed and enjoyed while being belittled. Again, homosexuality ought not to be made the scapegoat. Homosexuality can be enjoyed and disparaged because representations of heterosexuality have led the way. In this regard, *Will and Grace* follows the pattern of other sitcoms like *Seinfeld* and *Friends*. Sex and love in the market are already nomadic. When they become settled, they must be unseated in the romantic and contractual world of sexual experiences. As a sitcom with a heterosexual audience, it is Jack who is the satisfied homosexual, but he represents the heterosexual libertine. For market heterosexuality, the experience of "gayishness" is simply a new frontier. Orientation is irrelevant. In a restless world, ironic disparagement is the best way for love and sexual pleasure to be possessed. Desire in the market is free from institutional constraints, and as sexuality becomes habituated, it must be set free from itself.

A place for the debate

Whether the result is civil unions or marriage, the legal debate on same-sex unions will be settled by indifference, which is fostered by contractual habits of sex and love. This indifference to private unions is not possible in the church, for the unity of Christ's body is always a central concern. Sex in the church is not public in the sense that it is open to view, as it is in markets and media. However, sexual practices are sustained institutionally, to the degree that marriage and family conform to wider institutional practices and are called upon to support goods that are not particular to marriage or private family life. For example, couples married in the Catholic Church commit themselves to raising their children in a common faith. Likewise, marriage is not considered an autonomous sphere, but is set in the image of Christ's love for the church. The relationship between husband and wife is called to live out practices of love and care that are definable apart from marriage (like fraternal

correction and forgiveness). Marriage is only a particular instantia-
tion of common practices of the Christian life.

Before we move on to theological arguments for and against
same-sex unions, we should recall key elements of a modern conception of marriage. The first is twentieth-century personalism,
which finds a reflection and sign of God's love in the interpersonal
subjectivity of man and woman. This theological theme has developed in a particularly modern social context. With the modern
detachment of family from social and economic institutions, it
becomes a non-public social space (a world created by two) where
we find our true selves in relation to another. The relationship
between a man and a woman in marriage is understood as a social
world in itself. In effect, the common personalist account of
marriage is both a product of the world of "the pure relationship"
and a reaction against it.

Most theological accounts of marriage have also been shaped by
efforts to deny, on the one hand, that procreation is a necessary end
of marriage and, on the other hand, that homosexual acts can be
justified. The dismissal of procreation as necessary to sex is usually
taken as common sense and receives little argument. With procreation unnecessary, virtually all the weight of marriage is carried
by the communion of husband and wife. This shift of theological
weight marks an innovation in terms of both tradition and
Scripture, where procreation and quelling desire are always in view.
The creation of humanity as male and female, in Genesis 1—2,
becomes central for the personalist account. But only recently has
"creation as male and female" been understood as an egalitarian
union, and for Paul, marriage is a distraction from the fellowship of
the kingdom (1 Cor. 7).

The personalist account of marriage is on firm biblical and
traditional ground in its rejection of homosexuality. Some biblical
scholars have argued that scriptural prohibitions depend upon
ancient understandings of homosexual acts, which have no correspondence to modern practices of faithful, egalitarian same-sex
unions.[57] However, it is also obvious that all known forms of homosexual acts are rejected and that what we moderns call heterosexuality is assumed as a given.[58] By developing this biblical given in a
particularly modern way, personalist theology appeals to the
creation of humanity as male and female in order to show that
a heterosexual orientation (communion with the other sex) is a

fundamental aspect of the Creator's design and our fulfillment as human beings.

The personalist account of marriage and human communion seems to exclude homosexuality by definition. Nevertheless, theological arguments in support of same-sex unions readily use personalist arguments. Oddly, the rejection implies the defense. The reason for this contrasting use of similar arguments is that a focus on interpersonal union (by both sides) allows a consideration of the psycho-social relationship to subsume judgments about the physical structure of sex. By and large, personalist arguments against homosexuality also discount procreation as a necessary end of sexual intercourse. Likewise, personalist arguments for homosexuality discount the gender complementarity of male and female as necessary to spousal union. On the one hand, arguments against homosexuality appeal to the ontological structure of a heterosexual orientation (rather than procreation). On the other hand, arguments for same-sex unions also appeal to the givens of a person's homosexual orientation – a psycho-social orientation to the other. Each utilizes personalist arguments that transcend traditional arguments from nature.

The argument for same-sex unions proceeds in this way. If a homosexual orientation points to how a person is unavoidably and irreversibly oriented to others, then the orientation entails a corresponding mode of interpersonal and psycho-sexual fulfillment. Even if a homosexual orientation is considered abnormal or anomalous, proponents argue that the way we should deal with this abnormality is to support same-sex unions.[59] If the orientation is irregular, an irregular union is implied as well.

Further, advocates argue that Scripture and tradition do not comment directly on the modern understanding of a homosexual orientation and that same-sex unions certainly can sustain the theological and biblical structure of steadfast fidelity and intimate fellowship in the image of God's love. Same-sex marriage would establish a set of practices through which a person's sexual identity and fundamental orientation can be disciplined, formed, and incorporated into God's love and plan of salvation.[60]

Advocates of same-sex unions hold that marriage is a means through which people with homosexual orientations can unite bodily desires and spirit in a faithful life in Christ's body – the church. Opponents argue that gays and lesbians already have a traditional and biblical route to holiness, one that is common to hetero- and homosexuals, that is, celibacy. In making this counter-argument, however, personalists are caught in a quandary. If a homosexual orientation is an abnormality that must be resisted, how is it that all those who have this abnormality will also have the gifts required to live a celibate life? The personalist account assumes that the sexual union of male and female is the standard course of human fulfillment, and that celibacy is a special gift. If celibacy is not the usual course, then all those with a homosexual orientation are wanting in the sense of orientation, but would have to be exceptionally able in matters of chastity. Personalists help create this problem by making sexuality fundamental to human identity and fulfillment, and they have no answer for the quandary, except to assert again that all people with a homosexual orientation are either called to celibacy or to heterosexual marriage.

By pointing out that homosexual desire and acts follow from a fundamental orientation, advocates for same-sex unions incorporate, theologically, a homosexual union of bodies through a faithful and steadfast bodily expression of this desire. Opponents answer that homosexuality cannot express sexual union as it is represented in the very structure of human sexuality. In other words, they explain that male–female anatomy represents a physical complementarity that sets the necessary context for a psychological and social one. From this point of view, sex between men or between women looks, physically and psychologically, like nothing more than mutual masturbation – nothing more than a selfish pursuit of desire.

However, from a traditional point of view, the non-procreative sex of modern personalism looks self-centered as well. This negative view of non-procreative heterosexuality is important to note because the argument is put forward in social terms and cannot be accused of a naïve attachment to nature. For example, Jacques Ellul, in his *Ethics of Freedom*, rejects traditional procreative arguments and grimly accepts the wide use of contraceptives, but he also holds that we should hardly see non-procreative practices as a cultural advance. Ellul argues that sex, when free from procreation, "brings to expression . . . self-centeredness" and "an extremely narrow and mediocre view of life."[61] If procreation is excluded from the structure and meaning of sex, what distinguishes a one-night stand from sex within marriage if not a social relationship that corresponds to the nature of an act that is life-giving by its nature and structure? Sexual practices that are open to procreation fit logically with family and the household. If not generative, what social function might sex have except to become part of a market of desire? Ellul assumes that sexual desire is rightly ordered when it is open to the creation of new life.

The official Roman Catholic theology of marriage presupposes that the unifying (personalist) end of sexuality cannot be separated from its life-giving purposes. Pope John Paul II is a personalist philosopher, and he gives arguments much like the personalist account of marriage outlined above.[62] But he also understands the procreative end of marriage as a necessary and vital aspect of the unity between husband and wife. According to this view, contraception undermines the self-giving of spouses because it removes an intrinsic capacity of the sexual self. Natural family planning (NFP) differs fundamentally from contraception, which blocks or denies the procreative nature of sex and sexual unity. NFP resists or blocks nothing, but only corresponds to a woman's rhythms of fertility and infertility. The generative structure of sex is not removed but respected, and a woman's bodily nature sets the context for desire and union.

By defining sexuality by its unitive and procreative ends, this Catholic position offers a far more coherent rejection of homosexual acts than the typical personalist theology of marriage. But it is also seen as far too ascetic for most of those who reject same-sex unions. It is far less hospitable to typically modern conceptions and practices of sexual, economic, and personal freedom. In effect, the Catholic view is far less tied to the modern notion of sexual fulfillment as the restlessness of consumption and market desire. In practice, the Catholic sexual ethics assumes an intimate connection between sex and the productive home. This emphasis on the generative character of sexuality does leave room for exceptions, for instance, in the case of a couple who find that they are unable to conceive. According to the teaching of the Catholic Church, homosexual relationships cannot be justified. But if they were, then same-sex relationships, within the generative framework, would not be equivalent to heterosexual unions which are procreative. Same-sex unions would be considered as exceptions in the particular case, as an option for those who are gay or lesbian and cannot remain celibate, similar to Paul's concession to marriage in 1 Corinthians

7.6–7.6.[63] As it stands, church teaching does not allow for this kind of exception.

As debates about homosexuality advance, as they have among Anglicans, more divisions will come within and among church bodies. After a two-day meeting with Anglican primates (October 15–16, 2003), Archbishop Rowan Williams could only conclude that the issue "will continue to be difficult and divisive . . . it will continue to cause pain and anger and misunderstanding and resentment all round."[64] Unity is one of the primary theological problems at stake – unity of our bodies with the groaning of creation, of our desires with the love of God, and our lives with God's communion of the church. What is at stake is our very course of life and faith.

In times like this, it is clear that interest group politics, majority rule, the polity of modern sexual freedom, and the "pure relationship" are far too shallow and divisive to meet the tasks of faith. We are called to be formed by God into God's own people. What is at stake, it seems to me, is hospitality, obedience, and prayer. We will have to make our arguments plain and forceful, but we should recognize that arguments do not transform our lives. We (on opposing sides) who see ourselves as strong should attend to the worries, needs, and souls of the weak. We should see that we are in a terrible state together, and we cannot make our way through with private relationships and a politics of indifference. The common task of all Christians is to accept God's invitation to share Christ's body in the Eucharist, which means to have our bodies be formed by our call to discipleship and by our place in the one body of the church. God's invitation is our call to live out God's hospitality as members of the body of Christ.

Home repair

The sacrament of marriage sets conditions for unconditional love, but as a basis or goal of a relationship the idea of unconditional love is deceptive. "Marriage is a contract to a noncontractual relationship."[65] In a romantic sense, we might feel an unconditional sense of total abandon. In a dutiful sense, we might want to dedicate our lives to learning true self-giving. In each case, we want to give ourselves to each other unconditionally and without reservation. We are beyond contractual limits. Our love exceeds our usefulness to each other, beyond superficial notions of pleasure and happiness.

We promise to endure the good and bad, poverty and plenty, all the way to the end of our lives.

Unconditional love is promising. However, outside the limits of social controls, unrestricted love and unconditional relationships are far more unstable, and we (statistically women in particular) are made far more vulnerable. If we abandon ourselves to another, he or she may as easily diminish as enliven us. And if dominant cultural conceptions of love are post- or extra-marital, then the constraints of unconditional love in marriage and family are especially daunting. We live in an era when marriage is based on conceptions of interpersonal intimacy, but there is little evidence that faithful and enduring relationships are practices that we, in broad cultural terms, are qualified to fulfill. In this sense, the popular notion that marriage "starts" a family is misleading. It implies that we have the tools and skills, and we are ready to build. We will do better, perhaps, to enter marriage with an eye to learning a craft. Marriage and family set the context for a journey (a shared quest) that highlights our interpersonal shortcomings and points the way to learning steadfast love.

While considering sex and love in the context of "home repair," mention should be made of widespread domestic violence.[66] Despite legal and social advances for women in public and private life, violence against women, especially sexual violence, continues to be common. Statistically speaking, women in the U.S. are more likely to be abused if they are in an intimate relationship. They are safer with strangers. According to a survey in 1998, "nearly one-third of American women (31 percent) report being physically or sexually abused by a husband or boyfriend at some point in their lives."[67] In 1999 alone, over 670,000 women reported that they suffered assault or rape at the hands of their husband or boyfriend, ostensibly in the name of love or in the context of a loving relationship.[68]

In the pathology of domestic violence, the abuser and victim agree that violence does not undermine or contradict love and sometimes is motivated by loving concern.[69] The batterer strikes out while in love, and the abused submits also in the name of love. This apparent coexistence of violence and love puts great weight behind the hypothesis that domestic and sexual violence do not contradict contemporary conceptions and practices of love as much as they are a consistent outcome of dominant cultural practices.[70] It is an ironic coincidence that, at the beginning of the twentieth century, the main cause of death for women of childbearing age was childbirth, and now, in a time when love has become the basic good of sex, the primary reason for an early death is domestic violence. The prevalence of abuse is liable to be attributed to traditional gender roles in traditional forms of marriage. However, contemporary incidences of spouse and child abuse are higher amid practices of cohabitation.[71]

Three social factors that contribute to domestic violence also suggest why abuse is more likely outside of marriage.[72] The factors are an increased privacy of relationships, inequality of partners, and a legitimization of violence. First, the isolation of an abused partner makes her or him more vulnerable, with less recourse to external relationships, and the abuser is allowed more control. The second factor, an inequality of the partners, has a connection to this isolation. Intimate relationships, generally, tend to be defined by couples on their own terms, apart from impersonal standards of fairness and equality.[73] These adjustments are common. Couples work out the everyday household matters in ways suited to their personalities, talents, and shortcomings. But when two people are isolated from networks of family, their judgments are more likely to be askew. Unconditional love, apart from social investment, paves the way for self-deception. Violence may be seen as justified in the eyes of a couple, if not in general terms then in the context of their particular relationship (e.g., "He is not really aggressive, but under a great deal of stress at work").

The third social factor, the legitimization of violence, is available at every turn in our culture. Violence is commonly considered a means to solve problems and assert power and control. Sex has a similar function. Both sexual charisma and skills of conquest give social status and are considered a means for economic and social mobility. Given that physical power and sexual availability are social currency, it is not surprising to find that violence, if unchecked, becomes part of intimate relationships. In these terms, institutions and social practices that shape life at home are supposed to function as constraints on market violence and sexual conquest. No doubt, the privatized home will be especially vulnerable to wider cultural expressions of violence.

The problem of domestic violence helps put the more general question of "home repair" in social terms. If we are to make good on Christian claims about marriage and family, we will work to sustain a full picture of human fulfillment and equality for women and men in basic social institutions. We will build networks of family that resist unrealistic and destructive attitudes toward the body, particularly the female body which is marketed pervasively in terms of male sexual needs and fantasies. We will build neighborhoods where family is not isolated as a private institution, but is a counter-weight to market desire and to widespread habits of violence. Family and neighborhood will be a site where alternative habits of forgiveness and reconciliation are sustained.

Thinking about social pressures contributing to domestic violence may illuminate more benign instances of marital breakdown as well. People, especially women suffering abuse, hold together relationships and marriages that should be separated. At the same time, marriages are dissolved that should have been sustained. This judgment, "should have been sustained," implies a commitment to, not simply *a* marriage, but to marriage as a set of practices that carry basic goods of human life. A common contributing factor to divorce is that divorce itself is seen as a solution to disagreements and the logical resolution to static or weakened interpersonal connections. In other words, disagreements, expressions of anger, and dissatisfaction with a husband's or wife's role in the family should not undermine marriage.[74] In fact, learning to confront one's spouse, resolve conflicts, and overcome dissatisfaction foster marital love.[75] Not anger but disdain, not conflict but coercion, and not confrontation but withdrawal, bring a bad end to married life.

Christian marriage has a place to flourish when set in terms of steadfast fidelity, forgiveness, and reconciliation, and other practices of the Christian life. The roles of family – being a husband, mother, brother-in-law, or daughter – are learned over time, and communities develop ways to judge and to form these relationships of family. As an aside, I should note that ongoing, institutional judgments about familial relationships are a key virtue of the formal process of annulment (granting that criticism of the process can be made). In the church, judgments about family are made in terms of wider conceptions of discipleship, aptitude or the personal capacity for marriage, and the habits of living out the love of God.

Families and marriages are fragmented for various reasons, some petty and some grave. Sometimes it is not easy to tell the difference. Marriages, from the start, are often troubled by immaturity, differences in family background, personality differences, and financial worries.[76] A couple might have divergent views about the nature of marriage itself. During a romantic courtship, lively notions of a pure relationship may be indifferent to problems like these, but quickly, the spouses will find that "love as passion" alone will not overcome the troubles of marriage. Marriages and families are also troubled by obviously severe problems like violence, alcoholism, drug abuse, and mental illness. Amid these struggles, it is not clear whether individuals and families can overcome fractures and build a happy household. But it is clear in these situations that a couple or family cannot make their way through alone.

Social networks and a common commitment to the institution of marriage are required to open marriage and family to the blessings of home. Problems in marriage may require that we see our relationships in a new way, acquire new habits of day-to-day life, or commit ourselves to becoming different kinds of persons. This is the age-old pathway of conversion. Either it is undertaken in small steps over time, or it is marked by radical change. In each case, an ongoing journey of transformation is part of all family life, as ongoing conversion is an inextricable part of Christian discipleship. The wisdom of good marriages and healthy families will have to be passed on, and individuals will have to submit themselves to self-evaluation and appropriate disciplines of growth. Married couples and families will have to risk hearing how they are seen in the eyes of others. We can take these risks in faith that the struggles of confrontation, repentance, forgiveness, and reconciliation lay a family vulnerable and open to grace.

Dying at home

Dying among family and friends is an apt way to conclude a discussion of family, especially when emphasizing the miscellaneous (or heterogeneous) elements of kinship and the adoptive character of making a home. Among the middle class, the majority of elderly die in a hospital, in a nursing facility, or when living alone at home.[77] The elderly who die while in professional care have often been living alone just before entering a health care institution. This isolation of the aged underlines problems of the closed home. Set apart from practical networks of family and neighborhood, we stay holed up in our own homes until the end. Aging and dying in the company of others requires hard work of vulnerability and dependence.

Weakened by age or disabled by illness, we are no longer the capable and active person we were. We have a diminished role, and we will have to find a new place among others. Likewise, the work of caring for the aged or dying is difficult. Caregivers themselves become dependent, and they can hardly expect to sustain hospice care alone.

The economic and cultural forces that impinge upon dying also press upon marriage, family, and the household. Modern aging and dying have undergone a process of "biomedicalization." They are treated like diseases, as "phenomena fundamentally alien to life and therefore to be controlled, or if possible, defeated by medical technology."[78] Economic and contractual freedom allows greater access to services and technological control. However, as we are drawn more deeply into the need for contractual care and services of the market, aging becomes an increasing burden. Without their own marketability, the elderly cannot provide for themselves. In fact, "planning for retirement" means storing up enough reserve income so that the independence and control provided by the market can be maintained as one becomes a burden to oneself.[79] We pay a high price for growing old.

In effect, the economic and contractual habits of our fight against dying and dependency are the same habits as those that attenuate the family and neighborhood networks that might have provided an alternative to dying alone (cf. Chapters 4 and 5). Dying among family, as well as hospitality to the aged, are heavy loads to be carried by a household. Practical matters, like eating and hygiene, cannot be taken for granted. Emotional strains intensify, financial burdens arise, and a sick loved one may seem like a stranger in the house. The stresses of aging and dying among family are not unlike struggling through the strains of a difficult marriage. Caring for the dying requires attention to the depths of ordinary matters of life, to eating and sleep, to bathrooms and comfortable chairs. At the same time, hospice care makes extraordinary emotional and physical demands. We continue on in hope that love will endure, and that, as the years pass, we look back and see that we have been opened to grace. Dying at home is, indeed, a test case for the church, neighborhood, and hospitable home.

Sexual Practices and Social Reproduction

Introduction

After several years of teaching Moral Theology to undergraduates, I have developed some reliable ways to instigate lively discussions. For instance, I might begin class by asking, "Isn't it great when a young woman, say sixteen years old, becomes pregnant? Don't babies make life wonderful?" The questions are so troublesome that the students, especially young women, do not recognize my obvious attempt to provoke them. A passionate conversation ensues, and we quickly come to the idea that procreation is a social question. According to the logic of family values (Chapter 4), childbearing is a private matter for the closed home. Because this logic and its social reality are firmly in place, young women react to my questions fervently. They suspect that the pregnant sixteen-year-old will be alone with the responsibilities of raising and supporting her child. By and large, their suspicions are correct.[1] During our class discussion, it is inevitable that at least one young woman will protest, "If I were to have a baby now, it would ruin my life."

This chapter links sexual practices with procreation and a social grammar of hospitality. The second half of the chapter considers sexual fidelity in marriage as a set of bodily activities where we come to belong and to be set, irreplaceably, within an expanding context of family, friends, and neighbors. Conjugal union, in other words, does not set us apart (through romantic moments), but uniquely in the middle of things, in connections through time and generations and to a place. From the side of romantic love and "reproductive desire," marriage is a threat to sexual passion insofar as sexual practices become routine and ordinary. I take these accusations to be true. Marriage and family life domesticate sex. Recalling themes from Chapter 2, I propose that sexual union has a protracted character that is analogous to procreation and childrearing. Within marriage, sex is vulnerable to everyday life, and through the course of our lives together we come to belong and to discover who we are. During pregnancy a bodily relationship is cultivated, not through words, but through months of day-to-day connection that make the coming-to-be of a person possible. Likewise, sex in marriage is enduring bodily presence.

Before the constructive proposal, the chapter attends to wide-ranging social questions. I will draw contrasts through categories similar to previous chapters, between contractual social management and neighborhood reciprocity, consumptive and generative social economies, and the inhospitable (closed) and hospitable (open) home. The fundamental problem with teen pregnancies and unwanted babies is that these "situations" are considered failures or dilemmas for individual girls and women. In fact, the dominant contractual economy is inhospitable to children even when a particular home or sixteen-year-old girl wants one intensely. In social and economic (rather than sexual) terms, this young woman is thought to have done something wrong. Her desire for a child is irresponsible; she imposes an unnecessary burden upon society. In the first part of the chapter, I hope to link procreation to the very logic of common life, and to do so, I will begin with grand issues of greenhouse gases, fossil fuels, and managing the global household.

Habitat and home

For years, environmental desolation has been troubling Al Gore.[2] In 1997, when Vice-President, he invited over one hundred TV weather forecasters to the White House for a conference and lecture.[3] With an international conference impending in Kyoto, Gore wanted to talk about the environment, and he lectured extensively, like a school teacher, on the scientific evidence for global warming. He wanted to persuade the weather-casters to help make the threat of global warming a prominent public issue. "Maybe they can make the subject . . . a little more lively for their audiences."[4] According to *The Washington Times*, questions from his guests brought Gore to the problem of overpopulation. It is interesting how readily a problem brought on by fossil fuel can be diverted to worry about someone else's children.

Gore dealt with overpopulation in customary fashion. Booming numbers in Third World and developing countries are an obvious threat. A solution will come through cutting infant mortality rates, empowering women with reproductive choices, making birth control information and technology available, and freeing up access to abortion. Gore's comments on population control were considered newsworthy only by *The Washington Times*, which highlighted the issue with its headline, "Third World Birth Control Tops Gore's List of 'Greenhouse' Cures."[5] The ideological leaning of the *Times* is obvious here, insofar as the paper considers birth control an issue at all.[6] It is likely that *The Washington Times* reporter put the issue at the center, when, in fact, Gore and his guests passed over the population issue as a matter of course.[7] It is fair to say that Gore's proposals for population control were not news inasmuch as he was rehashing economic and political common sense.

Industrial pollution, automobiles, and deforestation are at the heart of the global warming debate. Nevertheless, typical analyses of global warming invite questions about population growth – given projections that by 2050 more than three billion people will be added to the over six billion in the world during the millennial year.[8] More people means fewer trees, more cars, and more production powered by fossil fuels. The question about overpopulation must have delighted Mr. Gore, as any lecturer will be pleased and likely to hop around a bit when students show interest. Afterward, the White House spokesperson, Michael McCurry, reported that the TV personalities "appreciated being treated as something other than airheads."[9] Imagine an eager hand raised and the thoughtfulness with which the question was prefaced. "With world population growth out of control, and with the birthrate in developing countries showing little sign of abating, what, Mr. Vice President, can we do?"

Mr. Gore's consultation with the men and women of TV weather is full of incongruities. I do not pretend to know what obsessions animate the Weather Channel's target audience, but I do know that television weather is entertainment, and for the most part, its target audience hopes to be entertained by it, that is, by the weather and nature, ski slopes, lakes, fall foliage, sunny days, and summer breezes. A few summers ago, in the dead of a long drought, one local weatherman would give us a big smile and happily report that there would be no rain to ruin the weekend. Occasionally, a weekday news segment, not related to the weather report, might show interviews with frustrated suburbanites shaking their heads over their brown lawns.

Accusing our weatherman of being an airhead misses the point. It might be closer to the point that television stations in our region are located in urban areas, either Washington, DC, or Baltimore, Maryland. Those who produce on the land do not attract the press. At bottom, the incongruities of the White House weather conference come from the fact that TV weather is generated by an economy of consumption. Talk about global warming might be good now and then, but on the whole, fears about greenhouse gases cannot be allowed to cast a cloud over our sunny days. Heat indexes and "Red" days on the ozone scale give us something to do, to stay close to our air conditioners or to cover ourselves with sun block. Threats of global warming, on the other hand, suggest that we should not do anything at all, or that we should do less than we normally would. The threat suggests that we should park our cars and slow down oil-burning and coal-burning factories. It is much easier to worry about someone else's children.

Despite White House hopes, global warming has not become a lively topic in TV weather reporting. Greenhouse gases simply cannot be a persistent topic for weather forecasts that are sandwiched between car advertisements and ads for countless products dependent on fossil fuels for production and trucking for transport. In the end, the gloom of global warming does not fit with television weather reporting because it contradicts the pleasant nature of the activity. Global warming is depressing, and it renders us helpless. We have insurance for hurricanes and floods, but what good will it do me if I do not drive my car? What kind of insurance is that? To make any difference at all, we would have to change the very structure of everyday life. Every other kind of disaster implies some form of growth and rebuilding, and in this regard, hurricanes are not a challenge to our market economy. Reducing greenhouses gases, on the other hand, seems to imply simple reduction.

Global warming occasions questions about population growth, because population reduction allows us to carry on as before. Having less children is the kind of reduction we can live with, and we are perplexed with the persistence of Third World birth rates. Poor people do not seem to know that their children are keeping them down. The irony is this. While we are frightened by numbers, we are training our own children to be voracious consumers. The more we work to make our world a wonderful place for our children, the less hospitable to children we become. An American household is likely to have more cars than children.[10] The world population may increase 50 per cent by 2050, but our fuel dependent economy is likely to increase between fivefold and tenfold.[11] Concern for the poor in developing nations may be legitimate, but there is no evidence that population increases in these countries are stifling or eating up *their* economic growth.[12] There is no evidence that fewer children will make their lives better. A poor child in Central America goes hungry not because her brother has eaten her bananas. Her bananas are on a ship to the U.S.A. We are eating up Third World growth, which is precisely the goal of centuries-long European, North American, and now corporate colonialism.

These environmental dilemmas and worries fit with the economy of desire discussed in Chapter 2. Sex in the dominant market must be detached not only from marriage and home, but also from procreation. In the dominant social economy, good sex is required to reproduce unfulfilled desire, and to do so, "making love" must be freed from making babies. Child rearing domesticates sex and settles desire. For this reason, procreative sexual practices threaten to oppress women and to repress social well-being and economic growth. The modern sexual economy is contingent on access to the kind of contraceptives that free desire. I take this point to be obvious. Natural family planning is inferior as a technique, not because it fails to avoid conception, but because it does not free desire sufficiently. Conforming sexual activity to a woman's cycle of fertility is proven to be as effective as the best contraceptive methods.[13] However, unlike condoms and contraceptive pills, NFP also regulates desire. It is considered unrealistic.

The economy of desire promises to free our bodies, especially the female body, from the toils of children. Ironically, reproductive desire fosters an antagonism between a woman and her bodily agency. While the contemporary man enjoys greater access to sexual fulfillment, a woman must contend with her fertility for most of her life time. Her autonomy as a social agent in the world of work and career depends upon this struggle against childbearing. Likewise, the cultural code of sexual desire continues to be worked out on the site of a woman's body, where women mourn for pre-pubescent hips, and men desire full breasts not ruined by child rearing and lactation.[14] The same struggle puts the modern household in an ironic light. We enjoy freedom from hordes of children, but we are constrained even more by the few we have. The practices of reproductive desire are unable to sustain a habitat where our desires fit with our everyday embodiment, and where sexual practices cultivate our belonging.

The inhospitality of home

Our economic advancement is increasingly inhospitable to children.[15] Any aspiring middle-class couple knows that children are a liability, and it is almost inconceivable to us that poor Malaysian and Indian parents do not experience the same. Children impose divided loyalties between family and productive work.[16] In American culture, the parents of large families are considered irresponsible because they impose an inordinate strain on our limited resources.[17] They are irresponsible also because they must portion their time and personal investment among too many children who will have to compete for their attention.[18] Our homes have become emotionally child-centered, but oddly inhospitable to raising children.[19] The analogy with weather is found in the problem of consumption. The very economic environment that structures childhood as an economic drain conceives of raising children in terms of consumption and entertainment. Whether or not greenhouse gases are a real threat and whether or not they are caused by our use of fossil fuels are moot questions. The point is that our economy is structured such that we need growth, expanding markets, increased production, and increased consumption for the sake of encouraging more production. Children are an accessory. Parenting is supposed to be wonderful, but, paradoxically, child rearing is a continuous problem of economic damage control and risk management.[20] Upwardly mobile families, with one or two children, will attempt to ensure that no more children will become part of their household, for everyone's sake, especially for the children.

Our children are learning well. Growing up in the market economy can now be plotted as a narrative of consumption. Before they can read, most children are educated consumers.[21] Market analyst James McNeal outlines five stages of childhood development: children observe their parents shopping, ask for products, choose products, purchase products with assistance, and purchase products independently. McNeal claims that these stages are market universals, inasmuch as they transcend family background or economic class. Most children are independent shoppers before they enter their first year of school; basic consumer skills have become basic life skills. The narrative of consumption measures personal growth in terms of market savvy, and it envisions empowerment in terms of purchasing power. In 1999, it was reported that "children [in the U.S.] spend $25 billion a year directly and influence $190 billion of their parents' spending."[22] Our children have come of age, and now they are able to make an important contribution to common life. They spend.

The narrative of the maturing consumer fits with the development of a particular kind of household. Insofar as the economic power of children is on the rise and the purchasing power of their parents is declining, McNeal refers to the creation of "'filiarchies' in households where matriarchies would ordinarily exist."[23] Where consumer activity is a basic measure of power, the rule of home has shifted. In other words, parents make peace at home by ceding buying decisions to children, from fast food to clothes. Certainly, parents feel the weight of this shift when they take family outings to the shopping mall. A definite familial harmony sets in when surrounded by the pleasant, comfortable atmosphere of little shops, video arcades, toy stores, fountains, restaurants, and child-friendly department stores. The harmony is contingent, of course, on purchasing power. There is more to the shift than trips to the mall. Personal identity is formed, in part, through a connection between young consumers and corporations, their product lines, logos, and images. To this end, advertising strategies are increasingly directed at nurturing children as customers and cultivating brand-name loyalty.[24] Parents want to be a part of it. We bond with our children at the Disney Store and McDonald's, and as an auxiliary practice, we offer purchasing incentives for cooperative behavior (e.g., cleaning one's room).[25] Brand-name products give us leverage to be good parents.[26]

It seems healthy, or at least innocuous, when our children learn how to inhabit the market. Consumers are the commodity upon which the health of the economy rests. Jean Kilbourne has made this theme central to her studies of advertising, media, and corporate marketing strategies. She reveals that addiction, (symbolic) violence against women, and the objectification of persons are promoted as basic sales techniques.[27] The goal of any company that sells goods or services is to possess us, to have ownership of a demographic: to know us, classify us, and makes us its own.[28] The best marketing strategies are the ones that look good for us, like technological equipment donated to schools in exchange for free advertising and exclusive contracts (e.g., televisions and Pepsi machines).[29] In effect, our underfunded schools are selling access to our children, so that fidgety students can pump themselves up with Mountain Dew or some other caffeine source between classes. Our consumptive structure of life makes for an environment inhospitable to us and our children.

Social reproduction

It may seem odd, in this chapter on sexual practices, to brood over marketing strategies and greenhouse gases, but these questions about habitat provide means to locate sexual practices within broad and interconnected matters of household management. As the conversation between Al Gore and the weather forecasters suggests, managing a global household is bound up with our conception of things and what people are for, with our economy and how people are managed. Fears about ozone depletion naturally lead to questions about population control because our global economy is a means of structuring social relations. The dominant means of managing reproductive practices are an essential part of the overarching systems of production and distribution.[30] Likewise, the dominant grammar of sexual practices is sustained by an economy, and recalcitrant procreative practices, particularly in poor countries, must be tamed and managed in order to protect our style of life. In effect, sexual practices correspond to a means of social reproduction. The systems of social exchange make certain sexual opportunities possible and impose particular necessities and constraints.

Previous chapters on "Sexual Desire" and "Romantic Love" have already argued the point that common conceptions of sex and love fit with a nomadic economy of desire. The dominant currency of desire defies domestication; however, unsettled desire is our means for establishing and sustaining personal connections (through love as passion). Sexual practices place us on a social landscape and give texture to our belonging. The dilemma of romantic passion is that the inner connection of desire is ephemeral and elusive (see Chapter

2). On the outside, sexual expression has become an important part of modern personal entitlement and a basic marker of one's identity and politics. More often than not, these communities of identity will not provide concrete relationships of reciprocity, but a contractual space for common individual concerns. An individual's sexual expression is usually located within a demographic category, a voting block and style of consumption, like "two-parent families" and the "gay community."[31]

In the contractual market, reproduction has also become a right, and one quite distinct from sexual experiences and relationships. Like sexual desire (cf. Chapter 2), sexual reproduction, in the dominant grammar of desire, has an unsettling effect. Those who have a stake in the commerce of procreation have a stake in the pain of sterility, or at least in the profound emptiness that is ready to be filled by fertility treatment. This stake in the despair of would-be parents need not be cynical. Growth capitalism simply cultivates its markets by drawing attention to what we lack. Once infertile couples become a market, real grief over children not born becomes a necessary market condition. No doubt, a profound desire for off-spring is not merely a market construction, but it is particularly troublesome when children are conceptualized as a kind of self-possession. While the nobility of ages past would go to great lengths to secure legitimate heirs, we will spare no expense to have our own children because they bring personal fulfillment. Procreation takes on the character of love as passion. It is a desire for fulfillment through a romantic, inner connection.

In the market, infertile couples are in the same compromised bargaining position as grieving families who deal with funeral homes and other economic aspects of dying. Purse strings are loosened when the sense of lack rises, especially when a person is plagued by the prospect of a future without a clear sense of connection. "'It's very hard,' says a 34-year-old woman . . . who has made several attempts at *in vitro* fertilization, 'You start to feel that everyone else is going to have a good life except you. For some reason, the world has passed you by, and it's very depressing.'"[32] The promises of reproductive technology only heighten this sense of exclusion and failure. In light of what science can do, procreation has the aura of always being a choice that is contingent only on our persistence. With an endless number of technological options at our disposal, our bodies will fail us in many more ways. "Why won't fertility drugs or in vitro fertilization work on me?"[33] Infertility, in the economy of desire, is a failure of self-possession.

Sexual practices and identity take a different shape when set within the social economy of the household. Certainly, frustrated attempts to conceive a child will always be painful. However, when sexual practices are domesticated, they are likely to be of a piece with a wider sense of belonging. Neighborhood reciprocity (as opposed to a consumptive economy) will tend to give all adults a parenting role. Reproduction, as a fundamental activity of the household, implies more than conceiving children. Households reproduce themselves by sustaining and advancing the interests of their members, by providing for food, shelter, clothing, education, and investment in vocational training. In the open household, the social form of family is extended and reproduced. In this regard, patronage is regular practice of local reciprocity. It is simply part of the protracted context of exchange and gift-giving, where an elder or superior uses his or her influence, power, and resources for the benefit of an inferior. Patronage is essential to the neighborhood economy, and as gift-exchange, its character is necessarily informal and improvised. Benefaction is a basic gift-imbalance that extends common life. Like parenting, it delays reciprocity, perhaps for a generation. It is an ad hoc form of adoption that depends, for the most part, on patrons who have dispensable resources because they do not have their own children at home. In the neighborhood economy, all adults have children.

The closed suburban home, in comparison, can be seen as a defensive strategy in a contractual market. The social placement of the upwardly mobile home is narrowed in order to carry itself forward by means of the dominant economy, by self-sufficiency and individual interests. In order to advance, the closed home evades the entanglements of neighborhood reciprocity and non-voluntary commitments. This closed ideal intends to reproduce an attenuated social economy. The family looks to secure outward contractual agreements and to heighten its internal emotional intensity. In the process, the suburban ideal brings children into a tight circle of self-possession, and it is likely to interpret patronage as a threat. In the context of local community, it is a responsibility of parents to encourage sponsorship relationships for their children, if for no other reason than to diffuse parental authority and to offer children alternative avenues of dependence. A child establishes his or her social identity not through independence, but through maintaining his or her own lines of interdependence. When all is said, patronage as adoptive parenting is fundamental to community, particularly as common life is extended through time.

Childbearing and rearing do not constitute a freestanding foundation of the open household, but they are key purposes within a constellation of reciprocity and domestic belonging. Sexual practices within the household are shaped by its grammar of deepening and extending common life. Put normatively, a habitat inhospitable to children is an inferior context for sex, and for this reason, the procreative meaning of sex ought to be sustained as essential to good sexual practices. This is not to say that every sexual act ought to produce children or that a couple ought to intend conception during every sexual encounter. It means that, in contrast to an economy set on reproducing desire, sexual practices fit with the purposes of producing people – of making us who we are and placing us as individuals in community. I take this to be John Paul II's meaning when he sets marriage and family in the context of "the genealogy of persons."[34]

Sexual practices between husband and wife have an adoptive character insofar as our bodies come to belong through day-to-day presence, through sharing a kitchen and a bed, through illness and good health. Within the household, conjugal union is not an unparalleled form of love. It is possible that enduring friendships and parent–child relationships might be unique and intense in their own right. Marriage, in fact, needs the support of parallel loves and commitments of reciprocity; conjugal union flourishes when opened outward to a wider order of love (see Chapters 7 and 8). Marital love is unique in a different way, in its possibilities for intimate bodily presence over time. Through marriage, our bodies become irreplaceable in relation to one another. In Chapter 2, I argued that isolated sexual acts have variable significance and that a critical problem with romantic views is that sex is expected to carry meaning that transcends its particular place and time. In contrast, I proposed that sexual practices in marriage are significant because particular acts are variable. As sex takes on the course of time, a husband and wife communicate the ebb of flow of their common life and "live into" a complexity of bodily presence. Here, I am proposing that this enduring bodily presence brings involvement in an intricate social network. Through our belonging in marriage, we become deeply set within a network of loves. The communion between husband and wife is not set apart, but located in the middle of things.

Domestic life invests sexual practices with the rich complexity of a familial order of love. Likewise, childbearing and rearing form a nexus, a "genealogy of persons," where the social body is reproduced. A spouse is adopted into generations not his or her own and into networks of friends by way of association. Kin and neighbors have a stake in the home, and they will work to bring a couple into an extension of common life through mutual dependence. While love as passion forges an inner connection, sexual practices in the home attach and link us through fixtures of everyday life. As a spouse takes her place at the dinner table, she cannot untangle her relationship to her husband from the children who are squirming in their chairs. She cannot disentangle the marriage from neighbors who will be waving through the window or her mother who will be calling on the phone. Neighbors and kin would find it difficult to separate her from her spouse as well. They share everyday life. As this couple lies down in bed, everyday entanglements are there: annoyances, ailments, intimacies and joys. Sexual practices cultivate a deep sense of belonging and identity because they are part of day-to-day connections that carry our lives.

As bodily presence, it seems to me that there is a connection between conjugal union and care for the body. There is a connection, for instance, between sexual belonging and the grammar of parental care for infants and toddlers. Bathing, diapering, and feeding the young are everyday routines that bind beyond declarations of love or the apparent virtues of our sons and daughters. My mother is pointing to something important when, in anger, she tells me that she knows me better than I know myself because she held me as a baby on her knee. Her agency of bodily care has set us within a network of relationships (mother–son, brother–sister) that exceeds voluntary association. The body leads. Likewise, care for the infirm requires habitual intimacy that carries a knowing and a belonging that are fully consistent with a husband's lifelong sexual relationship with his wife. Long-term nursing care is likely to bring routines of bodily presence that surpass the relationship of patient to professional nurse. Religious communities, as well, operate by means of bodily presence and care. The vows of poverty, chastity, and obedience generate concrete relationships of bodily dependence that endure through personality differences and frustrations.

The body belongs, and becomes the nexus of common life. Marriage, in this sense, offers a particular avenue of social reproduction, where a person's bodily presence is communicated through sexual practices. Through time, a person becomes physically irreplaceable to another, and that "place" is set within a network of family, friends, and neighbors. In a popular view, it is thought that domestication deadens sexual desire, but the household economy actually "re-socializes" and transforms it. In a popular view, marriage is no match for sheer (adolescent) passion. This is true. As passing years bring sagging shoulders and widening torsos, the body gains a different kind of attraction. Hands and face, hips and arms are invested with common endeavors, joys and pains, with who we have become, and with our being – claimed by another. Our desires are satisfied in our belonging.

Unitive and procreative ends

Theologically, the two intrinsic goods of marriage are unity and procreation. Sexual union, in current parlance, is considered an expression of interpersonal love, which provides the context for bearing and raising children. "Context," here, is the critical term. Strictly speaking, the good of procreation is not expressed when sperm meets egg, but when a couple is open to procreation. This "openness," even when considered essential to every sexual act, is typically set within the context, not of isolated acts, but of the marriage as a whole.[35] Sex does not always end in conception, but it ought always to unite husband and wife in love and interpersonal communion. This emphasis on interpersonal love provides a way to highlight the "life-giving" and "self-giving" character of sex in contrast to older (Augustinian) views that emphasized external and impersonal purposes of marriage, such as civic duty and procreation. In Chapter 2, I argued that the standard conception of interpersonal union offers an inadequate context for sexual practices. Up to this point, the current chapter has reversed the typical order of things by locating the unitive end of marriage within the procreative good. The environment suited to sexual union is characterized by a "genealogy of persons," where sex is set within practices of "making" people.

Openness to procreation implies a way of organizing social life, as an alternative, particularly, to the consumptive household management discussed at the beginning of the chapter. The productive home is opened outward through common endeavors (see Chapters 5 and 8) and through its connection to wider social networks (see Chapters 6 and 7). Theologically, family comes in relation to the world through the church, which is gathered as a community in terms of God's relation to the world. A family in Maryland, for instance, does not have a specific relation to poor children in Honduras, but it does have a role and vocation in terms of the church's relation to Honduran poor. A priest recently visited our parish and reminded us of what the church is called to do. He gave my wife a photograph of an eight-year-old girl, Zandy, and asked us to support her family by sending money each month, from now on. Our daughter has written a letter. We have not entered a contractual obligation. Through exchanges like this, the household is a site for overlapping roles and systems of reciprocity. Family, in this regard, does not stand on its own, but is oriented toward interminable exchanges, gift-giving, and benefaction that carry its procreative character. The household is a site of social reproduction because it is formed by the grammar of belonging, of making persons, of bearing and raising children.

In this regard, procreation depends first of all upon a network of social practices before it can be understood fully as the character of a particular act. If a couple is childless, their relationship can be open to children in a concrete and practical way inasmuch as their relationship is sustained by a community of hospitality. The "fruitfulness" and outward orientation of their love for each other can be structured by the extended commitments and the vulnerability of being open to new life, to the stranger, and to relationships that are not merely a matter of choice and mutual regard.[36] The same holds for people who are not married. In fact, the open household depends upon relationships that diffuse parent–child relationships and provide alternative routes for patronage and other forms of reciprocity. It can be argued that the household depends upon single people to convey the procreative goods of family and marriage, especially in a context where family is inclined toward a consumptive social economy. The procreative family is a heavier load than marriage can bear.

This understanding of procreation parallels common agreement in Catholic debates about sexual practices in marriage. Pope Paul VI, in *Humanae vitae,* proposes that the procreative meaning of sexual intercourse is sustained not by the intention to have a child during each sexual encounter, but by a couple's openness to the natural rhythms of fertility and infertility. Regulating births and intending to avoid conception are permissible if, among other things, both conceptive and non-conceptive intercourse are set within the natural generative process.[37] Paul VI's arguments depend upon a strong connection between our sexual and social nature, between "the natural generative process" and the social form of marriage.

Paul VI argues that natural family planning is a means for limiting births while sustaining procreative character of marital union. He holds that artificial contraception breaks with the procreative context of human sexuality, and in doing so, removes sex from the biological setting of a woman's fertility and our (society's) parental vocation. He fears that sex will have "no place" (i.e., will be nomadic) when detached from procreative givens. Sexual practices will be shaped instead by the consumptive practices of advanced nations over against developing countries, and the power of men over against women.[38] Paul VI thinks of "nomadic desire" as one way among others to undermine the context required to sustain hospitality to the stranger and economic justice. Among the disagreements about "artificial" contraception, Paul VI's worries about social consequences are widely considered to have been correct.

Humanae vitae is associated with a variety of dissenting views, but these objections, in the main, do not dispute the procreative character of marriage. Bernard Häring, for example, defends the use of contraceptives when spousal union sustains a parental vocation, when household practices of raising children are sustained and enhanced through a limited use of contraceptives.[39] Dissent, here, is an internal dispute, and when viewed from the outside, these arguments represent more agreement than disagreement, especially in contrast to a "contraceptive" culture. Häring sets the use of "artificial" contraceptives within wider procreative purposes, insofar as the procreative good is considered essential to the sexual and social economy of marriage and home. In other words, for Häring's objections to *Humanae vitae* to work, he must conceive of procreation as a social good that binds people and points to the character of sexual union.[40]

My emphasis on agreement between *Humanae vitae* and its opponents is not meant to minimize the divisiveness of the debate, but to highlight the character of my proposal. Typically, the procreative good of marriage is understood as extended over time and through enduring relationships. A couple conceives, and then the meaning of this event is worked out over a lifetime. Even for couples who do not have children, openness to procreation signifies a course of life and the character of home. Even single people are connected to the procreative social form through a genealogy of persons and a communion of generations.[41] In contrast, the unitive goal of sex, typically conceived, is isolated in time and considered a closed communion. In Chapter 2, I referred to this "liminal" setting as a wedding day or honeymoon conception of conjugal union. Fitting with a modern otherworldliness of sexual desire, this isolated context detaches the moment of consummation from the quotidian matters of home. This common "personalist" view gives sexual intercourse transcendent meaning so that it can locate a lifelong marriage in every act. I have argued, in contrast, that each sexual act is likely to mean very little, that individual acts will communicate a multitude of significant and insignificant things. Over time and through the little things, we come to belong, irreplaceably with another and in a complex web of social relations. This is the procreative meaning of steadfast love and sexual fidelity. Sexual practices in marriage shape us as people, as sex and love are vested with and vulnerable to the everyday.

Conclusion:

Marriage and Family

This book is an attempt to envision domestic life as an adventure and to consider the household as "other than – more than – a feck-less haven, a commodity, or a personal hobby."[1] Throughout, my concern is to highlight the ordinary, to recognize, for instance, that good sex is routine and is significant precisely when we are able to take the presence of another for granted. This kind of domestication is hardly the making of a "feckless haven," but is a risky venture that strikes fear in many who hope for the freedoms of social detach-ment. In contrast to an economy of desire and romantic ideals, I seek to widen the ground of marriage beyond a loving couple's "I–Thou" encounter, and to show that the grammar of interpersonal love is dependent on the day-to-day operations of neighborhood and home. Marriage, in other words, is not a merely personal endeavor. Along these lines, I challenge the notion of the autonomous, nuclear family purveyed by proponents of family values. Family, I argue, is a dependent social institution that requires a fit within broader systems of reciprocity, patronage, and gift-exchange. Its openness and vulnerability to the depth and the binding of common life constitute the adventure of marriage and family.

My proposal for venturesome housekeeping engages opponents on two fronts. First, I sustain a critique of market capitalism and the contractual social economy. The market requires that our desires be nomadic, that our longings never find a resting place. In the market, our experiences of things and people are considered ideal when they conjure up more desire, and drive us incessantly onward to new things. In order to enliven us, our desires must be continually unsettled. Accordingly, the dominant social sphere sustains a market rationality that offers few interesting places to settle down. Throughout the book, I use the term "social economy" in order to highlight the grammar of exchange that underlies social life. In terms of exchange, modern contractual government has become the dominant grammar of neighborhood and home. It is a grammar of suburban detachment, limited cooperation, and temporary arrangements that intend to serve pre-social self-interests (rather than a mutual binding in common life). By design, the contractual home is set apart and safe from social entanglements. I have argued that the open household, by contrast, is open to unmanageable and interminable forms of gift-exchange and reciprocity. Life in the neighborhood economy is a rich and risky venture, and for this reason, the simple matters of everyday life are key forms of resistance to the dominating market.

On the second front, I challenge a standard theology of marriage: what could be called a personalist or inter-subjective account of nuptial love and unity. Certainly, the personalist's focus on the interpersonal "I and Thou" is not pernicious, but too often its ideal of marriage gives us little chance to resist the pitfalls of modern romanticism. Contemporary romanticism is not the selfless love of Medieval troubadours. It is a calculated way to enliven the self through personal (inner and subjective) connections. This form of romanticism is a complement to market desire and the contractual social economy. "Love as passion" (Chapter 2) and "the pure relationship" (Chapter 10) are defined by their ability to regenerate desire, so that the enemy of love is considered to be the practical matters of life that bring a domestication or settling of desire. Romantic love purports to form deep connections, but it is always frustrated insofar as its very character resists our belonging. Love, in the dominant economy, is the continual reproduction of passion, and like market desire, romantic love is unsettling. This economy of desire carries difficulties for theological personalism. When personalism confines itself to an inter-subjective view of marriage, it is unable to raise questions about the social conditions that make romantic love functional and indispensable. Love is thought to transcend the limits of our social world; romantic abandonment is considered necessary in order to overcome what is thought to be our natural isolation within contractual and utilitarian relationships.[2] Why is it that the self is conceived in isolation only to be saved from the ordinary struggles of life by irrational passion? When personalism falls within this romantic framework, its account of marital love and sex transcends day-to-day matters of good housekeeping and the struggles of home. Love continues to require a displacement of domestic life.

In contrast to personalism and over against the contractual market, I give a detailed account of the social economy of the neighborhood and household. While doing so, I work around a common dilemma. Political proposals about family usually exaggerate its social role by locating the home within the dominant social and economic discourse. Family is put on the world or national stage where it is expected to either buttress or transform the basic structures of society. This overstated role of family constitutes one side of the dilemma: the household is displaced, once again, from its very ordinary environment, and then it is given the impossible (romantic) task of saving the world. The other side of the dilemma is that an ordinary account of family is likely to have little social or economic importance. A commonplace proposal about family is likely to be politically tedious and dull. The home, on this side of the dilemma, is practically an asocial space. Facing this dilemma, my goal is to present everyday life as a modest but complex economy that makes a critical difference to how the social body is formed. I attempt an understated proposal that, if taken seriously, will challenge dominant systems of exchange and encourage a form of community-building that comes naturally to the home.

This household economy is central to the book. Notice, for instance, that the book's middle chapter, "Two Households," is wedged between dominant political conceptions of the home, in "Family Values," and a prominent theological understanding of "The Social Role of Family." Chapter 5, "Two Households," is the pivot point between the critical and constructive projects of the book. For instance, I wager a critique of romantic love in Chapter 2; however, after the meaning of love has passed through Chapter 5's presentation of the open home, I admit and develop the proper role of "love as passion" in Chapter 8. My concern in Chapter 8, "The Happy Home," is to place marital love within a larger context of family, friends, and neighborhood reciprocity. In contrast to romantic personalism, it is my view and experience that so-called outside relationships are necessary to the internal health of family. This theme is developed further in Chapter 10. Typical descriptions of marriage are so concerned to defend family that they imagine a husband and wife making each other wonderfully complete (giving to the other "totally" and exhausting the other self). This defense of marriage seems to be a formula for failure. It requires spouses to be interpersonally heroic, and ironically, its conception of the self (as completed by a single "other") is thin and lonely. A similar binary logic characterizes popular guides for parenting. The parent–child relationship is isolated with a romantic intensity, and brothers and sisters are considered intrusions and obstacles to healthy childhood development.

The constructive part of the book (Chapters 7 to 11) reinterprets marriage and family by following the logic of what I develop, in Chapter 5, as the social economy of neighborhood and home. Chapter 7, "The Order of Love," argues that mutuality and preferential regard are the basic and highest expressions of love, grounded theologically in the love of God. I build a case for love as a set of virtues and dispositions of common life that are not only local in orientation, but also spread out and are transformed through the family's (still local) placement in the church. I do not provide an extended discussion of the church; for the purposes of the argument, church needs only to be defined as the social body that is called to live out and express God's love for the world. Families are called to be part of this social body, but strictly speaking, transforming the world is not the social role of the home. In Chapter 9, "Order, Gender, and Function," the economy of the open household is used to identify gender-identity as important to social life, while at the same time making the relationship between gender and function inexact and diffuse. It seems to me that the social complexity of the neighborhood economy militates against simple gender roles. I take the so-called traditional nuclear home to be a construction of contractual governance in the dominant public sphere.

Sex and Love in the Home is not the typical book on marriage and family. As noted in Chapter 10, Michael Lawler defines marriage as "a partnership of love for the whole life, ordered equally to the well-being of the spouses and to the generation and nurture of children."[3] I take this definition to be exactly right. My purposes have been to widen the context of this definition beyond the narrow marital dyad. I make a decisive break with recent theology by arguing that marriage is not the foundation of family or the household. In the final chapter, for instance, I do not suggest that conjugal union establishes and sustains a communion. On the contrary, I propose that marriage does not set a couple apart in order to begin a family, but puts a husband and wife in the middle of a larger network of preferential loves. In the household (in contrast to the market), sexual practices have a grammar of belonging. Sexual fidelity and the enduring love of marriage are a course of life through which a person becomes irreplaceable and intimately known within a complex set of social relations.

The book does not begin with the usual terms like fidelity, covenant, and sacrament. Marital fidelity, for example, is not mentioned until the last two chapters. This apparent oversight is deliberate. *Sex and Love in the Home* is social groundwork for the practices of marriage as a faithful, generative, and steadfast union. It is an argument that intends to make sense of marriage as a sacrament; that is, marriage as a set of practices that do not stand in isolation, but are open to be transformed by God's gracious communion as it is routinized in the social body of the church. I expect that the reader will recognize the book's underlying grammar of steadfast love and faithfulness. Too often, we use the concepts of marriage without the practical grammar. The traditional vows of marriage continue to be professed at an astounding pace even though their meaning is often hollow from the start. Many do not inhabit a place where such vows are good promises. A theology of marriage and family does little if it works only with the concepts. What is needed is a sociology of faith. This book has been an attempt to renarrate the home and the domestication of love and sex as the venture of a rich social life.

Notes

Introduction

1. Dietrich von Hildebrand, *Marriage: The Mystery of Faithful Love*, Manchester, NH: Sophia Institute Press 1984, pp. 1–30.

2. Immanuel Wallerstein and Joan Smith, "Households as an Institution of the World Economy," *Creating and Transforming Households: The Constraints of the World-Economy*, ed. Joan Smith and Immanuel Wallerstein, New York: Cambridge University Press 1992, pp. 4–7.

3. Michael Walzer, *Spheres of Justice*, New York: Basic Books 1983, pp. 227–42.

4. M. Patricia Fernández-Kelly and Anna M. García make a distinction between family as a theoretical notion (to which few families measure up) and the household as a practical and economic structure of life. "Informalization at the Core: Hispanic Women, Homework, and the Advanced Capitalist State," *The Informal Economy: Studies in Advanced and Less Developed Countries*, ed. Alejandro Portes, et al., Baltimore: The Johns Hopkins University Press 1989, p. 261.

5. James U. McNeal, *The Kids Market, Myths and Realities*, Ithaca, NY: Paramount Market Publishing, Inc. 1999.

6. See Theodore Mackin, S.J., *What Is Marriage?* New York: Paulist Press 1982, pp. 225–47.

7. Dale B. Martin, *The Corinthian Body*, New Haven: Yale University Press 1995; Michael J. Schuck, *That They Be One: The Social Teaching of the Papal Encyclicals 1740–1989*, Washington, DC: Georgetown University Press 1991.

8. Cf. Stephanie Coontz, *The Way We Never Were: American Families and the Nostalgia Trap*, New York: Basic Books 1992.

9. Lisa Sowle Cahill, *Sex, Gender, and Christian Ethics*, New York: Cambridge University Press 1996, p. 164.

10. Consider, for instance, T. Berry Brazelton, M.D., *Touchpoints: Your Child's Emotional and Behavioral Development*, New York: Perseus Press 1994.

11. Brazelton, *Touchpoints*, pp. 390–7. Brazelton does not integrate siblings into his conception of childhood development, but puts them toward the end of a long list of challenges to development.

12. Stanley Hauerwas, *A Community of Character*, Notre Dame: University of Notre Dame Press 1981, pp. 22–7.

13. Alasdair MacIntyre argues that the flight, in modern moral philosophy, from locating the moral life in social roles and functions is basic to the fragmentation of the discipline and to its distance from conversation with ordinary people – a flight to the meta-ethical and to an obsession with procedural concerns. See his *A Short History of Ethics: A History of Moral Philosophy from the Homeric Age to the Twentieth Century*, 2nd edn. Notre Dame: University of Notre Dame Press 1998.

14. Christopher Lasch, *Women and the Common Life: Love, Marriage, and Feminism*, ed. Elisabeth Lasch-Quinn, New York: W. W. Norton & Company 1997.

15. Arlie Hochschild, *The Time Bind: When Work Becomes Home and Home Becomes Work*, New York: Metropolitan Books 1997.

Chapter 1

1. Lesley Dormen, "Love and Partnership: How to Get Both," *Glamour* 95, Nov. 1, 1997, p. 268.

2. Dormen, "Love and Partnership," p. 268.

3. Denis de Rougemont, *Love in the Western World*, Princeton: Princeton University Press 1983.

4. Dormen, "Love and Partnership," pp. 269, 319.

5. Dormen, "Love and Partnership," pp. 269, 319.

6. Miranda Wells, "16 Ways to Free Your Mind for Great Sex," *Redbook* 190, no. 3, Jan. 1, 1998, p. 88.

7. Wells, "16 Ways to Free Your Mind for Great Sex," p. 88.

8. I am thinking of magazines not like *Playboy* or *Penthouse*, but more respectable publications that are displayed up front in grocery stores and newsstands, magazines like *Maxim* and *Men's Health*. The subtext for most of the articles is that women are to be had for sex, and "relationships" are women's work.

9. Contrast David Blankenhorn, *Fatherless America*, New York: HarperCollins 1995, with Arlie Russell Hochschild, *The Time Bind: When Work Becomes Home and Home Becomes Work*, New York: Metropolitan Books 1997.

10. Frances and Joseph Gies, *Marriage and the Family in the Middle Ages*, New York: HarperCollins 1989.

11. Edward Shorter, *The Making of the Modern Family*, New York: Basic Books 1975.

12. Robert N. Bellah, et al., *Habits of the Heart*, Berkeley: University of California Press 1985, pp. 56–62.

13. There is a widespread use of Martin Buber's "I and Thou" (*I and Thou*, New York: Scribner 1970) to refer to the relationship between spouses. Popular use in reference to marriage does not have the precise meaning that Buber gives to "I–Thou," but means something more equivalent to the two of us are a complete whole (two in one flesh). I am using "Me and You" as a reference to the popular use of "I and Thou."

14. Consider Dietrich von Hildebrand, *Marriage: The Mystery of Faithful Love*, Manchester, NH: Sophia Institute Press 1984, and Bernard Cooke, *Sacraments and Sacramentality*, rev. edn. Mystic, CT: Twenty-Third Publications 1994.

15. The only love that is prior to particular ways of organizing human community is the love of God, a point spelled out in Chapter 7.

16. Chapters 2 and 3 will discuss the economic and social interests in making fulfilling sex and true love impossible.

17. See an interesting account of envy in Henry Fairlie, *The Seven Deadly Sins Today*, Notre Dame: University of Notre Dame Press 1978.

18. Andrew M. Greeley and Mary Greeley Durkin, *How to Save the Catholic Church*, New York: Viking Penguin 1984, pp. 107–19. Cf. Mary Greeley Durkin, *Feast of Love: Pope John Paul II on Human Intimacy*, Chicago: Loyola University Press 1983.

19. James P. Hanigan, *What Are They Saying About Sexual Morality?* New York: Paulist Press 1982, p. 113. Cf. John Paul II, *The Original Unity of Man and Woman: Catechesis on the Book of Genesis*, Boston: Daughters of St. Paul 1981.

20. Michael A. Fahey, "The Christian Family as Domestic Church at Vatican II," *The Family*, Concilium 1995/4, ed. Lisa Sowle Cahill and Dietmar Mieth, Maryknoll, NY: Orbis Books 1995, pp. 85–93.

21. Consider the editors' introduction to a selection of Chrysostom's sermons on marriage, in *On Marriage and Family Life*, trans. Catharine P. Roth and David Anderson, Crestwood, NY: St. Vladimir's Seminary Press 1997, pp. 7–24.

22. See Peter Brown, *The Body and Society*, New York: Columbia University Press 1988, pp. 305–22.

23. "Homily 12, On Colossians 4:18," *On Marriage and Family Life*, p. 74.

24. "Homily 12," *On Marriage and Family Life*, pp. 73–80.

25. "How to Choose a Wife," *On Marriage and Family Life*, p. 96.

26. Christopher Brooke, *The Medieval Idea of Marriage*, Oxford: Oxford University Press 1989, pp. 119ff.

27. Florence Kaslow and James A. Robison, "Long-Term Satisfying Marriages: Perceptions of Contributing Factors," *The American Journal of*

Family Therapy 24, no. 2, Summer 1996, pp. 153–70.

28. Christopher Lasch, *Haven in a Heartless World*, New York: Basic Books 1977.

29. Nelson W. Aldrich, *Old Money: The Mythology of Wealth in America*, New York: Allworth Press 1996; David Brooks, *Bobos in Paradise: The New Upper Class and How They Got There*, New York: Simon & Schuster 2000; Paul Fussell, *Class: A Guide through the American Class System*, New York: Summit 1983; Lewis H. Lapham, *Money and Class in America: Notes and Observations on Our Civil Religion*, New York: Weidenfeld & Nicolson 1988.

30. See Shorter, *The Making of the Modern Family*; William R. Garrett, "The Protestant Ethic and the Spirit of the Modern Family," *The Journal for the Scientific Study of Religion* 37, no. 2, June 1998, pp. 222–34; and especially Stephanie Coontz, *The Social Origins of Private Life*, New York: Verso 1988.

31. Coontz, *The Social Origins of Private Life*, p. 178.

32. See Willemien Otten's comments on Western and Eastern monasticism in "Augustine on Marriage, Monasticism, and the Community of the Church," *Theological Studies* 59, 1998, pp. 385–405.

33. Brown, *The Body and Society*, p. 313; also pp. 307–9.

34. *On Virginity*, in *John Chrysostom: On Virginity; Against Marriage*, trans. Sally Rieger Shore, New York: Edwin Mellon Press 1983, XVI.2.

35. "Homily LV: Matthew 16.24," *Saint Chrysostom: Homilies on the Gospel of Saint Matthew*, Nicene and Post-Nicene Fathers X, ed. Philip Schaff, Grand Rapids: Eerdmans 1983, p. 344.

36. *On Virginity*, X.3.

37. *On Virginity*, XI.

38. Michael Moffatt gives an interesting account of the new sexual orthodoxy and its constraints in *Coming of Age in New Jersey*, New Brunswick, NJ: Rutgers University Press 1989, pp. 181–230.

39. "And today our race is not increased by the authority of marriage, but by the word of our Lord, who said at the beginning: 'Be fruitful and multiply. . .' For marriage will not be able to produce many men if God is unwilling, nor will virginity destroy their number if God wishes there to be many of them [consider the time of Noah]. (XV.1)", John Chrysostom, *On Virginity*, pp. 22–3.

40. "How to Choose a Wife," *On Marriage and Family Life*, p. 99.

41. *On Virginity*, IX.1.

42. "Homily 19," *On Marriage and Family Life*, p. 41.

43. "[L]et us seek just one thing in a wife, virtue of soul and nobility of character, so that we may enjoy tranquility, so that we may luxuriate in harmony and lasting love" ("How to Choose a Wife," *On Marriage and Family Life*, p. 97).

44. See the interplay of eros and agape in Homily 20, On Ephesians 5:22–33, in *Homiliae in Epist. ad Ephesios, Patrologiae Graeca 62*, ed. J. P. Migne, Parisiis 1862, pp. 135–49.

45. The notion of family roles introduces the question of gender roles. These issues will be discussed in Chapter 9: Order, Gender, and Function.

46. Eva Illouz, *Consuming the Romantic Utopia: Love and the Cultural Contradictions of Capitalism*, Berkeley: University of California Press 1997, pp. 25–47.

Chapter 2

1. An ad like this is one of many in the movie, *Crazy People* (1990). Dudley Moore is an advertising executive who decides to tell the truth in his advertisements and as a consequence is shipped off to an insane asylum. The patients at the hospital start a successful and truthful advertising business.

2. Consider, for instance, Ronald Primeau, *Romance of the Road: The Literature of the American Highway*, Bowling Green, OH: Bowling Green State University 1996.

3. Julia A. Ericksen and Sally A. Steffen, *Kiss and Tell: Surveying Sex in the Twentieth Century*, Cambridge, MA: Harvard University Press 1999. The book provides an interesting history of sex surveys, particularly biases of the social scientists who do the surveying and the desire of the public to know the sexual practices of others.

4. Stephen Heath, *The Sexual Fix*, New York: Schocken Books 1982.

5. Robert T. Michael, et al., *Sex in America: A Definitive Survey*, New York: Warner Books 1995.

6. Alan Soble, *Sexual Investigations*, New York: New York University Press 1996.

7. Soble, *Sexual Investigations*, p. 87.

8. Soble, *Sexual Investigations*, p. 88.

9. Soble, *Sexual Investigations*, p. 90.

10. Soble, *Sexual Investigations*, p. 90.

11. Colin Beavan, "Sin-sational Advice: Passion Pumper Uppers: Reboot sexual tension with these tips for making six-months later sex as memorable as it was the first night," *Glamour* 97, April 1, 1999, p. 206.

12. Beavan, "Sin-sational Advice", p. 206.

13. Susan Block, *The Ten Commandments of Pleasure: Erotic Keys to a Healthy Sexual Life*, New York: St. Martin's Press 1996.

14. Barbara Keesling, *Getting Close: A Lover's Guide to Embracing Fantasy and Heightening Sexual Connection*, New York: HarperCollins 1999.

15. Block, *The Ten Commandments of Pleasure*, pp. xxiv–xxv.

16. Beavan, "Sin-sational Advice," p. 209.

17. Keesling, *Getting Close*, p. vii.

18. Keesling, *Getting Close*, p. 85.

19. The sexual work ethics is consistent in my review of various magazines that span about four years, from 1996 to early 2000. For a more extensive analysis see Eva Illouz, *Consuming the Romantic Utopia: Love and the Cultural Contradictions of Capitalism*, Berkeley: University of California Press 1997.

20. "31 Ways to Feel Sexy," *Mademoiselle*, February 2000, p. 124.

21. Jennifer Baumgardner, "When Good Girls Go Bad," *Maxim*, January 2000, pp. 54–6.

22. Megan Fitzmorris McCafferty, "Are You a Perfect (Sexual) Match?" *Cosmopolitan*, May 1, 1999, p. 220.

23. McCafferty, "Are You a Perfect (Sexual) Match?", p. 221. Also see, "Sex Tricks That Always Work," *Men's Health*, September 1999.

24. Julie Taylor, "Cosmo's 20 Favorite Sex Tips Ever," *Cosmopolitan*, January 2000, p. 154.

25. "Ten Dates Before Sex . . . and other habits of highly effective daters," *Mademoiselle*, February 2000, p. 105.

26. For a detailed discussion of contemporary philosophy on sex, see my "Sexual Utterances and Common Life," *Modern Theology* 16, no. 4, October 2000, pp. 443–59.

27. Jean Kilbourne, *Deadly Persuasion: Why Women and Girls Must Fight the Addictive Power of Advertising*, New York: Free Press 1999; *Killing Us Softly: How Advertising Changes the Way We Think and Feel*, New York: Touchstone 2000.

28. Philippe Ariès, "Thoughts on the History of Homosexuality," *Western Sexuality: Practice and Precept in Past and Present Times*, ed. Philippe Ariès and André Béjin, London: Basil Blackwell 1985.

29. Ariès, "Thoughts on the History of Homosexuality," p. 70.

30. Michael Moffat, *Coming of Age in New Jersey: College Life and American Culture*, New Brunswick, NJ: Rutgers University Press 1989, pp. 181–230.

31. William E. Kraft, *Sexual Dimensions of Celibate Life*, Kansas City, KS: Andrews & McMeel, Inc. 1979, p. 52. Cited in David Bohr, *Catholic Moral Tradition*, 2nd edn. Huntington, IN: Our Sunday Visitor 1999, p. 241.

32. Bohr, *Catholic Moral Tradition*, p. 239.

33. John A. Sanford, *Invisible Partners*, New York: Paulist Press 1980, p. 89. Cited in Bohr, *Catholic Moral Tradition*, p. 239.

34. Andrew M. Greeley and Mary Greeley Durkin, *How to Save the Catholic Church*, New York: Viking Penguin 1984, p. 120.

35. James P. Hanigan, *What Are They Saying About Sexual Morality?*

New York: Paulist Press 1982, pp. 116–20. Also see James P. Hanigan, *Homosexuality: The Test Case for Christian Sexual Ethics*, New York: Paulist Press 1988, pp. 89–112; André Guindon, *The Sexual Language*, Ottawa: University of Ottawa Press 1977; Stanley J. Grenz, *Sexual Ethics: An Evangelical Perspective*, Louisville, KY: Westminster John Knox Press 1990, pp. 15–54; Dietrich von Hildebrand, *Marriage: The Mystery of Faithful Love*, Manchester, NH: Sophia Institute Press 1984.

36. Consider essays by Thomas Nagel, Robert Solomon, Janice Moulton, and Alan Goldman in Alan Soble (ed.), *The Philosophy of Sex*, Savage, MD: Rowman & Littlefield Publishers, Inc. 1991.

37. Vincent J. Genovesi, *In Pursuit of Love: Catholic Morality and Human Sexuality*, 2nd edn. Collegeville, MN: The Liturgical Press 1996. A host of other texts would suffice as representative as well, such as Grenz, *Sexual Ethics: An Evangelical Perspective* and Hanigan, *What Are They Saying About Sexual Morality?*.

38. Genovesi, *In Pursuit of Love*, p. 151.

39. Genovesi, *In Pursuit of Love*, p. 151.

40. Genovesi, *In Pursuit of Love*, p. 154.

41. Genovesi, *In Pursuit of Love*, p. 152.

42. John F. Derek, *Contemporary Medical Ethics*, New York: Sheed & Ward 1975, pp. 82–3, cited in Genovesi, *In Pursuit of Love*, pp. 152–3.

43. Genovesi, *In Pursuit of Love*, p. 153. He is discussing the work of James Gaffney in *Moral Questions*, New York: Paulist Press 1974, pp. 16–27.

44. Genovesi, *In Pursuit of Love*, p. 153.

45. See notes 28, 30, 31, 32, 39, 40. Also John Paul II, *The Original Unity of Man and Woman: Catechesis on the Book of Genesis*, Boston, MA: Daughters of St. Paul 1981.

46. Genovesi, *In Pursuit of Love*, pp. 157–67.

47. Genovesi, *In Pursuit of Love*, p. 157.

Chapter 3

1. R. Vance Fitzgerald, M.D., et al., "What Are the Essential Ingredients for a Long, Happy Marriage?," *Medical Aspects of Human Sexuality* 19, no. 3, March 1985, pp. 237–57.

2. Fitzgerald, "What Are the Essential Ingredients for a Long, Happy Marriage?," pp. 238–9.

3. I am not referring precisely to romantic love as it is understood in the work of Denis de Rougemont, *Love in the Western World*, Princeton: Princeton University Press 1983.

4. Eva Illouz, *Consuming the Romantic Utopia: Love and the Cultural*

Contradictions of Capitalism, Berkeley: University of California Press 1997, pp. 153–84.

5. Illouz, *Consuming the Romantic Utopia*, p. 157.

6. Illouz, *Consuming the Romantic Utopia*, pp. 160–4.

7. Illouz, *Consuming the Romantic Utopia*, pp. 166–70.

8. Illouz, *Consuming the Romantic Utopia*, pp. 175–6.

9. *The Washington Post*, Sunday, January 30, 2000, F4–5.

10. Niklas Luhmann, *Love as Passion: The Codification of Intimacy*, trans. Jeremy Gaines and Doris L. Jones, Stanford: Stanford University Press 1998.

11. Luhmann, *Love as Passion*, p. 20.

12. Luhmann, *Love as Passion*, p. 26.

13. Luhmann, *Love as Passion*, p. 28.

14. John Alan Lee, "Ideologies of Lovestyles and Sexstyles," *Romantic Love and Sexual Behavior: Perspectives for the Social Sciences*, ed. Victor C. de Munck, Westport, CT: Praeger 1998, pp. 33–76.

15. Lee, "Ideologies of Lovestyles and Sexstyles," p. 69.

16. John Alan Lee, *Colours of Love*, Toronto: New Press 1973; "A Typology of Styles of Loving," *Personality and Social Psychology Bulletin* 3, no. 2, 1977, pp. 173–82.

17. Lee, "Ideologies of Lovestyles and Sexstyles," pp. 36–7.

18. Lee, "Ideologies of Lovestyles and Sexstyles," pp. 37–8.

19. Lee, "Ideologies of Lovestyles and Sexstyles," p. 39.

20. John Alan Lee, "The Romantic Heresy," *Canadian Review of Sociology and Anthropology* 2, no. 4, 1975, pp. 514–28.

21. Lee, "Ideologies of Lovestyles and Sexstyles," p. 62.

22. *The Bodyguard* (1992), director Mick Jackson, starring Kevin Costner and Whitney Houston.

23. *Titanic* (1997), director James Cameron, starring Leonardo Di Caprio and Kate Winslet.

24. *Pretty Woman* (1990), director Garry Marshall, starring Julia Roberts and Richard Gere.

25. Illouz, *Consuming the Romantic Utopia*.

26. "Whatever else romantic love may be, when the experience strikes, it involves a series of feeling states, physiological symptoms, and preoccupation of attention" (Susan S. Hendrick and Clyde Hendrick, *Romantic Love*, Newbury Park, CA: Sage Publications 1992, p. 19). Here, Susan and Clyde Hendrick attempt to summarize recent philosophical and sociological literature on falling in love. See D. Van de Vate, Jr., *Romantic Love: A Philosophical Inquiry*, University Park, PA: Penn State University Press 1981; R. Brown, *Analyzing Love*, New York: Cambridge University Press 1987; R. Solomon, *Love: Emotion, Myth, and Metaphor*, New York: Anchor Books 1981. One main effect of romantic feeling states and

physical sensations is a decision, some kind of commitment of self, that "may not be consciously recognized by the two lovers." In other words, "romantic love involves choice (often disguised as non-choice) and is increasingly linked historically to sexual expression and selection of a marriage partner (thus combining elements of both biological and socio-logical perspectives)." Cultural sanctioning, according to Peter Berger, suggests why people tend to "fall for" others who are much like themselves in social and economic class, race, education, and religious attitudes (*Invitation to Sociology: A Humanistic Perspective*, New York: Anchor Books 1963, p. 35). Wider, and also unrecognized, social constraints place individuals in a social field where they can safely fall in love (i.e., be drawn irresistibly rather than decide for another).

27. Luhmann, *Love as Passion*, p. 147.

28. Luhmann, *Love as Passion*, p. 147.

29. Andrew M. Greeley and Mary Greeley Durkin, *How to Save the Catholic Church*, New York: Viking Penguin 1984, p. 115. Also see Mary Greeley Durkin, *Feast of Love: Pope Paul II on Human Intimacy*, Chicago: Loyola University Press 1983.

30. Greeley and Durkin, *How to Save the Catholic Church*, p. 115.

31. Dietrich von Hildebrand, *Marriage: The Mystery of Faithful Love*, Manchester, NH: Sophia Institute Press 1984.

32. von Hildebrand, *Marriage: The Mystery of Faithful Love*, p. 5.

33. von Hildebrand, *Marriage: The Mystery of Faithful Love*, pp. 5–6.

Chapter 4

1. Marite Burwell, "Celebrity Wedding Trends: What's Hot in Tinseltown," *About Weddings*, http://weddings.about.com.

2. William J. Clinton, "Parents' Day, 1999," Office of the Press Secretary: http://www.pub.whitehouse.gov/, July 23, 1999.

3. George W. Bush, "Parents' Day, 2001," Office of the Press Secretary: http://www.pub.whitehouse.gov/, July 21, 2001.

4. George W. Bush, "Parents' Day, 2003," Office of the Press Secretary: http://www.pub.whitehouse.gov/, July 25, 2003.

5. See William T. Cavanaugh, "The World in a Wafer," *Modern Theology* 15, no. 2, April 1999, pp. 181–96. Also John Milbank, "On Complex Space," *The Word Made Strange: Theology, Language, Culture*, Oxford: Basil Blackwell 1997, pp. 268–92, and Cavanaugh's use of Robert Nisbet, *The Quest for Community*, London: Oxford University Press 1953, pp. 75–152.

6. The point is made by Michele Barrett and Mary McIntosh while dis-cussing Jacques Donzelot, *The Policing of Families,* trans. Robert Hurley

(New York: Pantheon Books 1979), in their *The Anti-Social Family*, 2nd edn. New York: Verso 1991, p. 96.

7. Barrett and McIntosh, *The Anti-Social Family*, p. 49. Susan Moller Okin, *Women in Western Political Thought*, Princeton: Princeton University Press 1979, shows that classical liberalism considered the male-head of household as an individual unit and that the internal relations of family were considered outside political/public consideration. "Where as the liberal tradition appears to be talking about individuals, as components of political systems, it is in fact talking about male-headed families" (p. 202).

8. James Davison Hunter, *Culture Wars: The Struggle to Define America*, New York: Basic Books 1991, pp. 176–98.

9. Carole Pateman, *The Sexual Contract*, Stanford: Stanford University Press 1988.

10. This point is stated plainly in the welfare reform of 1996, H.R. 3734: "Personal Responsibility and Work Opportunity Reconciliation Act of 1996" (http://thomas.loc.gov/). Paula Allen-Meares and Eric M. Roberts argue that recent welfare policy actually sets an ethics of work over against an ethics of family, in "Public Assistance as Family Policy: Closing Off Options for Poor Families," *Social Work* 40, no. 4, July 1995, pp. 559–65. Also Felicia Kornbluh, "Subversive Potential, Coercive Intent: Women, Work, and Welfare in the 90's," *Social Policy* 21, no. 4, Spring 1991, pp. 23–40.

11. Clinton, "Parents' Day, 1999."

12. Bush, "Parents' Day, 2003."

13. Hunter, *Culture Wars*, p. 180.

14. David Blankenhorn, *Fatherless America: Confronting Our Most Urgent Social Problem*, New York: HarperCollins 1995; Andrew J. Polsky, *The Rise of the Therapeutic State*, Princeton, NJ: Princeton University Press 1993.

15. See Frances E. Olsen, "The Myth of State Intervention in the Family," *University of Michigan Journal of Law Reform*, 18, no. 4, 1985, pp. 835–65, and her "The Family and the Market: A Study of Ideology and Legal Reform," *Harvard Law Review* 96, no. 7, May 1983, pp. 1497–1578.

16. David Wagner, "The Family and the Constitution," *First Things* 45, August/September 1994. Wagner depends heavily upon the analysis by Polsky in *The Rise of the Therapeutic State*. Also see Dana Mack, *The Assault on Parenthood*, New York: Simon & Schuster 1997. A movement has emerged for a Parental Rights Amendment to the Constitution. The two provisions of the amendment show how close a call for parental rights is, in fact, to the power of state. "1. The rights of parents to direct the upbringing and education of their children is a fundamental right. 2. The state maintains a compelling interest in investigating, prosecuting, and punishing

child abuse and neglect as defined by statute." (*Of the People Foundation*, founded in 1993 and based in Arlington VA, is working for the Parental Rights Amendment (www.ofthepeople.org/).)

17. Michael Walzer, *Spheres of Justice: A Defense of Pluralism and Equality*, New York: Basic Books 1983, pp. 227–42.

18. Walzer, *Spheres of Justice*, pp. 231–2.

19. John Rawls, *A Theory of Justice*, Cambridge, MA: Belknap Press 1971; *Political Liberalism*, New York: Columbia University Press 1993.

20. Rawls, *A Theory of Justice*, p. 463; cf. pp. 74, 301, 511.

21. The problem of incompatible conceptions of human nature is generated by the modern divide between public and private, between work/politics and home. See Robert Paul Wolff, "There is Nobody Here but Us Persons," *Women and Philosophy*, ed. Carol C. Gould and Marx W. Wartofsky, New York: Putnam 1976, pp. 128–44.

22. Family, for Rawls, is a place where inequality can be located and separated from the basic structure of liberal theory and practice. In this regard, family will be sustained as somewhat justifiable, but essentially unequal and politically flawed. This strategy is pronounced in Rawls' *Political Liberalism* where he protects family, church, synagogue, and other associations as non-public institutions with their own reasonableness. He cordons off non-public institutions from the public sphere and narrows his theory of justice to a distinct public or political usefulness. In this later work, he will prescind entirely from questions about the internal justice of family. His intention is to allow for a plurality of traditions (non-public) while maintaining a singular structure of political liberalism. A corresponding benefit to narrowing the purview of liberalism is that social inequalities can be located within non-public practices. Political liberalism does not need to establish equality, only mitigate non-public inequalities.

23. Rawls, *A Theory of Justice*, p. 303.

24. Rawls, *A Theory of Justice*, p. 461.

25. Rawls, *A Theory of Justice*, pp. 460 n. 6, 461 n. 8.

26. Carol Gilligan, *In a Different Voice*, Cambridge: Harvard University Press 1982, p. 156.

27. Susan Moller Okin argues, in *Justice, Gender, and the Family*, New York: Basic Books 1989, that women are socially and economically vulnerable in the family and that Rawls' contractual conception of justice ought to be applied to the household.

28. Feminists like Germaine Greer, *The Whole Woman*, New York: Alfred A. Knopf 1999, are not troubled by this dilemma insofar as she critiques contractual politics along with sexism.

29. Pateman, *The Sexual Contract*.

30. Rawls, *A Theory of Justice*, p. 465.

31. Rawls, *A Theory of Justice*, pp. 467–8.

32. Rawls, *A Theory of Justice*, p. 473.

33. Rawls, *A Theory of Justice*, p. 474.

34. Rawls, *A Theory of Justice*, p. 476.

35. The basic tenor of the following paragraphs is shaped by the work of Christopher Lasch, in his *Haven in a Heartless World*, New York: Basic Books 1977, and *Women and the Common Life: Love, Marriage, and Feminism*, ed. Elisabeth Lasch-Quinn, New York: W. W. Norton & Company 1997.

36. Lasch, *Haven in a Heartless World*, pp. 3–8.

Chapter 5

1. Mary C. Howell, *Helping Ourselves: Families and the Human Network*, Boston: Beacon Press 1975, p. 71.

2. Christopher Lasch, *Women and the Common Life: Love, Marriage, and Feminism*, ed. Elisabeth Lasch-Quinn, New York: W. W. Norton & Company 1997.

3. For a more recent book by Howell, see *Serving the Underserved: Caring for People who Are both Old and Mentally Retarded: A Handbook for Caregivers*, Exceptional Parent Press 1989.

4. The U.S. Bureau of the Census (1997) puts the marriage rate at 8.9 per thousand in 1995 and the number of divorces at 4.4 per thousand.

5. Arlie Hochschild, *The Time Bind: When Work Becomes Home and Home Becomes Work*, New York: Metropolitan Books 1997, pp. 15–24, 45–52.

6. Stephanie Coontz, *The Way We Never Were: American Families and the Nostalgia Trap*, New York: Basic Books 1992.

7. Edward Shorter, *The Making of the Modern Family*, New York: Basic Books 1997, p. 3.

8. Shorter, *The Making of the Modern Family*, p. 3.

9. Christopher N. L. Brooke, *Marriage in Christian History*, Cambridge: Cambridge University Press 1977; Edmund S. Morgan, *The Puritan Family: Religion and Domestic Relations in Seventeenth-Century New England*, New York: Harper & Row 1944.

10. Stephanie Coontz provides an interesting account of changes in family, among different classes, that were directed toward sustaining its members socially and economically. *The Social Origins of Private Life: A History of American Families 1600–1900*, New York: Verso 1988.

11. Sharon Hays, *The Cultural Contradictions of Motherhood*, New Haven: Yale University Press 1996; Robert Bellah, et al., *Habits of the Heart*, Berkeley: University of California Press 1985; Christopher Lasch, *Haven in a Heartless World*, New York: Basic Books 1977.

12. Shorter, *The Making of the Modern Family*, pp. 5–6.

13. Shorter, *The Making of the Modern Family*, p. 5; Hays, *The Cultural Contradictions of Motherhood*, p. 64.

14. Jean Bethke Elshtain, *Public Man, Private Woman*, Princeton: Princeton University Press 1981.

15. Eva Illouz, *Consuming the Romantic Utopia: Love and the Cultural Contradictions of Capitalism*, Berkeley: University of California Press 1997, pp. 25–78.

16. Hays, *The Cultural Contradictions of Motherhood*, pp. 8–10, 64–8.

17. Hays, *The Cultural Contradictions of Motherhood*, p. 68.

18. Wendell Berry, *Home Economics*, San Francisco: North Point Press 1987; *Sex, Economy, Freedom, and Community*, New York: Pantheon Books 1992.

19. Saskia Sasse-Koop, "New York City's Informal Economy," *The Informal Economy: Studies in Advanced and Less Developed Countries*, ed. Alejandro Portes, Manuel Castells, and Lauren A. Benton, Baltimore: The Johns Hopkins University Press 1989, p. 61.

20. Sasse-Koop, "New York City's Informal Economy," p. 71.

21. M. Patricia Fernández-Kelly and Anna M. Garcia, "Informalization at the Core: Hispanic Women, Homework, and the Advanced Capitalist State," Portes et al. (eds), *The Informal Economy*, p. 260.

22. Fernández-Kelly and Garcia, "Informalization at the Core," p. 262.

23. Howell, *Helping Ourselves*, pp. 75–6.

24. Howell, *Helping Ourselves*, p. 72.

25. The image of the suburbs is not just a trope but key to the history of the middle-class family. See Lasch, *Haven in a Heartless World*.

26. Alasdair MacIntyre offers an interesting critique of the therapist, expert, and manager in *After Virtue,* 2nd edn. Notre Dame: University of Notre Dame Press 1984, pp. 75–8.

27. In *Helping Ourselves,* Howell adds work (pp. 95–118) and health-care (pp. 169–94) to childcare (pp. 119–45) and education (pp. 146–68) to the list of professionalized areas of family life.

28. James L. Nolan, *The Therapeutic State: Justifying Government at Century's End*, New York: New York University Press 1998.

29. This account depends partly on Immanuel Wallerstein's contributions to *Creating and Transforming Households: The Constraints of the World-Economy*, ed. Joan Smith and Immanuel Wallerstein, Cambridge: Cambridge University Press 1992, pp. 3–23, 253–62.

30. Howell, *Helping Ourselves*, p. 76.

31. Howell, *Helping Ourselves*, p. 77.

32. Howell, *Helping Ourselves*, pp. 77–8.

33. Howell, *Helping Ourselves*, p. 80.

34. Howell, *Helping Ourselves*, p. 82.

35. Howell, *Helping Ourselves*, p. 82.

36. The foregoing account of place and the idea of a home economy is gleaned from the wide-ranging writings of Wendell Berry. See, for instance, his *Home Economics*, San Francisco: North Point Press 1987.

37. Alvin W. Gouldner, *For Sociology: Renewal and Critique in Sociology Today*, New York: Basic Books 1973, pp. 241–2.

38. Pierre Bourdieu, *Outline of a Theory of Practice*, New York: Cambridge University Press 1977, pp. 4–6; D. Stephen Long, *Divine Economy: Theology and the Market*, London: Routledge 2000, pp. 144–6.

39. John Milbank, "Can a Gift Be Given? Prolegomena to a Future Trinitarian Metaphysic," *Modern Theology* 11, no. 1, January 1995, pp. 119–61.

40. Thomas Aquinas, *Summa Theologiae* I.2, qq. 109–14, Blackfriars edn. vol. 30, New York: McGraw-Hill Book Company 1972; II.2, qq. 23–7, Blackfriars edn. vol. 34, 1975.

41. Susan Moller Okin's arguments in *Justice, Gender, and the Family*, New York: Basic Books 1989, pp. 134–69.

42. Okin, *Justice, Gender, and the Family*, p. 3.

43. Peter Meikins, "Confronting the Time Bind: Work, Family, and Capitalism," *Monthly Review* 49, no. 9, February 1998, pp. 1–13.

44. Malia McCawley Wyckoff and Mary Snyder, *You Can Afford to Stay Home with Your Kids*, Franklin Lakes, NJ: Career Press 1999.

45. Studies of working-class women are interesting in this regard. Christine Stansell, *City of Women: Sex and Class in New York 1789–1860*, Chicago: University of Illinois Press 1987; Julie A. Matthaei, *An Economic History of Women in America: Women's Work, the Sexual Division of Labor, and the Development of Capitalism*, New York: Schocken Books 1982.

Chapter 6

1. Kathleen and James McGinnis, "Family as Domestic Church," *One Hundred Years of Catholic Social Thought: Celebration and Challenge*, ed. John A. Coleman, S.J., Maryknoll, NY: Orbis Books 1991, p. 133. Parenting for Peace and Justice Network: Jim and Kathy McGinnis, PPJN, Institute for Peace and Justice, 4144 Lindell Blvd, St. Louis, MO 63108.

2. McGinnis and McGinnis, "Family as Domestic Church," pp. 120–34.

3. See National Conference of Catholic Bishops, *Brothers and Sisters to Us*, Washington, DC: United States Catholic Conference 1979.

4. Kathleen and James McGinnis, *Parenting for Peace and Justice: Ten Years Later*, Maryknoll, NY: Orbis Books 1990. Cf. *Parenting for Peace and Justice*, Maryknoll, NY: Orbis Books 1981.

5. McGinnis and McGinnis, *Parenting for Peace and Justice: Ten Years Later*, p. 129.

6. See John Milbank's discussion of social teaching in "On Complex Space," *The Word Made Strange: Theology, Language, Culture*, Oxford: Blackwell 1997, pp. 268–92.

7. Lisa Sowle Cahill, "Marriage: Institution, Relationship, Sacrament," in Coleman (ed.), *One Hundred Years of Catholic Social Thought*, pp. 103–19; and "Sex, Gender, and the Common Good: Family," *Religion, Ethics, and the Common Good*, The Annual Publication of the College Theology Society 41, ed. James Donahue and M. Theresa Moser, R.S.C.J., Mystic, CT: Twenty-Third Publications 1996, pp. 145–67.

8. Cahill, "Marriage," pp. 108–9, citing John Pawlikowski, O.S.M., "Modern Catholic Teaching on the Economy: An Analysis and Evaluation," *Christianity and Capitalism: Perspectives on Religion, Liberalism and the Economy*, ed. Bruce and David A. Krueger, Chicago: Center for the Scientific Study of Religion 1984, p. 4.

9. Cahill, "Marriage," p. 109.

10. John Paul II, *Familiaris consortio*, in *Origins: CNS Documentary Service* 11, nos. 28–29, December 24, 1981, pp. 438–66.

11. Mary Aquin O'Neill, "The Mystery of Being Human Together," *Freeing Theology: The Essentials of Theology in Feminist Perspective*, ed. Catherine Mowry LaCugna, New York: HarperCollins 1993, pp. 139–59.

12. Cahill, "Marriage," p. 115.

13. Cahill, "Marriage," p. 115.

14. Michael A. Fahey provides a review of the concept in "The Christian Family as Domestic Church at Vatican II," *The Family*, Concilium 1995/4, ed. Lisa Sowle Cahill and Dietmar Mieth, Maryknoll, NY: Orbis Books 1995, pp. 85–92.

15. Fahey, "The Christian Family," p. 91.

16. Vatican II documents are cited from Austin Flannery, O.P. (ed.), *Vatican Council II, The Conciliar and Post Conciliar Documents*, Northport, NY: Costello Publishing Company 1987.

17. Norbert Mette, "The Family in the Teaching of the Magisterium," *The Family*, ed. Cahill and Mieth, p. 81.

18. Fahey, "The Christian Family," p. 91.

19. Cahill, "Sex, Gender, and the Common Good: Family," p. 160.

20. Leo XIII, *Arcanum, On Christian Marriage*, no. 26, in Claudia Carlen (ed.), *The Papal Encyclicals,* vol. 2, Wilmington, NC: McGrath Publishing 1981.

21. Pius XI, *Casti connubii* (Gerald Treacy, S.J., ed., *Five Great Encyclicals*, New York: Paulist Press 1939) follows the same order of goods. Michael J. Schuck, *That They Be One: The Social Teaching of the Papal Encyclicals 1740–1989*, Washington, DC: Georgetown University Press 1991, treats Leo XIII and Pius XI together (along with Benedict XV and Pius XII) in what he calls the Leonine Period: 1878–1958.

22. Leo XIII, *Arcanum,* no. 26.

23. Consider Leo XIII, *Immortale dei,* in Carlen (ed.), *The Papal Encyclicals,* pp. 107–20.

24. This point is emphasized by Pius XI in *Quadragesimo anno,* in Treacy, *Five Great Encyclicals,* nos. 76–80.

25. In *Rerum novarum* (Treacy, *Five Great Encyclicals*), Leo XIII will propose, for example, that rich and poor, capital and labor each has "its duties to the other, and especially the duties of justice" (no. 16). The duty of the laborer to work and to earn what is required to live is matched by the employer's duty to safeguard the worker's physical and spiritual well-being (nos. 32–3) and to pay wages based on standards of justice, "enough to support the wage-earner in reasonable and frugal comfort" (no. 34). The state, for its part, has a duty to maintain justice, and justice "demands that the interests of the poorer population be carefully watched over by the administration, so that they who contribute so largely to the advantage of the community may themselves share in the benefits they create, that being housed, clothed, and enabled to support life, they may find their existence less hard and more endurable." In this regard, the well-being of laborers ought to receive special consideration, "for it cannot but be good for the commonwealth to secure from misery those on whom it so largely depends" (no. 27).

26. John Paul II, *Letter to Families,* in *Origins: CNS Documentary Service* 23, no. 37, March 3, 1994, pp. 638–59; *Acta Apostolicae Sedis* 86, no. 11, November 7, 1994, pp. 868–925.

27. John Paul II uses "person" to spell out the meaning of human beings as made in the image and likeness of God. At its core, the "image" is not found primarily in reason or human creativity and capacity for self-making. God's image and likeness is, from the beginning, the person as a human being in community. Before creation, "the Creator withdraws as it were into himself, in order to seek the pattern and inspiration in the mystery of his Being, which is already here disclosed as the divine 'We'" (*Letter to Families,* no. 6).

28. Human parents participate with God, who "is present in human fatherhood and motherhood quite differently than he is present in all other instances of begetting 'on earth'." Parenthood gives life to a human being "for his or her own sake," and in doing so forms a community of persons and the heart of the civilization of love. "Bound up with the family is the genealogy of every individual: *the genealogy of the person*" (*Letter to Families,* no. 9). "*Through the family passes the primary current of the civilization of love,* which finds therein its social foundation" (*Letter to Families,* no. 15).

29. *Acta Apostolicae Sedis* 86, no. 11, November 7, 1994, p. 890.

30. See John A. Coleman, S.J., "Neither Liberal nor Conservative: The

Originality of Catholic Social Teaching," in Coleman (ed.), *One Hundred Years of Catholic Social Thought*, pp. 25–42.

31. Paul J. Weithman, "Complementarity and Equality in the Political Thought of Thomas Aquinas," *Theological Studies* 59, no. 2, June 1998, pp. 277–9.

32. In John Paul's personalism, the intrinsic form of complementarity and the inner character of our sexual difference establish an outer complement of roles and responsibilities. The union of husband and wife is not merely a union of individuals, but a completion of persons, in God's image, as male and female, in a non-identical other. John Paul II proposes that this completion in complementarity is not a single act but an ongoing enrichment and discovery of ourselves in reciprocal self-giving. The life-span of the union (not merely vows at the altar) is a sacrament of Christ and the church. As the origin of persons, the "conjugal communion constitutes the foundation on which is built the broader communion of family, of parents and children, of brothers and sisters with each other, of relatives and other members of the household" (*Familiaris consortio*, no. 21, in *Origins: CNS Documentary Service* 11, nos 28–29, December 24, 1981, pp. 438–66).

33. In *Evangelium vitae*, the Pope speaks of a "veritable 'culture of death'." Here, he refers to "powerful cultural, economic, and political currents which encourage an idea of society excessively concerned with efficiency." For the "culture of death," efficiency is a utilitarian value, where persons, once again, are defined by productivity and use and where usefulness and value coincide. Greater value is given to the powerful, and the life of the weak is considered meaningless. "A life which would require greater acceptance, love and care is considered useless or held to be an intolerable burden . . . [and] a person who, because of illness, handicap or, more simply, just by existing, compromises the well-being or lifestyle of those who are more favored tends to be looked upon as an enemy to be resisted or eliminated" (*Evangelium vitae*, no. 12, in *Origins: CNS Documentary Service* 24, no. 42 (April 6, 1995, pp. 1–24). In *Sollicitudo rei socialis*, John Paul takes up the same theme from a different angle. He refers to a civilization of consumption and consumerism, which makes people slaves of "possession" and immediate gratification (*Sollicitudo rei socialis*, no. 28, in *Origins: CNS Documentary Service* 17, no. 38, March 3, 1988, pp. 641–60). The civilization of consumption is sustained by its waste, where no things or people are considered to have lasting value in themselves.

34. John Paul II, *Centesimus annus*, nos. 22–29, in *Origins: CNS Documentary Service* 21, no. 1, May 16, 1991, pp. 1–24.

35. *Sollicitudo rei socialis*, in *Acta Apostolicae Sedis* 80, no. 5, May 7, 1988, p. 565.

36. John Paul II, *Sacred in All Its Forms*, ed. James V. Schall, S.J., Boston: Daughters of St. Paul 1984, p. 138.

37. John Paul II, *Sacred in All Its Forms*, pp. 92–3.

38. Cahill, "Marriage," p. 110.

Chapter 7

1. Chip Brown and Blaine Harden, "THE SCENE: Ice Hampers Rescue Attempts; Night Falls as Rescue Crews Attempt to Find Victims," *The Washington Post*, January 14, 1982, A1.

2. William McPherson, "The Crash: Looking at Courage," *The Washington Post*, January 17, 1982, D8.

3. McPherson, "The Crash: Looking as Courage," D8.

4. Paul Hendrickson, "Fame and Fate: Skutnik Copes with Celebrity," *The Washington Post*, June 28, 1982, C1.

5. Mary McGrory, "Lenny Skutnik Gave Us All a Lifeline," *The Washington Post*, January 17, 1982, D1.

6. Joseph Fitzmyer, *The Gospel According to Luke (X–XXIV)*, Anchor Bible 28A, Garden City, NY: Doubleday 1985, p. 878.

7. Gene Outka, "Universal Love and Impartiality," *The Love Commandments: Essays in Christian Ethics and Moral Philosophy*, ed. Edmund N. Santurri and William Werpehowski, Washington, DC: Georgetown University Press 1992), pp. 89–90.

8. Gene Outka, *Agape: An Ethical Analysis*, New Haven: Yale University Press 1972, pp. 13–14.

9. Outka, *Agape*, p. 260.

10. Outka, *Agape*, p. 282.

11. Outka, *Agape*, p. 9.

12. Outka, *Agape*, pp. 34–44.

13. Fitzmyer, *Luke*, p. 563; Hans Conzelmann, *The Theology of St. Luke*, trans. Geoffrey Buswell, Philadelphia: Fortress Press 1982, pp. 42–3.

14. Lawrence C. Becker, *Reciprocity*, New York: Routledge & Kegan Paul 1986.

15. Becker, *Reciprocity*, p. 74.

16. Becker, *Reciprocity*, pp. 140–1.

17. Becker, *Reciprocity*, p. 3.

18. Becker, *Reciprocity*, p. 138.

19. Becker, *Reciprocity*, p. 139.

20. The accusation that mutual love leads to treating God as lacking something is articulated by Gene Outka against defining love as communion, "Universal Love and Impartiality," pp. 88–9.

21. Thomas Aquinas, *Summa Theologiae* II.2, q. 23, Blackfriars edn. 34, trans. R. J. Batten, O.P., New York: McGraw-Hill Book Company 1975.

22. Becker, *Reciprocity*, p. 89.

23. Becker, *Reciprocity*, pp. 105–24.

24. Dorothy Day, *By Little and By Little*, ed. Robert Ellsberg, New York: Alfred A. Knopf 1984, p. 97.

25. Day, *By Little and By Little*, p. 95.

26. The same can be said in relation to Becker's second and third propositions, "Evil received (2) should not be returned with evil and (3) should not be resisted." If evil is a privation of good, then resisting evil, even passively, has a positive character – directed toward the reign of good and the transformation of common life – canceling out one form of social exchange in favor of another. Evil is received but not accepted and not returned. The teaching of Jesus in Matthew 5.38–48, on non-retaliation and the love of enemies, provides means to resist not only evil but also victim status. Turning the other cheek, walking an extra mile, loving your enemies, and praying for those who persecute you imply that one rejects a state of affairs – or the reigning grammar of social life. Each rejects established rules of exchange by performing what appears to be absurd.

I am knocked down by a blow. Within the grammar of retaliation, there are two options. Either I can strike back and I do, or I cannot and I am victim. I am victim because I have no means to challenge the evil done to me. If I resist evil without returning it, on the other hand, the social possibilities are changed. Either I can strike back and I do not, or I cannot and I do not. The evil done to me no longer determines or negates my agency. Violence loses value as social currency, so that it cannot be justified (even for me). The abused wife can no longer justify the violence done to her, by blaming herself, imagining that it will not happen again, convincing herself that "he really loves me," or attempting to change her own behavior so as to avoid his wrath and take on responsibility for the agency of his violence. Resisting evil is not being deferential to it. Violence itself becomes absurd and her husband's abuse is unmasked. It will become clear, at least to her, that either he must change or she must go. She has already inhabited a new language of social life. The challenge for the church is to provide the networks of support so that she has the means to enter a new life.

27. Stephen Post, *A Theory of Agape*, Lewisburg: Bucknell University Press 1990, p. 116.

28. See, for example, Richard Dawkins, *The Selfish Gene*, New York: Oxford University Press 1976; and Edith Wyshogrod, *Saints and Postmodernism: Revisioning Moral Philosophy*, Chicago: University of Chicago Press 1990.

29. This view of obligations to self are in line with Immanuel Kant's categorical imperative in his *Foundations of the Metaphysics of Morals*, trans. Lewis White Beck, New York: Macmillan Publishing Company 1959.

30. Post, *A Theory of Agape*, pp. 22–30.

31. Valerie Saiving, "The Human Situation," *Womanspirit Rising: A Feminist Reader in Religion*, ed. Carol P. Christ and Judith Plaskow, New York: Harper & Row 1979, pp. 25–42.

32. Robert Bellah, et al., *Habits of the Heart*, Berkeley: University of California Press 1985.

33. Post, *A Theory of Agape*, p. 54. Wyschogrod, *Saints and Post-modernism*, presents this kind of radically altruistic and ultimately anti-social moral exemplar. See her discussion of Nelson Mandela's imprisonment, pp. 151–5. Compare the community orientation of moral exemplars in Robert Inchausti's wonderfully written, *Ignorant Perfection of Ordinary People*, Albany, NY: State University of New York Press 1991.

34. Anders Nygren, *Agape and Eros*, trans. Philip S. Watson, New York: Harper & Row 1969, has been profoundly influential in this regard. For a representative sample, see pp. 115–33.

35. Herbert McCabe, *God Matters*, Springfield, IL: Templegate 1987, p. 17.

36. Cf. Nygren, *Agape and Eros*, pp. 532–5, 621–6.

37. Aquinas, *Summa Theologiae* II.2, q. 23.2.

38. William J. Hill, O.P., *The Three-Personed God: The Trinity as Mystery of Salvation*, Washington, DC: The Catholic University of America Press 1982, pp. 273–4.

39. Hill, *The Three-Personed God*, p. 286.

40. McCabe, *God Matters*, p. 20.

41. Post, *A Theory of Agape*, p. 54; cf. pp. 59–61.

42. Aquinas, *Summa Theologiae* II.2, q. 26.

43. Stephen J. Pope, *The Evolution of Altruism and the Ordering of Love*, Washington, DC: Georgetown University Press 1994, pp. 62, 64.

44. Pope, *The Evolution of Altruism*, pp. 35–6.

45. Pope, *The Evolution of Altruism*, p. 36.

46. Pope, *The Evolution of Altruism*, p. 34.

47. See Bernard Cooke, "Human Friendship: Basic Sacrament," in his *Sacraments and Sacramentality*, rev. edn. Mystic, CT: Twenty-Third Publications 1994, pp. 78–91. Also, William Johnson Everett, *Blessed Be the Bond*, Philadelphia: Fortress Press 1985.

48. Pope, *The Evolution of Altruism*, p. 39.

49. Charles Taylor, *Sources of the Self: The Making of the Modern Identity*, Cambridge, MA: Harvard University Press 1989. Alasdair MacIntyre, *A Short History of Ethics: A History of Moral Philosophy from the Homeric Age to the Twentieth Century*, 2nd edn. Notre Dame, IN: University of Notre Dame Press 1998.

50. Aquinas criticizes a similar view in *Summa Theologiae* II.2, q. 26.6.

51. Herbert McCabe, *What Is Ethics All About?*, Washington, DC: Corpus Books, 1969), pp. 110–13.

52. McCabe, *What Is Ethics All About?*, p. 113.

53. McCabe, *What Is Ethics All About?*, p. 145.

54. Stanley Hauerwas, *The Peaceable Kingdom*, Notre Dame: University of Notre Dame Press 1983, pp. 72–95.

55. Hauerwas, *The Peaceable Kingdom*, p. 76.

56. Post, *A Theory of Agape*, p. 116.

Chapter 8

1. The recent idea of "having a relationship" is noted by John Alan Lee in his "Ideologies of Lovestyles and Sexstyles," *Romantic Love and Sexual Behavior: Perspectives from the Social Sciences*, ed. Victor C. de Munck, Westport, CT: Praeger 1998, p. 63.

2. Mihaly Csikszentmihalyi and Eugene Rochberg-Halton, *The Meaning of Things: Domestic Symbols and the Self*, New York: Cambridge University Press 1981, pp. 146–71.

3. Csikszentmihalyi and Rochberg-Halton, *The Meaning of Things*, p. 147.

4. Csikszentmihalyi and Rochberg-Halton, *The Meaning of Things*, pp. 148–9.

5. Csikszentmihalyi and Rochberg-Halton, *The Meaning of Things*, p. 150.

6. Mihaly Csikszentmihalyi, *Flow: The Psychology of Optimal Experience*, New York: Harper & Row 1990, pp. 43–70.

7. Csikszentmihalyi and Rochberg-Halton, *The Meaning of Things*, p. 84.

8. Csikszentmihalyi and Rochberg-Halton, *The Meaning of Things*, p. 84.

9. Csikszentmihalyi, *Flow*, pp. 45–6.

10. Csikszentmihalyi, *Flow*, pp. 48–52.

11. Csikszentmihalyi and Rochberg-Halton, *The Meaning of Things*, p. 155.

12. Csikszentmihalyi and Rochberg-Halton, *The Meaning of Things*, p. 158.

13. Csikszentmihalyi and Rochberg-Halton, *The Meaning of Things*, p. 162.

14. Csikszentmihalyi and Rochberg-Halton, *The Meaning of Things*, p. 163.

15. See Theodore Mackin, S.J., *What Is Marriage?* New York: Paulist Press 1982, pp. 332–3.

16. Germain Grisez, et al., *The Way of the Lord Jesus*, Vol. 2: *Living a*

Christian Life, Quincy, IL: Franciscan Press 1993, pp. 555–69.

17. *Gaudium et spes, Pastoral Constitution on the Church in the Modern World*, in *Vatican Council II, The Conciliar and Post Conciliar Documents*, ed. Austin Flannery, O.P., Northport, NY: Costello Publishing Co. 1987, no. 49.

18. Brennan R. Hill, "Reformulating the Sacramental Theology of Marriage," *Christian Marriage and Family: Contemporary Theological and Pastoral Perspectives*, ed. Michael G. Lawler and William P. Roberts, Collegeville, MN: The Liturgical Press 1996, pp. 12–13.

19. Cf. Thomas Aquinas, *Summa Theologiae* II.2, q. 108, Blackfriars edn. 42, New York: McGraw-Hill 1966.

20. Augustine, "The Good of Marriage," *Saint Augustine, Treatises on Marriage and Other Subjects, The Fathers of the Church* 27, ed. Roy J. Deferrari, New York: Fathers of the Church, Inc. 1955, ch. 9.9; *Patrologia Latina* 40, ed. J. P. Migne, Parisiis 1841, pp. 374–96.

21. See Grisez, *Living a Christian Life*, p. 558.

22. Peter Brown, *The Body and Society*, New York: Columbia University Press 1988, p. 401.

23. "The Good of Marriage," chs. 17–23.

24. Augustine, *Confessions*, in *The Works of Saint Augustine: A Translation for the 21st Century* I/1, trans. Maria Boulding, O.S.B., Hyde Park, NY: New City Press 1997, ch. 4.8 (4.13).

25. Cf. "The Good Marriage," chs 3, 7, 8, 14, 16; Brown, *The Body and Society*, pp. 402–3.

26. I am presenting the main points of a study on friendship by Marie Aquinas McNamara, O.P., *Friends and Friendship for Saint Augustine*, Staten Island, NY: Society of St. Paul 1964.

27. Cicero, "Laelius De Amicitia," *De Senectute, De Amicitia, De Divinatione, with an English Translation*, trans. William Armistead Falconer, The Loeb Classical Library, Cambridge, MA: Harvard University Press 1964, pp. 127–9, 163–4.

28. Cicero, "Laelius De Amicitia," pp. 177–9.

29. Augustine, *Confessions*, 4.4.9.

30. Cf. William J. Collinge, "Christian Community and Christian Understanding: Developments in Augustine's Thought," *Catholic Authority and Dialogue with the World*, The Annual Publication of the College Theology Society 1986, ed. Bernard P. Prusak, Lanham, MD: University Press of America 1988, pp. 24–40; Lewis Ayres, "Augustine on God as Love and Love as God," *Pro Ecclesia* 5, no. 4, Fall 1996, pp. 470–87.

31. *Homilies on the First Epistle of John*, Nicene and Post-Nicene Fathers X, ed. Philip Schaff, Grand Rapids: Eerdmans 1983, 7 (524). Cited in McNamara, *Friends and Friendship*, p. 233.

32. Michael G. Lawler, *Marriage and Sacrament: A Theology of*

Christian Marriage, Collegeville, MN: The Liturgical Press 1993. Lawler is a prominent writer and educator on both marriage and sacrament, and he is the director of the Center for Marriage and Family, Creighton University, Omaha, NE.

33. Lawler, *Marriage and Sacrament*, p. 1.
34. Lawler, *Marriage and Sacrament*, p. 2.
35. Lawler, *Marriage and Sacrament*, p. 2.
36. Aristotle, *Nicomachean Ethics*, chs 8 and 9.
37. Cicero rejects the notion that friendship ought to be sought "for the sake of defense and aid" (although defense and aid are included as a benefit). If mutual aid were the foundation, then "those least endowed with firmness of character and strength of body [would] have the greatest longing for friendship . . . helpless women, more than men, [would] seek its shelter, the poor more than the rich, and the unfortunate more than those who are accounted fortunate." Cicero, "Laelius De Amicitia," pp. 157–9.
38. Augustine, *City of God*, bk 19, ch. 27.

Chapter 9

1. *The New Cana Manual*, ed. Walter Imbiorski, Chicago: The Cana Conference of Chicago 1957, pp. 161–2. Also see, Jeffrey M. Burns, *Disturbing the Peace: A History of the Christian Family Movement*, Notre Dame: University of Notre Dame Press 1999, p. 162.
2. *The New Cana Manual*, pp. 159–61.
3. Michael G. Lawler, *Marriage and Sacrament: A Theology of Christian Marriage*, Collegeville, MN: The Liturgical Press 1993, pp. 41–7. I take Lawler's treatment of Ephesians 5 to be representative. He shows that the hierarchy of the passage is undone by the mutual subjection of husband and wife along with the identity of the husband with the lowering of Christ. However, his interpretative strategies deal with the body metaphor in isolation from the New Testament as a whole.
4. Melvin Konner, *The Tangled Wing: Biological Constraints of the Human Spirit*, New York: Holt, Rinehart, & Winston 1982, pp. 106–26.
5. Rosemarie Putnam Tong, *Feminist Thought: A More Comprehensive Introduction*, 2nd edn. Boulder, CO: Westview Press 1998; Graham Ward, *Theology and Contemporary Critical Theory*, 2nd edn. New York: St. Martin's Press 2000; Fergus Kerr, *Immortal Longings: Versions of Transcending Humanity*, Notre Dame: University of Notre Dame Press 1997.
6. Thomas Aquinas, *Summa Theologiae* I.41.1, Blackfriars edn. 7, New York: McGraw-Hill Book Company 1976; I.99.2, Blackfriars edn. 13, 1964.
7. William Johnson Everett, *Blessed Be the Bond*, Philadelphia: Fortress Press 1985.

8. Everett, *Blessed Be the Bond*, p. 115.

9. Once again, I am thinking in terms of John Milbank's "On Complex Space," *The Word Made Strange: Theology, Language, Culture*, Oxford: Blackwell 1997.

10. Julia Kristeva, "Women's Time," *The Kristeva Reader*, ed. Toril Moi, New York: Columbia University Press 1986; *Revolution in Poetic Language,* trans. Margaret Waller, New York: Columbia University Press 1984.

11. Zillah R. Eisenstein, *The Female Body and the Law,* Berkeley: University of California Press 1988; See Susan Okin's commentary on Robert Nozick in *Justice, Gender, and the Family*, New York: Basic Books 1989.

12. Carole Pateman, *The Sexual Contract*, Stanford: Stanford University Press 1988.

13. Sharon Hays, *The Cultural Contradictions of Motherhood*, New Haven: Yale University Press 1996.

14. Thomas J. McCarthy, "Stay-at-Home Dad: 'My life is a series of foibles and episodes of comic inadequacy,' " *America* 182, no. 6, Feb. 26, 2000, p. 6.

15. Julie A. Matthaei, *An Economic History of Women in America: Women's Work, the Sexual Division of Labor, and the Development of Capitalism*, New York: Schocken Books 1982; Christine Stansell, *City of Women: Sex and Class in New York 1789–1860*, Chicago: University of Illinois Press 1987.

16. Christopher Lasch, *Haven in a Heartless World*, New York: Basic Books 1977.

17. Lisa Sowle Cahill, *Between the Sexes: Foundations for a Christian Ethics of Sexuality*, Philadelphia: Fortress Press 1985, p. 84.

18. Richard B. Hays, *The Moral Vision of the New Testament*, New York: HarperCollins 1996, p. 52.

19. Elisabeth Schüssler Fiorenza, *In Memory of Her,* New York: Crossroad 1983, pp. 226–33.

20. Phil. 4.2–3; Rom. 16.1–16 includes several women, including Junia and Andronicus (who might be her husband). Both are counted "prominent among the apostles."

21. Richard B. Hays, *The Moral Vision of the New Testament*, p. 132.

22. Richard B. Hays, *The Moral Vision of the New Testament*, p. 132.

23. Richard B. Hays, *The Moral Vision of the New Testament*, p. 132.

24. Elizabeth Achtemeier, *The Committed Marriage*, Philadelphia: Westminster Press 1976.

25. Carolyn Osiek, "The New Testament and the Family," *The Family*, Concilium 1995/4, ed. Lisa Sowle Cahill and Dietmar Mieth, Maryknoll, NY: Orbis Books 1995, p. 8.

Chapter 10

    1. "Nephew Payments," *Morning Edition*, National Public Radio (www.npr.org), December 3, 2003.

    2. Julie Hanlon Rubio, *A Christian Theology of Marriage and Family*, New York: Paulist Press 2003, pp. 54–5, 148–9.

    3. Elinor B. Rosenberg, *The Adoption Life Cycle: The Children and Their Families Through the Years*, New York: The Free Press 1992, p. 10.

    4. Rosenberg, *The Adoption Life Cycle*, pp. 10–11.

    5. Maureen A. Sweeney, "Between Sorrow and Happy Endings: A New Paradigm of Adoption," *Yale Journal of Law and Feminism*, vol. 2, 1990, pp. 350–2.

    6. Stephen G. Post, "Adoption Theologically Considered," *Journal of Religious Ethics*, vol. 25, no. 1, Spring 1997, p. 149.

    7. Stephen G. Post, "The Moral Meaning of Relinquishing an Infant: Reflections on Adoption," *Thought*, vol. 67, no. 265, June 1992, pp. 209–10, 213–15.

    8. Kathy S. Stolley, "Statistics on Adoption in the United States," *The Future of Children*, vol. 3, no. 1, Spring 1993, p. 29.

    9. Stolley, "Statistics on Adoption in the United States," p. 32.

    10. Post, "Adoption Theologically Considered," p. 158. Post draws his historical perspective from John Boswell, *The Kindness of Strangers*, New York: Random House 1988.

    11. Post, "Adoption Theologically Considered," p. 151.

    12. Anne B. Brodzinsky, "Surrendering an Infant for Adoption: The Birthmother Experience," in *The Psychology of Adoption*, ed. David M. Brodzinsky and Marshall D. Schechter, New York: Oxford University Press 1990, pp. 295–315.

    13. Matthew McGuire, Personal Interview on Adoption and Adoption Policy, American University, Washington D.C., February 1, 2004.

    14. Annette Baran and Reuben Pannor, "Open Adoption," in *The Psychology of Adoption*, p. 317.

    15. Ann Hartman and Joan Laird, "Family Treatment After Adoption: Common Themes," in *The Psychology of Adoption*, pp. 221–39.

    16. Peter L. Benson, et al., *Growing Up Adopted: A Portrait of Adolescents and Their Families*, Minneapolis: The Search Institute 1994, cited in Post, "Adoption Theologically Considered," pp. 164–5.

    17. Benson, et al., cited in Post, "Adoption Theologically Considered," p. 164.

    18. Jay D. Teachman, Lucky M. Tedrow, and Kyle Crowder, "The Changing Demography of America's Families," *Journal of Marriage and the Family*, vol. 62, no. 4, November 2000; Sheila Fitzgerald and Andrea H. Beller, "Educational Attainment of Children From Single-Parent Families,"

Demography, vol. 25, no. 2, May 1988, pp. 221–34.

19. Michael G. Lawler, "Marriage and the Sacrament of Marriage," in *Christian Marriage and Family: Contemporary Theological and Pastoral Perspectives*, ed. Michael G. Lawler and William P. Roberts, Collegeville, MN: The Liturgical Press 1996, p. 33.

20. Lawler, "Marriage and the Sacrament of Marriage," p. 30. Lawler develops this definition from the 1983 Code of Canon Law and *Gaudium et spes*, The Pastoral Constitution on the Church in the Modern World (1965).

21. Lawler, "Marriage and the Sacrament of Marriage," p. 30.

22. David Matzko McCarthy, "Becoming One Flesh: Marriage, Remarriage, and Sex," in *The Blackwell Companion to Christian Ethics*, ed. Stanley Hauerwas and Samuel Wells, Oxford: Blackwell Publishing 2004, p. 283. See John Paul II, *Familiaris consortio*, in *Origins: CNS Documentary Service* 11, nos 28–29, December 24, 1981, pp. 438–66.

23. Jo-Ann Heaney-Hunter, "Living the Baptismal Commitment in Sacramental Marriage," in *Christian Marriage and Family: Contemporary Theological and Pastoral Perspectives*, pp. 106–24.

24. Heaney-Hunter, "Living the Baptismal Commitment in Sacramental Marriage," p. 115.

25. The next three paragraphs are a reworking of two paragraphs in David Matzko McCarthy, "Becoming One Flesh: Marriage, Remarriage, and Sex," p. 282.

26. Richard B. Hays, *The Moral Vision of the New Testament: A Contemporary Introduction of New Testament Ethics*, New York: HarperCollins 1996, pp. 352–7.

27. McCarthy, "Becoming One Flesh: Marriage, Remarriage, and Sex," p. 282.

28. Julie Hanlon Rubio, *A Christian Theology of Marriage and Family*, New York: Paulist Press 2003, pp. 26–9, 33.

29. Lisa Sowle Cahill, "Marriage: Institution, Relationship, Sacrament," in *One Hundred Years of Catholic Social Thought: Celebration and Challenge*, ed. John A. Coleman, Maryknoll: Orbis Press 1991, p. 117, cited in Rubio, *A Christian Theology of Marriage and Family*, p. 39.

30. Anthony Giddens, *The Transformation of Intimacy: Sexuality, Love, and Eroticism in Modern Societies*, Stanford: Stanford University Press 1992, p. 58.

31. Adrian Thatcher, *Living Together and Christian Ethics*, Cambridge: Cambridge University Press 2002, pp. 4–8.

32. Thatcher, *Living Together and Christian Ethics*, p. 5. The point is confirmed by the Secretariat for Family, Laity, Women and Youth, *Marriage Preparation and Cohabiting Couples*, Washington, DC: United States Conference of Catholic Bishops 1999, <www.usccb.org/laity/marriage/cohabiting.htm>.

33. Lee A. Lillard, Michael J. Brien, and Linda J. Waite, "Premarital Cohabitation and Subsequent Marital Dissolution: A Matter of Self-Selection?," *Demography*, vol. 32, no. 3, August 1995, p. 438.

34. Lillard, et al., "Premarital Cohabitation and Subsequent Marital Dissolution," p. 438.

35. Susan L. Brown and Alan Booth, "Cohabitation versus Marriage: A Comparison of Relationship Quality," *Journal of Marriage and Family*, vol. 58, no. 3, August 1996, p. 674.

36. Frances K. Goldscheider and Gayle Kaufman, "Fertility and Commitment: Bringing Men Back In," *Population and Development Review*, vol. 22, *Supplement: Fertility in the United States*, 1996, p. 89.

37. Goldscheider and Kaufman, "Fertility and Commitment," p. 89.

38. Goldscheider and Kaufman, "Fertility and Commitment," p. 89.

39. Wendy D. Manning and Daniel T. Lichter, "Parental Cohabitation and Children's Economic Well-Being," *Journal of Marriage and Family*, vol. 58, no. 4, November 1996, pp. 1008–9.

40. Thatcher, *Living Together and Christian Ethics*, pp. 15–17; Secretariat for Family, Laity, Women and Youth, *Marriage Preparation and Cohabiting Couples*, p. 13.

41. Brown and Booth, "Cohabitation versus Marriage," p. 677; Manning and Lichter, "Parental Cohabitation and Children's Economic Well-Being," p. 1009.

42. Lillard, "Premarital Cohabitation and Subsequent Marital Dissolution," p. 439.

43. Lillard, "Premarital Cohabitation and Subsequent Marital Dissolution," pp. 439–40.

44. Lillard, "Premarital Cohabitation and Subsequent Marital Dissolution," p. 455.

45. Kathleen Burge, "Gays have right to marry, SJC says in historic ruling, Legislature given 180 days to change law," *The Boston Globe*, November 19, 2003, A1. "The Gay Marriage Ruling, Court Opinions: Excerpts, Majority Opinions," *The Boston Globe*, November 19, 2003, B8.

46. Scott Barclay and Shaunna Fisher, "The States and the Differing Impetus for Divergent Paths of Same-Sex Marriage, 1990–2001," *The Policy Studies Journal*, vol. 31, no. 3, 2003, p. 348.

47. Donald M. Lowe, *The Body in Late-Capitalism USA*, Durham: Duke University Press 1995, pp. 127–37.

48. John D'Emilio, *Sexual Politics, Sexual Communities: The Making of a Homosexual Minority in the United States 1940–1970*, Chicago: University of Chicago Press 1983, p. 248.

49. Dennis Altman, *The Homosexualization of America, The Americanization of the Homosexual*, New York: St. Martin's Press 1982.

50. The TV show features "Five gay men, out to make over the world –

one straight guy at a time. They are the Fab Five: an elite team of gay men dedicated to extolling the simple virtues of style, taste, and class. Each week their mission is to transform a style-deficient and culture-deprived straight man from drab to fab in each of their respective categories: fashion, food & wine, interior design, grooming and culture." <http://www.bravotv.com/ Queer_Eye_for_the_Straight_Guy/>.

51. Laura Sessions Stepp, "Partway Gay?," *The Washington Post*, January 4, 2004, D1. Also see Lisa Diamond, "What does Sexual Orientation Orient? A Biobehavioral Model Distinguishing Love and Sexual Desire," *Psychological Review*, vol. 110, no. 1, 2003, pp. 173–92, and Diamond, "Was It a Phase? Young Women's Relinquishment of Lesbian/Bisexual Identities Over a 5-Year Period," *Journal of Personality and Social Psychology*, vol. 84, no. 2, 2003, pp. 352–64.

52. Also see Edward Ingebretsen, "Gone Shopping: The Commercialization of Same-Sex Desire," *Journal of Gay, Lesbian, and Bisexual Identity*, vol. 4, no. 2, 1999, pp. 125–47.

53. Altman, *The Homosexualization of America*, pp. 98–9.

54. Christopher Carrington, *No Place Like Home: Relationships and Family Life Among Lesbian and Gay Men*, Chicago: University of Chicago Press 1999.

55. National Catholic Bishop's Committee on Marriage and Family, *Always Our Children: A Pastoral Message to Parents of Homosexual Children*, Washington, DC: United States Catholic Conference, Inc. 1997.

56. See David F. Greenberg, *The Construction of Homosexuality*, Chicago: University of Chicago Press 1988.

57. Robin Scroggs, *New Testament and Homosexuality*, Philadelphia: Fortress Press 1983.

58. Richard B. Hays, *The Moral Vision of the New Testament*, New York: HarperCollins 1996.

59. Andrew Sullivan, *Virtually Normal*, New York: Alfred A. Knopf 1995.

60. Eugene F. Rogers, *Sexuality and the Christian Body*, Oxford: Blackwell Publisher 1999.

61. Jacques Ellul, *Ethics of Freedom*, trans. Geoffrey W. Bromiley, Grand Rapids: Eerdmans Publishing 1976, pp. 383–4.

62. John Paul II, *Familiaris consortio*, in *Origins: CNS Documentary Service* 11, December 24, 1981.

63. Philip S. Keane, *Sexual Morality: A Catholic Perspective*, New York: Paulist Press 1977.

64. "Primates say US gay bishop will split church," *TimesOnline*, October 16, 2003, <http://www.timesonline.co.uk>.

65. Robert N. Bellah, "The Church as a Context for the Family," in *Perspectives on Marriage*, ed. Kieran Scott and Michael Warren, New

York: Oxford University Press 1993, p. 162.

66. This section on domestic violence draws from a chapter on "Love in Fundamental Moral Theology," *Christian Living: Fundamental Issues and New Directions in Moral Theology*, ed. James Keating, New York: Paulist Press forthcoming.

67. The statistic is from a Commonwealth Fund survey in 1998, cited by the National Domestic Violence Hotline, "What is Domestic Violence?," <http://www.ndvh.org/dvInfo.html>.

68. Callie Marie Rennison, "Intimate Partner Violence and Age of Victim," United States Department of Justice: Bureau of Justice Statistics 2001, <http://www.ojp.usdoj.gov/bjs/pub/pdf/ipva99.pdf>, pp. 1–2. Put another way, "of the women who reported being raped and/or physically assaulted since the age of 18, three quarters (76 percent) were victimized by a current or former boyfriend." Patricia Tjaden and Nancy Thoennes, "Prevalence, Incidence, and Consequences of Violence Against Women: Findings From the National Violence Against Women Survey," United States Department of Justice: National Institute of Justice, Centers for Disease Control and Prevention, November 1998, <http://ncjrs.org/pdffiles/172837.pdf>, p. 12.

69. Al Miles, *Domestic Violence: What Every Pastor Needs to Know*, Minneapolis: Fortress Press 2000.

70. Marie Fortune, *Sexual Violence*, New York: Pilgrim Press 1983.

71. Thatcher, *Living Together and Christian Ethics*, p. 23.

72. Kirk R. Williams, "Social Sources of Marital Violence and Deterrence: Testing an Integrated Theory of Assaults between Partners," *Journal of Marriage and Family*, vol. 54, no. 3, August 1992, pp. 620–9.

73. Laura Sanchez and Constance T. Gager, "Hard Living, Perceived Entitlement to a Great Marriage, and Marital Dissolution," *Journal of Marriage and Family*, vol. 62, no. 3, August 2000, pp. 708–22.

74. The point about dissatisfaction is made by Sanchez and Gager in "Hard Living, Perceived Entitlement to a Great Marriage, and Marital Dissolution."

75. Daniel Coleman, "Want a Happy Marriage? Learn to Fight a Good Fight," in *Perspectives on Marriage*, ed. Scott and Warren, pp. 254–8.

76. Jack Dominian, *Make or Break: A Guide to Marriage Counselling*, Wilmington: Michael Glazier 1985.

77. David Matzko McCarthy, "Generational Conflict: Continuity and Change," in *Growing Old in Christ*, ed. Stanley Hauerwas, Carole Bailey Stoneking, Keith G. Meador, and David Cloutier, Grand Rapids: Eerdmans Publishing Company 2003, p. 234.

78. Joel James Shuman, "The Last Gift: The Elderly, the Church, and the Gift of a Good Death," in *Growing Old in Christ*, ed. Hauerwas, et al., p. 153–4.

79. D. Stephen Long, "The Language of Death: Theology and Economics in Conflict," in *Growing Old in Christ*, p. 131.

Chapter 11

1. "In the 50 largest U.S. cities, an average of 43 percent of all births are by unmarried women." Some of this number represents women who are not married but cohabitate. One effect of cohabitation is that boyfriends who leave are not legally (or socially) bound to support their children. "The poverty rate for single-parent families headed by a never-married mother is 55 percent, compared to 35 percent for families headed by a divorced or separated mother." Rebecca Gardyn, "And Baby Makes Two," *American Demographics*, March 2000.

2. Albert Gore, *Earth in Balance: Ecology and the Human Spirit*, Boston: Houghton Mifflin Company 2000.

3. Joby Warrick, "Gore's Environmental Stake, White House Stance on Global Warming Could Seriously Affect Political Climate Too," *Washington Post*, October 21, 1997, A4.

4. Paul Bedard, "Third World Birth Control Tops Gore's List of 'Greenhouse' Cures, Warming Blamed on Overpopulation," *The Washington Times*, October 2, 1997.

5. Bedard, "Third World Birth Control."

6. News stories on the 1994 conference, in Cairo, on population and development raised issues of birth control in the context of stories on the politics of the Vatican. Birth control is not interesting, but seemingly irrational (religious) efforts to oppose it are, apparently, fascinating.

7. Letter to *The Washington Times* on October 12, 1997.

8. U.S. Bureau of the Census, International Data Base.

9. Bedard, "Third World Birth Control."

10. In 1995, there were just about 76 million children nineteen years old and under (U.S. Department of Commerce). There were close to 135 million passenger cars and over 200 million total vehicles (American Automobile Manufacturers Association).

11. Bill McKibben, *The End of Nature*, New York: Doubleday 1999, p. 13.

12. Germaine Greer, *Sex and Destiny*, New York: Harper & Row 1984, pp. 480–1.

13. John and Sheila Kippley, *The Art of Natural Family Planning*, 4th edn. Cincinnati: Couple to Couple League International 1996, pp. 139–54.

14. Germaine Greer, *The Whole Woman*, New York: Alfred A. Knopf 1999, pp. 23–61.

15. Greer, *Sex and Destiny*, pp. 1–35.

16. Paula Allen-Meares and Eric M. Roberts, "Public Assistance as

Family Policy: Closing off Options for Poor Families," *Social Work* 40, no. 4, July 1995, pp. 559–65; Susan L. Thomas, "Women, Welfare, Reform and the Preservation of a Myth," *The Social Science Journal* 34, no. 3, 1997, pp. 351–68; Rosanna Hertz and Faith I. T. Ferguson, "Childcare Choice and the Constraints in the United States: Social Class, Race, and the Influence of Family Views," *Journal of Comparative Family Studies* 27, Summer 1996, pp. 249–80.

17. Bill McKibben, *Maybe One: A Case for Smaller Families*, New York: Plume 1999.

18. Intensive one-on-one parenting is the logic behind such manuals as Arlene Eisenberg and Sandee Hathaway, *What to Expect: The Toddler Years*, New York: Workman Publishing Company 1996.

19. Sharon Hays, *The Cultural Contradictions of Motherhood*, New Haven: Yale University Press 1996.

20. See Zygmunt Bauman's account of risk management as an economy in *Postmodern Ethics*, Oxford: Blackwell 1993.

21. James U. McNeal and Chyon-Hwa Yeh, "Born to Shop," *American Demographics* 15, no. 6, June 1993, pp. 34–40. McNeal's work (various books and articles) on the children's market is not a critique of the market but information and analysis given so that businesses can more effectively market to children. See, for instance, his *The Kids Market, Myths and Realities*, Ithaca, NY: Paramount Market Publishing, Inc. 1999.

22. Janet Bodnar, "How Kids 'Trick' Their Parents," *Kiplinger's Personal Finance Magazine* 53, no. 7, July 1999, p. 101.

23. James U. McNeal, "Tapping the Three Kids' Markets," *American Demographics* 20, no. 4, April 1998, p. 38.

24. McNeal, "Tapping the Three Kids' Markets," p. 39.

25. James U. McNeal, "Growing Up in the Market," *American Demographics* 14, no. 10 (October 1992), p. 48.

26. Bruce Crumley, et al., "Childhood's End? More than ever, advertisers are targeting campaigns at children as a way to tap parental spending power," *Time International* 154, no. 4, August 2, 1999, p. 36. Market analysts are developing a psychology and sociology of consumption, becoming experts in how to tap our buying impulses. See "Psychology's Child Abuse," *Psychology Today* 33, no. 2, March 2000, p. 13.

27. Jean Kilbourne is best known for films of her lectures on women and advertising, "Killing Us Softly." More recently she has published *Deadly Persuasion: Why Women and Girls Must Fight the Addictive Power of Advertising*, New York: Free Press 1999.

28. "According to Mike Searles, president of Kids 'R' Us, 'If you own this child at an early age, you can own this child for years to come. Companies are saying, Hey, I want to own the kid younger and younger'" (Kilbourne, *Deadly Persuasion*, p. 44).

29. Jill Wynns, "Yes: Selling Students to Advertisers Sends the Wrong Messages in the Classroom," *Advertising Age*, June 7, 1999, p. 26; Eli Lambert, Leah Plunkett, and Trish Wotowiec, "*Just the Facts* about Advertising and Marketing to Children," Center for a New American Dream 1999; "K-III's 'Channel One', the TV Show that Parents Can't Watch, Cheats School Kids," *Business Wire*, January 22, 1997.

30. Wendell Berry, *Sex, Economy, Freedom, and Community*, New York: Pantheon Books 1993.

31. Sex and gender have a political function. The "gay community" for instance, is an abstraction if not a political lobby. See John D'Emilio, *Sexual Politics, Sexual Communities: The Making of a Homosexual Minority in the United States 1940–1970*, Chicago: University of Chicago Press 1983. The people represented by the term "gay" are not a "community" in any usual sense, not sharing a place, common endeavors, goods, or practices. The "gay community" is made on the basis of legal rights and demands. In a more "traditional" example, Mother's Day 2000, in Washington, DC, witnessed its first Million Mom March. "We are giving birth to a movement," announced Rosie O'Donnell, and then she went about to denounce gun violence and the politics of the National Rifle Association (Susan Levine, "Rally Opposing Gun Violence Draws Thousands," *The Washington Post*, May 15, 2000, A1).

This is just the way gender and sexual politics work in the context of contractual individualism. One's identity becomes public through interest group politics, so that O'Donnell speaks of a "movement" coming to be as though she and the other mothers had been asocial up to that point. Sexual identity is abstracted from a local network and a setting of day-to-day practices so that it might become "public". After mothers become a lobby, they have a unified movement, even though everyone knows that many mothers do not have a stand on the issue, while others are members, or at least lovingly support members of the National Rifle Association. Their local or family attachments aside, motherhood is taken into contractual discourse and becomes the basis for political rights and demands. Watch any news program or talk show on sex, and you will see someone stating that his or her sexual expression is a right – swinging, cross-dressing, or whatever. In the household, sexual practices are not conceived in terms of rights as much as a set of roles, set in turn within particular relationships and goods of common life. There is no freestanding sexual identity; sexual expression, that is, is part of an ongoing conversation.

32. Patricia Chisholm, "For Infertile Couples, Heartache and Hope," *Maclean's*, December 8, 1999, p. 58.

33. In matters of reproduction, entitlement and consumption seem to coalesce. We ought to be able to have our own children because the market and technology make them widely available. The technological possibilities

imply entitlement and choice. A different, more striking example is provided by photographer Ron Harris who, apparently, is famous for his career in softcore pornography. He is called "the granddaddy of softcore" by *Playboy* magazine. Since he is already in the business of selling body images, Harris runs an egg and sperm auction on his web site www.ronsangels.com ("Ron's Angels.com"). He promotes the auction by means of eugenic arguments – creating more beautiful offspring. Beauty, Harris explains, almost insures personal success. "If you could increase the chance of reproducing beautiful children, and thus giving them an advantage in society, wouldn't you?" (Egg Auction, "Model" page, www.ronsangels.com). It makes sense that some-one already in the consumer industry of sex, would branch out to the commerce of reproduction. The consumers are ready to buy.

34. John Paul II, *Letter to Families*, February 2, 1994, no. 9. See Chapter 4 above.

35. See the different kinds of arguments concerning the end of procre-ation in "Contraception: A Symposium," *First Things* 88, December 1998, pp. 17–29.

36. Paul VI, "Pope Paul VI to the Teams of Our Lady (Rome, May 4, 1970)," nos 11–12, *Why Humanae Vitae Was Right: A Reader*, ed. Janet Smith, San Francisco: Ignatius Press 1993, pp. 87–103.

37. Paul VI, *Humanae vitae*, July 25, 1968, no. 16.

38. Paul VI, *Humanae vitae*, nos 2, 3, 17.

39. Bernard Häring, "The Inseparability of the Unitive-Procreative Functions on the Marital Act," *Contraception: Authority and Dissent*, ed. Charles E. Curran, New York: Herder & Herder 1969, pp. 187–92.

40. Häring's disagreements with magisterial teaching hinge on the relation, assumed necessary in *Humanae vitae*, between the natural and the social. Häring assumes, we could say, the priority of the social or inter-personal over the natural. Paul VI conceives of the natural as the landscape of social relations. Paul VI's arguments against artificial contraception are consistent with his arguments about social and economic life in *Populorum Progressio: On the Development of Peoples,* March 26, 1967.

41. John Paul II, *Letter to Families*, nos 9–10.

Conclusion

1. Rodney Clapp, "From Family Values to Family Virtues," *Virtues and Practices in the Christian Tradition: Christian Ethics After MacIntyre*, ed. Nancey Murphy, Brad Kallenberg, and Mark Thiessen Nation, Harrisburg, PA: Trinity Press International 1997, p. 201.

2. Andrew Greeley and Mary Greeley Durkin, *How to Save the Catholic Church*, New York: Viking Penguin 1984, pp. 105–29.

3. Michael G. Lawler, *Marriage and Sacrament: A Theology of Christian Marriage*, Collegeville, MN: The Liturgical Press 1993, p. 12.

Bibliography

Achtemeier, Elizabeth, *The Committed Marriage*, Philadelphia: Westminster Press 1976.

Aldrich, Nelson W., *Old Money: The Mythology of Wealth in America*, New York: Allworth Press 1996.

Allen-Meares, Paula, and Roberts, Eric M. "Public Assistance as Family Policy: Closing off Options for Poor Families," *Social Work* 40, no. 4, July 1995, pp. 559–65.

Altman, Dennis, *The Homosexualization of America, The Americanization of the Homosexual*, New York: St. Martin's Press 1982.

Aquinas, Thomas, *Summa Theologiae: Latin Text and English Translation*, Blackfriars edn. New York: McGraw-Hill Book Company 1964–80.

Ariès, Philippe, and Béjin, André (eds), *Western Sexuality: Practice and Precept in Past and Present Times*, London: Basil Blackwell 1985.

Augustine, *City of God*, trans. Demetrius B. Zema and Gerald G. Walsh, Fathers of the Church 8, 14, 24, New York: Fathers of the Church, Inc. 1950.

_____, *Confessions*, trans. Maria Boulding, O.S.B., *The Works of Saint Augustine: A Translation for the 21st Century* I/1, Hyde Park, NY: New City Press 1997.

_____, *De bono coniugali*, Patrologia Latina 40, pp. 374–96, ed. J. P. Migne, Parisiis 1845.

_____, *Treatises on Marriage and Other Subjects*, trans. Roy J. Deferrari, Fathers of the Church 27, New York: Fathers of the Church, Inc. 1955.

Ayres, Lewis, "Augustine on God as Love and Love as God," *Pro Ecclesia* 5, no. 4, Fall 1996, pp. 470–87.

Barclay, Scott, and Fisher, Shaunna, "The States and the Differing Impetus for Divergent Paths of Same-Sex Marriage, 1990–2001," *The Policy Studies Journal*, vol. 31, no. 3, 2003.

Barrett, Michele, and McIntosh, Mary, *The Anti-Social Family*, 2nd edn. New York: Verso 1991.

Bauman, Zygmunt, *Postmodern Ethics*, Oxford: Blackwell 1993.

Becker, Lawrence C., *Reciprocity*, New York: Routledge & Kegan Paul 1986.

Bellah, Robert N., et al., *Habits of the Heart*, Berkeley: University of California Press 1985.

Berger, Peter, *Invitation to Sociology: A Humanistic Perspective*, New York: Anchor Books 1963.

Berry, Wendell, *Home Economics*, San Francisco: North Point Press 1987.

_____, *Sex, Economy, Freedom, and Community*, New York: Pantheon Books 1993.

Blankenhorn, David, *Fatherless America: Confronting Our Most Urgent Social Problem*, New York: HarperCollins 1995.

Block, Susan, *The Ten Commandments of Pleasure: Erotic Keys to a Healthy Sexual Life*, New York: St. Martin's Press 1996.

Bohr, David, *Catholic Moral Tradition*, 2nd edn. Huntington, IN: Our Sunday Visitor 1999.

Bourdieu, Pierre, *Outline of a Theory of Practice*, New York: Cambridge University Press 1977.

Brazelton, T. Berry, M.D., *Touchpoints: Your Child's Emotional and Behavioral Development*, New York: Perseus Press 1994.

Brodzinsky, David M., and Schechter, Marshall D. (eds), *The Psychology of Adoption*, New York: Oxford University Press 1990.

Brooke, Christopher N. L., *Marriage in Christian History*, Cambridge: Cambridge University Press 1977.

_____, *The Medieval Idea of Marriage*, Oxford: Oxford University Press 1989.

Brooks, David, *Bobos in Paradise: The New Upper Class and How They Got There*, New York: Simon & Schuster 2000.

Brown, Peter, *The Body and Society*, New York: Columbia University Press 1988.

Brown, R., *Analyzing Love*, New York: Cambridge University Press 1987.

Brown, Susan L., and Booth, Alan, "Cohabitation versus Marriage: A Comparison of Relationship Quality," *Journal of Marriage and Family*, vol. 58, no. 3, August 1996, pp. 668–78.

Buber, Martin, *I and Thou*, New York: Scribner 1970.

Burns, Jeffrey M., *Disturbing the Peace: A History of the Christian Family Movement*, Notre Dame: University of Notre Dame Press 1999.

Cahill, Lisa Sowle, *Between the Sexes: Foundations for a Christian Ethics of Sexuality*, Philadelphia: Fortress Press 1985.

_____, *Sex, Gender, and Christian Ethics*, New York: Cambridge University Press 1996.

_____, "Sex, Gender, and the Common Good: Family," *Religion, Ethics, and the Common Good*, The Annual Publication of the College Theology

Society 41, ed. James Donahue and M. Theresa Moser, R.S.C.J., Mystic, CT: Twenty-Third Publications 1996.

Cahill, Lisa Sowle, and Mieth, Dietmar (eds), *The Family*, Concilium 1995/4, Maryknoll, NY: Orbis Books 1995.

Carlen, Claudia (ed.), *The Papal Encyclicals*, vols 1–5, Wilmington, NC: McGrath Publishing 1981.

Carrington, Christopher, *No Place Like Home: Relationships and Family Life Among Lesbian and Gay Men*, Chicago: University of Chicago Press 1999.

Christ, Carol P., and Plaskow, Judith, *Womanspirit Rising: A Feminist Reader in Religion*, New York: Harper & Row 1979.

Cicero, *De Senectute, De Amicitia, De Divinatione, with an English Translation*, trans. William Armistead Falconer, The Loeb Classical Library, Cambridge, MA: Harvard University Press 1964.

Coleman, John A., S.J. (ed.), *One Hundred Years of Catholic Social Thought: Celebration and Challenge*, Maryknoll, NY: Orbis Books 1991.

Collinge, William J., "Christian Community and Christian Understanding: Developments in Augustine's Thought," *Catholic Authority and Dialogue with the World*, The Annual Publication of the College Theology Society 1986, ed. Bernard P. Prusak, Lanham, MD: University Press of America 1988.

Conzelmann, Hans, *The Theology of St. Luke*, trans. Geoffrey Buswell, Philadelphia: Fortress Press 1982.

Cooke, Bernard, *Sacraments and Sacramentality*, rev. edn. Mystic, CT: Twenty-Third Publications 1994.

Coontz, Stephanie, *The Social Origins of Private Life: A History of American Families 1600–1900*, New York: Verso 1988.

_____, *The Way We Never Were: American Families and the Nostalgia Trap*, New York: Basic Books 1992.

Csikszentmihalyi, Mihaly, *Flow: The Psychology of Optimal Experience*, New York: Harper & Row 1990.

Csikszentmihalyi, Mihaly, and Rochberg-Halton, Eugene, *The Meaning of Things: Domestic Symbols and the Self*, New York: Cambridge University Press 1981.

Curran, Charles, E. (ed.), *Contraception: Authority and Dissent*, New York: Herder & Herder 1969.

Dawkins, Richard, *The Selfish Gene*, New York: Oxford University Press 1976.

Day, Dorothy, *By Little and By Little*, ed. Robert Ellsberg, New York: Alfred A. Knopf 1984.

D'Emilio, John, *Sexual Politics, Sexual Communities: The Making of a*

Homosexual Minority in the United States 1940–1970, Chicago: University of Chicago Press 1983.

de Munck, Victor C., *Romantic Love and Sexual Behavior: Perspectives for the Social Sciences*, Westport, CT: Praeger 1998.

de Rougemont, Denis, *Love in the Western World*, Princeton: Princeton University Press 1983.

de Vate, Jr., D. Van, *Romantic Love: A Philosophical Inquiry*, University Park, PA: Penn State University Press 1981.

Derek, John F., *Contemporary Medical Ethics*, New York: Sheed & Ward 1975.

Diamond, Lisa, "Was It a Phase? Young Women's Relinquishment of Lesbian/Bisexual Identities Over a 5-Year Period," *Journal of Personality and Social Psychology*, vol. 84, no. 2, 2003, pp. 352–64.

Diamond, Lisa, "What does Sexual Orientation Orient? A Biobehavioral Model Distinguishing Love and Sexual Desire," *Psychological Review*, vol. 110, no. 1, 2003, pp. 173–92.

Dominian, Jack, *Make or Break: A Guide to Marriage Counselling*, Wilmington: Michael Glazier 1985.

Donzelot, Jacques, *The Policing of Families*, trans. Robert Hurley, New York: Pantheon Books 1979.

Durkin, Mary Greeley, *Feast of Love: Pope John Paul II on Human Intimacy*, Chicago: Loyola University Press 1983.

Eisenberg, Arlene, and Hathaway, Sandee, *What to Expect: The Toddler Years*, New York: Workman Publishing Company 1996.

Eisenstein, Zillah R., *The Female Body and the Law*, Berkeley: University of California Press 1988.

Ellul, Jacques, *Ethics of Freedom*, trans. Geoffrey W. Bromiley, Eerdmans Publishing 1976.

Elshtain, Jean Bethke, *Public Man, Private Woman*, Princeton: Princeton University Press 1981.

Ericksen, Julia A., and Steffen, Sally A., *Kiss and Tell: Surveying Sex in the Twentieth Century*, Cambridge, MA: Harvard University Press 1999.

Everett, William Johnson, *Blessed Be the Bond*, Philadelphia: Fortress Press 1985.

Fitzgerald, Sheila, and Beller, Andrea, H., "Educational Attainment of Children From Single-Parent Families," *Demography*, vol. 25, no. 2, May 1988, pp. 221–34.

Fitzgerald, Vance, M.D., et al., "What Are the Essential Ingredients for a Long, Happy Marriage?" *Medical Aspects of Human Sexuality* 19, no. 3, March 1985, pp. 237–57.

Fitzmyer, Joseph, *The Gospel According to Luke (X–XXIV)*, Anchor Bible 28A, Garden City, NY: Doubleday 1985.

Flannery, Austin, O.P. (ed.), *Vatican Council II: The Conciliar and Post Conciliar Documents*, Northport, NY: Costello Publishing Co. 1987.

Fortune, Marie, *Sexual Violence*, New York: Pilgrim Press 1983.

Frankfurt Institute for Social Research, *Aspects of Sociology*, trans. John Viertel, Boston: Beacon Press 1972.

Freund, John, C. M., and Heaney-Hunter, Jo-Ann, *Mirror of God's Love: Sacramental Marriage and the Difference It Makes*, New York: Pueblo Publishing 1984.

Fussell, Paul, *Class: A Guide through the American Class System*, New York: Summit 1983.

Genovesi, Vincent J., *In Pursuit of Love: Catholic Morality and Human Sexuality*, 2nd edn. Collegeville, MN: The Liturgical Press 1996.

Giddens, Anthony, *The Transformation of Intimacy: Sexuality, Love, and Eroticism in Modern Societies*, Stanford: Stanford University Press 1992.

Gies, Frances, and Gies, Joseph, *Marriage and the Family in the Middle Ages*, New York: HarperCollins 1989.

Goldscheider, Frances K., and Kaufman, Gayle, "Fertility and Commitment: Bringing Men Back In," *Population and Development Review*, vol. 22, *Supplement: Fertility in the United States*, 1996, pp. 87–99.

Gould, Carol C., and Wartofsky, Marx W. (eds), *Women and Philosophy*, New York: Putnam 1976.

Gouldner, Alvin W., *For Sociology: Renewal and Critique in Sociology Today*, New York: Basic Books 1973.

Greeley, Andrew M., and Durkin, Mary Greeley, *How to Save the Catholic Church*, New York: Viking Penguin 1984.

Greenberg, David F., *The Construction of Homosexuality*, Chicago: University of Chicago Press, 1988.

Greer, Germaine, *Sex and Destiny*, New York: Harper & Row 1984.

_____, *The Whole Woman*, New York: Alfred A. Knopf 1999.

Grenz, Stanley J., *Sexual Ethics: An Evangelical Perspective*, Louisville, KY: Westminster John Knox Press 1990.

Grisez, Germain, *The Way of the Lord Jesus,* Vol. 2: *Living a Christian Life*, Quincy, IL: Franciscan Press 1993.

Guindon, André, *The Sexual Language*, Ottawa: University of Ottawa Press 1977.

Hagstrum, Jean H., *Esteem Enlivened by Desire: The Couple from Homer to Shakespeare*, Chicago: University of Chicago Press 1992.

Hanigan, James P., *Homosexuality: The Test Case for Christian Sexual Ethics*, New York: Paulist Press 1988.

_____, *What Are They Saying About Sexual Morality?* New York: Paulist Press 1982.

Hauerwas, Stanley, *A Community of Character*, Notre Dame: University of Notre Dame Press 1981.

_____, *The Peaceable Kingdom*, Notre Dame: University of Notre Dame Press 1983.

Hauerwas, Stanley and Wells, Samuel (eds), *The Blackwell Companion to Christian Ethics*, Oxford: Blackwell Publishing 2004.

Hauerwas, Stanley, et al. (eds), *Growing Old in Christ*, Grand Rapids: Eerdmans Publishing Company 2003.

Hays, Richard B., *The Moral Vision of the New Testament*, New York: HarperCollins 1996.

Hays, Sharon, *The Cultural Contradictions of Motherhood*, New Haven: Yale University Press 1996.

Heath, Stephen, *The Sexual Fix*, New York: Schocken Books 1982.

Hendrick, Susan S., and Hendrick, Clyde, *Romantic Love*, Newbury Park, CA: Sage Publications 1992.

Hertz, Rosanna, and Ferguson, Faith I. T., "Childcare Choice and the Constraints in the United States: Social Class, Race, and the Influence of Family Views," *Journal of Comparative Family Studies* 27, Summer 1996, pp. 249–80.

Hill, William J., O.P., *The Three-Personed God: The Trinity as Mystery of Salvation*, Washington, DC: The Catholic University of America Press 1982.

Hochschild, Arlie, *The Time Bind: When Work Becomes Home and Home Becomes Work*, New York: Metropolitan Books 1997.

Howell, Mary C., *Helping Ourselves: Families and the Human Network*, Boston: Beacon Press 1975.

_____, *Serving the Underserved: Caring for People Who Are Both Old and Mentally Retarded: A Handbook for Caregivers*, Exceptional Parent Press 1989.

Hunter, James Davison, *Culture Wars: The Struggle to Define America*, New York: Basic Books 1991.

Illouz, Eva, *Consuming the Romantic Utopia: Love and the Cultural Contradictions of Capitalism*, Berkeley: University of California Press 1997.

Imbiorski, Walter (ed.), *The New Cana Manual*, Chicago: The Cana Conference of Chicago 1957.

Inchausti, Robert, *Ignorant Perfection of Ordinary People*, Albany, NY: State University of New York Press 1991.

Ingebretsen, Edward, "Gone Shopping: The Commercialization of Same-Sex Desire," *Journal of Gay, Lesbian, and Bisexual Identity*, vol. 4, no. 2, 1999, pp. 125–47.

John Chrysostom, *Homiliae in Epist. ad Ephesios*, Patrologia Graeca 62, pp. 4–176, ed. J. P. Migne, Parisiis 1862.

_____, *John Chrysostom: On Virginity; Against Marriage*, trans. Sally Rieger Shore, New York: Edwin Mellon Press 1983.

_____, *On Marriage and Family Life*, trans. Catharine P. Roth and David Anderson, Crestwood, NY: St. Vladimir's Seminary Press 1997.

_____, *Saint Chrysostom: Homilies on the Gospel of Saint Matthew*, Nicene and Post-Nicene Fathers X, ed. Philip Schaff, Grand Rapids: Eerdmans 1983.

John Paul II, *Centesimus annus*, in *Origins: CNS Documentary Service* 21, no. 1, May 16, 1991, pp. 1–24.

_____, *Evangelium vitae*, in *Origins: CNS Documentary Service* 24, no. 42, April 6, 1995, pp. 1–24.

_____, *Familiaris consortio*, in *Origins: CNS Documentary Service* 11, nos 28–29, December 24, 1981, pp. 438–66.

_____, *Letter to Families*, in *Origins: CNS Documentary Service* 23, no. 37, March 3, 1994, pp. 638–59; *Acta Apostolicae Sedis* 86, no. 11, November 7, 1994, pp. 868–925.

_____, *The Original Unity of Man and Woman: Catechesis on the Book of Genesis*, Boston, MA: Daughters of St. Paul 1981.

_____, *Sacred in All Its Forms*, ed. James V. Schall, S.J., Boston, MA: Daughters of St. Paul 1984.

_____, *Sollicitudo rei socialis*, in *Origins: CNS Documentary Service* 17, no. 38, March 3, 1988, pp. 641–60; *Acta Apostolicae Sedis* 80, no. 5, May 7, 1988, pp. 513–86.

Kant, Immanuel, *Foundations of the Metaphysics of Morals*, trans. Lewis White Beck, New York: Macmillan Publishing Company 1959.

Keane, Philip S., *Sexual Morality: A Catholic Perspective*, New York, Paulist Press 1977.

Keesling, Barbara, *Getting Close: A Lover's Guide to Embracing Fantasy and Heightening Sexual Connection*, New York: HarperCollins 1999.

Kilbourne, Jean, *Deadly Persuasion: Why Women and Girls Must Fight the Addictive Power of Advertising*, New York: Free Press 1999.

Kippley, John, and Kippley, Sheila, *The Art of Natural Family Planning*, 4th edn. Cincinnati: Couple to Couple League International 1996.

Konner, Melvin, *The Tangled Wing: Biological Constraints of the Human Spirit*, New York: Holt, Rinehart, & Winston 1982.

Kraft, William E., *Sexual Dimensions of Celibate Life*, Kansas City, KS: Andrews & McMeel, Inc. 1979.

Kristeva, Julia, *The Kristeva Reader*, ed. Toril Moi, New York: Columbia University Press 1986.

_____, *Revolution in Poetic Language*, trans. Margaret Waller, New York: Columbia University Press 1984.

LaCugna, Catherine Mowry, *Freeing Theology: The Essentials of Theology in Feminist Perspective*, New York: HarperCollins 1993.

Lapham, Lewis H., *Money and Class in America: Notes and Observations on Our Civil Religion*, New York: Weidenfeld & Nicolson 1988.

Lasch, Christopher, *Haven in a Heartless World*, New York: Basic Books 1977.

_____, *Women and the Common Life: Love, Marriage, and Feminism*, ed. Elisabeth Lasch-Quinn, New York: W. W. Norton & Company 1997.

Lawler, Michael G., *Marriage and Sacrament: A Theology of Christian Marriage*, Collegeville, MN: The Liturgical Press 1993.

Lawler, Michael G., and Roberts, William P. (eds) *Christian Marriage and Family: Contemporary Theological and Pastoral Perspectives*, Collegeville, MN: The Liturgical Press 1996.

Lee, John Alan, *Colours of Love*, Toronto: New Press 1973.

_____, "The Romantic Heresy," *Canadian Review of Sociology and Anthropology* 2, no. 4, 1975, pp. 514–28.

_____, "A Typology of Styles of Loving," *Personality and Social Psychology Bulletin* 3, no. 2, 1977, pp. 173–82.

Lillard, Lee A., et al., "Premarital Cohabitation and Subsequent Marital Dissolution: A Matter of Self-Selection?," *Demography*, vol. 32, no. 3, August 1995, pp. 437–57.

Long, D. Stephen, *Divine Economy: Theology and the Market*, London: Routledge 2000.

Lowe, Donald M., *The Body in Late-Capitalism USA*, Durham: Duke University Press 1995.

Luhmann, Niklas, *Love as Passion: The Codification of Intimacy*, trans. Jeremy Gaines and Doris L. Jone, Stanford, CA: Stanford University Press 1998.

MacIntyre, Alasdair, *After Virtue*, 2nd edn. Notre Dame: University of Notre Dame Press 1984.

_____, *A Short History of Ethics: A History of Moral Philosophy from the Homeric Age to the Twentieth Century*, 2nd edn. Notre Dame: University of Notre Dame Press 1998.

Mackin, Theodore, S.J., *What Is Marriage?* New York: Paulist Press 1982.

Manning, Wendy D., and Lichter, Daniel T., "Parental Cohabitation and Children's Economic Well-Being," *Journal of Marriage and Family*, vol. 58, no. 4, November 1996, pp. 998–1010.

Martin, Dale B., *The Corinthian Body*, New Haven: Yale University Press 1995.

Matthaei, Julie A., *An Economic History of Women in America: Women's Work, the Sexual Division of Labor, and the Development of Capitalism*, New York: Schocken Books 1982.

McCabe, Herbert, *God Matters*, Springfield, IL: Templegate 1987.

_____, *What Is Ethics All About?* Washington, DC: Corpus Books 1969.

McCarthy, David M., "Sexual Utterances and Common Life," *Modern Theology* 16, no. 4, October 2000, pp. 443–59.

McGinnis, Kathleen, and McGinnis, James, *Parenting for Peace and Justice: Ten Years Later*, Maryknoll, NY: Orbis Books 1990.

McKibben, Bill, *The End of Nature*, New York: Doubleday 1999.

_____, *Maybe One: A Case for Smaller Families*, New York: Plume 1999.

McNamara, O.P., Marie Aquinas, *Friends and Friendship for Saint Augustine*, Staten Island, NY: Society of St. Paul 1964.

McNeal, James U., *The Kids Market, Myths and Realities*, Ithaca, NY: Paramount Market Publishing, Inc. 1999.

McNeal, James U., and Yeh, Chyon-Hwa, "Born to Shop," *American Demographics* 15, no. 6, June 1993, 34–40.

Michael, Robert T., et al., *Sex in America: A Definitive Survey*, New York: Warner Books 1995.

Milbank, John, "Can a Gift Be Given? Prolegomena to a Future Trinitarian Metaphysic," *Modern Theology* 11, no. 1, January 1995, pp. 119–61.

_____, *The Word Made Strange: Theology, Language, Culture*, Oxford: Blackwell 1997.

Miles, Al, *Domestic Violence: What Every Pastor Needs to Know*, Minneapolis: Fortress Press 2000.

Moffat, Michael, *Coming of Age in New Jersey: College Life and American Culture*, New Brunswick, NJ: Rutgers University Press 1989.

Morgan, Edmund S., *The Puritan Family: Religion and Domestic Relations in Seventeenth-Century New England*, New York: Harper & Row 1944.

Murphy, Nancey, Kallenberg, Brad, and Nation, Mark Thiessen (eds), *Virtues and Practices in the Christian Tradition: Christian Ethics After MacIntyre*, Harrisburg, PA: Trinity Press International 1997.

National Catholic Bishops' Committee on Marriage and Family, *Always Our Children: A Pastoral Message to Parents of Homosexual Children*, Washington, DC: United States Catholic Conference, Inc. 1997.

National Catholic Bishops' Secretariat for Family, Laity, Women and Youth, *Marriage and Cohabiting Couples*, Washington, DC: United States Catholic Conference, Inc. 1999.

Nolan, James L., *The Therapeutic State: Justifying Government at Century's End*, New York: New York University Press 1998.

Nygren, Anders, *Agape and Eros*, trans. Philip S. Watson, New York: Harper & Row 1969.

Okin, Susan Moller, *Justice, Gender, and the Family*, New York: Basic Books 1989.

_____, *Women in Western Political Thought*, Princeton: Princeton University Press 1979.

Olsen, Frances E., "The Family and the Market: A Study of Ideology and Legal Reform," *Harvard Law Review* 96, no. 7, May 1983, pp. 1497–578.

_____, "The Myth of State Intervention in the Family," *University of Michigan Journal of Law Reform* 18, no. 4, 1985, pp. 835–65.

Otten, Willemien, "Augustine on Marriage, Monasticism, and the Community of the Church," *Theological Studies* 59, 1998, pp. 385–405.

Outka, Gene, *Agape: An Ethical Analysis*, New Haven: Yale University Press 1972.

Pateman, Carole, "Feminist Critiques of the Public/Private Dichotomy," *Public and Private in Social Life*, ed. S. T. Benn and G. F. Gaus, New York: St. Martin's Press 1983.

_____, *The Sexual Contract*, Stanford: Stanford University Press 1988.

Paul VI, *Populorum Progressio: On the Development of Peoples*, in *The Gospel of Peace and Justice: Catholic Social Teaching Since Pope John*, ed. Joseph Gremillion, Maryknoll, NY: Orbis 1976.

_____, "To the Teams of Our Lady (Rome, May 4, 1970)," *Why Humanae Vitae Was Right: A Reader* ed. Janet Smith, San Francisco: Ignatius Press 1993.

Polsky, Andrew J., *The Rise of the Therapeutic State*, Princeton: Princeton University Press 1993.

Pope, Stephen P., *The Evolution of Altruism and the Ordering of Love*, Washington, DC: Georgetown University Press 1994.

Portes, Alejandro, Castells, Manuel, and Benton, Lauren A. (eds), *The Informal Economy: Studies in Advanced and Less Developed Countries*, Baltimore: The Johns Hopkins University Press 1989.

Post, Stephen, "Adoption Theologically Considered," *Journal of Religious Ethics*, vol. 25, no. 1, Spring 1997, pp. 149–68.

Post, Stephen, "The Moral Meaning of Relinquishing an Infant: Reflections on Adoption," *Thought*, vol. 67, no. 265, June 1992, pp. 207–20.

Post, Stephen, *A Theory of Agape*, Lewisburg: Bucknell University Press 1990.

Rawls, John, *Political Liberalism*, New York: Columbia University Press 1993.

_____, *A Theory of Justice*, Cambridge, MA: Belknap Press 1971.

Rennison, Callie Marie, "Intimate Partner Violence and Age of Victim," United States Department of Justice: Bureau of Justice Statistics 2001.

Rogers, Eugene F., *Sexuality and the Christian Body*, Oxford: Blackwell Publisher 1999.

Rosenberg, Elinor B., *The Adoption Life Cycle: The Children and Their Families Through the Years*, New York: The Free Press 1992.

Rubio, Julie Hanlon, *A Christian Theology of Marriage and Family*, New York: Paulist Press 2003.

Sanchez, Laura, and Gager, Constance T., "Hard Living, Perceived Entitlement to a Great Marriage, and Marital Dissolution," *Journal of Marriage and Family*, vol. 62, no. 3, August 2000, pp. 708–22.

Sandel, Michael J., *Liberalism and the Limits of Justice*, New York: Cambridge University Press 1982.

Sanford, John A., *Invisible Partners*, New York: Paulist Press 1980.

Santurri, Edmund N., and Werpehowski, William (eds), *The Love Commandments: Essays in Christian Ethics and Moral Philosophy*, Washington, DC: Georgetown University Press 1992.

Schuck, Michael J., *That They Be One: The Social Teaching of the Papal Encyclicals 1740–1989*, Washington, DC: Georgetown University Press 1991.

Schüssler Fiorenza, Elisabeth, *In Memory of Her*, New York: Crossroad 1983.

Scott, Kieran, and Warren, Michael (eds), *Perspectives on Marriage*, New York: Oxford University Press 1993.

Scroggs, Robin, *New Testament and Homosexuality*, Philadelphia: Fortress Press, 1983.

Senior, Donald (ed.), *The Catholic Study Bible*, New York: Oxford University Press 1990.

Shorter, Edward, *The Making of the Modern Family*, New York: Basic Books 1977.

Silverstone, Roger, and Hirsch, Eric, *Consuming Technologies: Media and Information in Domestic Spaces*, New York: Routledge 1992.

Smith, Joan and Wallerstein, Immanuel (eds), *Creating and Transforming Households: The Constraints of the World-Economy*, New York: Cambridge University Press 1992.

Soble, Alan (ed.), *The Philosophy of Sex*, Savage, MD: Rowman & Littlefield Publishers, Inc. 1991.

_____, *Sexual Investigations*, New York: New York University Press 1996.

Solomon, R., *Love: Emotion, Myth, and Metaphor*, New York: Anchor Books 1981.

Stansell, Christine, *City of Women: Sex and Class in New York 1789–1860*, Chicago: University of Illinois Press 1987.

Stolley, Kathy S., "Statistics on Adoption in the United States," *The Future of Children*, vol. 3, no. 1, Spring 1993, pp. 26–42.

Sullivan, Andrew, *Virtually Normal*, New York: Alfred A. Knopf, 1995.

Sweeney, Maureen A., "Between Sorrow and Happy Endings: A New

Paradigm of Adoption," *Yale Journal of Law and Feminism*, vol. 2, 1990, pp. 329–69.

Taylor, Charles, *Sources of the Self: The Making of the Modern Identity*, Cambridge, MA: Harvard University Press 1989.

Teachman, Jay D., Tedrow, Lucky M., and Crowder, Kyle, "The Changing Demography of America's Families," *Journal of Marriage and the Family*, vol. 62, no. 4, November 2000.

Thatcher, Adrian, *Living Together and Christian Ethics*, Cambridge: Cambridge University Press 2002.

Thomas, Susan L., "Women, Welfare, Reform and the Preservation of a Myth," *The Social Science Journal* 34, no. 3, 1997, pp. 351–68.

Tong, Rosemarie Putnam, *Feminist Thought: A More Comprehensive Introduction*, 2nd edn. Boulder, CO: Westview Press 1998.

Treacy, Gerald C., S.J., *Five Great Encyclicals*, New York: Paulist Press 1939.

von Hildebrand, Dietrich, *Marriage: The Mystery of Faithful Love*, Manchester, NH: Sophia Institute Press 1984.

Walzer, Michael, *Spheres of Justice: A Defense of Pluralism and Equality*, New York: Basic Books 1983.

Ward, Graham, *Theology and Contemporary Critical Theory*, 2nd edn. New York: St. Martin's Press 2000.

Weithman, Paul J., "Complementarity and Equality in the Political Thought of Thomas Aquinas," *Theological Studies* 59, no. 2, June 1998, pp. 277–9.

Williams, Kirk R., "Social Sources of Marital Violence and Deterrence: Testing an Integrated Theory of Assaults between Partners," *Journal of Marriage and Family*, vol. 54, no. 3, August 1992, pp. 620–9.

Wyckoff, Malia McCawley, and Snyder, Mary, *You Can Afford to Stay Home with Your Kids*, Franklin Lakes, NJ: Career Press 1999.

Wyshogrod, Edith, *Saints and Postmodernism: Revisioning Moral Philosophy*, Chicago: University of Chicago Press 1990.

Index